TEXAS CONFEDERATE, RECONSTRUCTION GOVERNOR

# TEXAS CONFEDERATE,

NUMBER SEVENTEEN
*Sam Rayburn Series on Rural Life*
Sponsored by Texas A&M University–Commerce
M. HUNTER HAYES, GENERAL EDITOR

# RECONSTRUCTION GOVERNOR

## JAMES WEBB THROCKMORTON

KENNETH WAYNE HOWELL

*Texas A&M University Press, College Station*

First edition

This paper meets the requirements of ANSI/NISO Z39.48-1992
(Permanence of Paper).
Binding materials have been chosen for durability.

LIBRARY OF CONGRESS CATALOGING-IN-PUBLICATION DATA

Howell, Kenneth Wayne, 1967–
Texas Confederate, Reconstruction governor : James Webb Throckmorton /
Kenneth Wayne Howell.—1st ed.
p. cm.—(Sam Rayburn series on rural life ; no. 17)
Includes bibliographical references and index.
ISBN-13: 978-1-60344-040-0 (cloth : alk. paper)
ISBN-10: 1-60344-040-2 (cloth : alk. paper)
1. Throckmorton, J. W. (James Webb), 1825–1894. 2. Governors—
Texas—Biography. 3. Texas—Politics and government—19th century.
4. Texas—History—Civil War, 1861–1865. 5. Reconstruction (U.S.
history, 1865–1877)—Texas. I. Title. II. Series.
F391.T55H85 2008
976.4'061092—dc22
[B]
2008005176

*For my mentors:*
*Dr. James Smallwood,*
*Dr. Walter Buenger,*
*Dr. Barry Crouch,*
*Dr. Ty Cashion,*
*and*
*Dr. Ralph Goodwin*

*I will forever be indebted to each of these gentlemen for their guidance and forbearance during my tenure as a graduate student.*

# CONTENTS

# ILLUSTRATIONS

# SERIES EDITOR'S FOREWORD

Since 1997 an abiding mission of the Sam Rayburn Series on Rural Life has been to provide new perspectives on the life, culture, and history of East Texas and the surrounding regions. Established at Texas A&M University–Commerce under the auspices of Texas A&M University Press in College Station and named in honor of Samuel Talafierro Rayburn, a Bonham native and longtime Speaker of the United States House of Representatives, the series conveys much of the richness of the area and its history. Each volume in the series presents readers with an opportunity to discover—or to rediscover—a facet of life in the area. Collectively, these volumes constitute a wide-ranging and finely-detailed mosaic, one centering on East Texas. Previous contributions to the Rayburn Series have focused on topics as diverse as outlaws, cotton, cinemas, and Mennonites communities.

The sixth volume in the series, *Murder and Mayhem* (2003), by James M. Smallwood, Barry A. Crouch, and Larry Peacock, examines Reconstruction, or the "Second Civil War," and its violent consequences in the Corners region of Northeast Texas. With *Texas Confederate, Reconstruction Governor: James Webb Throckmorton,* Kenneth Wayne Howell presents a paradox of sorts by examining a subject that will be both familiar and new to many readers. The inherent complexities and consequences of the Reconstruction era have been studied at length, but Howell's scholarship demonstrates that this period is continually open to fresh ways of understanding. In his examination of Throckmorton's political career during the mid- to late-nineteenth century, Howell astutely scrutinizes the man's life and deeds within their historical context. Moreover, Howell effectively explains and illustrates the key factors that have wrought this context. Rather than relying on an easy or formulaic signification of terms such as *racism,* Howell reveals the underlying motives and mindset, asking readers to define such terms from their own experiences. Howell also achieves the difficult task of reconstructing identity, not only the political characteristics of Throckmorton but those of the region and state as well.

It is with great pleasure that we include Howell's *Texas Confederate, Reconstruction Governor: James Webb Throckmorton* in the Sam Rayburn Series on Rural Life. As "Mr. Sam" once remarked, in a phrase that has been repeated countless times in many variations, "A jackass can kick a barn down, but it takes a carpenter to build one." Make no mistake: Howell is, in this figurative sense at least, a carpenter; his insights and explanations fashion anew the image of Throckmorton the politician and his culture. Howell and his fine book are welcome additions to the series.

M. HUNTER HAYES
*General Editor*

# PREFACE

In March 1997, I attended my first Texas State Historical Association meeting. It was at this meeting that the idea for this book was conceived. I really did not know anyone at the meeting and no one knew me, except for James M. Smallwood, my good friend and mentor who had suggested that it would be a good idea for me to attend the meeting. In an effort to make me feel more comfortable, Dr. Smallwood began introducing me to people he knew. Little did I know at that time, but the first introduction proved to be one of the most important—it was Barry Crouch, a longtime friend and colleague of my mentor. After just a few minutes of conversation, I took an immediate liking to Dr. Crouch, and I would like to think that the feeling was mutual. When he learned that I had just finished my M.A. and wanted to pursue a Ph.D., he asked, "What are you going to do your dissertation on?" His question came as a bit of a shock: I wasn't even sure that I would be accepted into a Ph.D. program, and here this gentleman was asking me about a dissertation topic. I suspect he already knew what my answer would be, because he had an immediate response: "It is not too early, and you better start thinking about it." This was the first (but not the last) sound advice that Dr. Crouch would eventually share with me over the brief time that I knew him. Most importantly, he suggested that I consider writing my dissertation on either E. M. Pease, A. J. Hamilton, or J. W. Throckmorton. I took his advice to heart, completing my dissertation on James Webb Throckmorton at Texas A&M University in the spring of 2005. Unfortunately, Dr. Crouch passed away before I began work on this manuscript, but I owe him special thanks for sparking my interest in Throckmorton and for convincing me that a biographical study of this nineteenth-century Texan was a worthwhile project.

This book is the direct result of my early efforts as a graduate student to understand Throckmorton's early life and political career. As readers and reviewers will undoubtedly note, this is not a full-length biography. I have intentionally focused on Throckmorton's career during three tumultuous decades of Texas history, primarily 1843 to 1874. In choosing not to include Throckmorton's post-Reconstruction political career, the most important consideration was that my interest in Throckmorton centered on his brief career as the first elected Reconstruction governor of Texas. As a prewar Unionist, Throckmorton should have embraced the Republican Party and should have aided the federal government's efforts to bring his state back into the Union. However, Throckmorton became a devoted member of the Democratic Party, and federal military authorities removed him from office because he proved to be an impediment to their Reconstruction efforts in Texas. How did Throckmorton, a staunch prewar Unionist, become an impediment to Reconstruction? Was he an actual impediment to Reconstruction? If so, how and to what degree? Did his post–Civil War political career represent a significant shift in his prewar political ideology? Or was there continuity in the two seemingly divergent positions? These are the questions that I attempt to answer. Thus, those seeking a detailed account of Throckmorton's congressional career between the late 1870s and 1880s are likely to be disappointed.

I am in awe of how many people aided me in the completion of this volume. I greatly appreciate the assistance and advice of numerous professors, historians, archivists, librarians, friends, and family members. When this study was in its early stages of development, Professors Walter Buenger, Charles Brooks, H. W. Brands, Henry Schmidt, and James Kracht provided many helpful comments. I thank all of them for their assistance, especially Professor Buenger, whose encouragement and guidance proved invaluable. On more than one occasion, Dr. Buenger's suggestions saved my work from being a mere biographical examination of an obscure nineteenth-century politician. He pushed me to think about my subject in new ways and forced me to look at questions that placed Throckmorton within the broader historical context of the Old South and the United States. For this, I owe Dr. Buenger my deepest gratitude.

Dr. James Smallwood deserves special thanks. He took time away from his own projects to read every word of the manuscript and offered many valuable insights.

I am also thankful to a number of close academic friends who listened patiently to my ideas regarding the development of Throckmorton's political ideology and character and offered their unwavering support for the project. Among those are Charles Spurlin, Ty Cashion, Carl Moneyhon, Bill Stein, Robert Wettemann, Keith Volanto, Kirk Bane, Dale Baum, Bruce Glasrud, and Tai Kreidler. I also owe a special debt of gratitude to Gregg Cantrell. He read my entire manuscript and offered many suggestions that improved its overall scholarly merit. While I have stretched my memory in an effort to include all that have aided my efforts, I am sure that I have left someone out. I apologize for any lapse in memory.

As most scholars realize, historical research is a financially draining adventure, especially for graduate students. I was fortunate to receive financial assistance from two valuable sources. The history department at Texas A&M University provided me with a research grant in the summer of 2003 and the East Texas Historical Association bestowed upon me the Ottis Lock Endowment Award for research in 2003. Both sources of financial assistance proved to be invaluable and made possible the completion of my research on Throckmorton.

Throughout this project I have received the help of numerous archivists and librarians. I am especially grateful for the help received from the staff of the Texas State Archives and Library in Austin, Texas. Donally Brice, a good friend and one of the most knowledgeable archivists at the state archives, provided extraordinary research assistance. Likewise the archivists and research assistants at the Center for American History, the Austin Public Library, and Texas A&M University's libraries deserve special thanks for all their help during my many visits to their depositories.

During my efforts to research information on Throckmorton's family background, the descendants of James Webb Throckmorton provided me with numerous genealogical documents related to the subject. Gary Throckmorton proved especially interested in the project. With his help, I believe we have been able to solve some of the mysteries of Throckmorton's childhood years.

Also, I greatly appreciate the staff and editors at Texas A&M University Press. Their efforts have greatly improved the overall quality and merit of this work. I want to especially thank editor-in-chief Mary Lenn Dixon for patiently guiding a young author through the tangled webs of the publishing industry. Her belief in this project and professionalism was very comforting during the process of waiting for the readers' reviews and of revising my original manuscript.

Finally, I want to express my deepest gratitude to my family for all their prayers, advice, encouragement, and moral support, and especially to my wife, Felesha, and my children, Zachary and Tyler. Their love, support, understanding, and countless daily acts of service allowed me to complete this manuscript. Despite all the professional assistance that I have received throughout the research and writing of this biography, all errors of fact, faulty interpretations, and mistaken conclusions remain my own.

# TEXAS CONFEDERATE, RECONSTRUCTION GOVERNOR

# INTRODUCTION

## *An Enigma in Nineteenth-Century Texas Politics*

On February 1, 1861, a crowd stood outside the state capitol. Most of those gathered around the entrance of the building had arrived too late to make their way inside. However, given the historical significance of what was about to transpire, they were unwilling to retreat to their homes before learning the fate of their state. Inside, delegates of the Secession Convention filed into the legislative chamber and prepared to vote on whether the state would remain in the Union or would follow the other states of the Lower South down the path of secession. The atmosphere was tense as all understood the gravity of the situation. The state's top officials were the last to enter the room. In front of a full gallery of onlookers, Gov. Sam Houston, Lt. Gov. Edward Clark, and the justices of the state Supreme Court took their seats beside the presiding officers of the convention. The president, Oran Roberts, called the delegates to order and issued instructions that they were to cast a simple ballot of "aye" or "nay," specifying that they were not allowed to explain their vote. Nevertheless, once the voting began, several delegates felt compelled to speak their minds.[1]

The first to explain his vote was Thomas J. Chambers, who justified his support for secession. Few in the gathering seemed to mind his grandiose comments. Following Chambers's vote, Thomas Hughes of Williamson County, W. H. Johnson of Lamar County, Joshua Johnson of Titus County, and A. P. Shuford of Wood County caused a stir among the delegates when they voted against leaving the Union. Perhaps due to intimidation, these gentlemen chose not explain their vote.[2] The next eight votes in favor of secession calmed the crowd, but tensions soon resurfaced when Roberts called James Webb Throckmorton's name.[3] The North Texas senator rose from his chair and stated, "In view of [my] responsibility, in the presence of God and my country, and unawed by the wild spirit of revolution around me, I vote no."[4] It was reported that an individual perched in the gallery hissed at the senator as he took his seat, prompting the North Texan to jump to his feet again and deliver with dramatic flare, "Mr. President, when the rabble hiss, well may patriots tremble."[5]

Out of respect for Throckmorton, others in the gallery quickly hushed the heckler. In fact, the senator's negative vote was no surprise to the other delegates because he had repeatedly announced that he was opposed to secession. Before the voting was completed, three more votes were cast against secession, including the ballots of L. H. Williams and George W. Wright, both of whom were from Lamar County. The final tally was 166 to 8 in favor of secession.[6] At the very apex of his career in state politics, Senator Throckmorton was unable to stem the tide of secession and his life was forever altered as a result.

JAMES WEBB THROCKMORTON was one of the most noted politicians of nineteenth-century Texas. Beginning in 1850, he orchestrated a political career that few Texas politicians have been able to match. By the end of his life, Throckmorton had served as a representative and senator in the state legislature, as the governor of Texas, and as a member of the United States Congress. Between 1850 and 1894, Throckmorton's political reputation and name recognition among Texans equaled that of other noted individuals of his times, including Sam Houston, Elisha M. Pease, John H. Reagan, Edmund J. Davis, and James S. Hogg. However, despite his notoriety, Throckmorton remains a neglected figure in the annals of Texas history.

Throughout his life, four primary factors influenced Throckmorton's political career: his experience of living within a frontier culture; his embrace of conservative Whig political ideology; his belief in white supremacy; and his desire to stimulate economic development in North Texas. Of these factors, his frontier experiences had the greatest overall impact on his life and career. Living on the frontier shaped Throckmorton's view of the world as he understood it, especially his concept of race, class, and patriotism. For example, Throckmorton's support of white supremacy directly corresponded to the common perception of white settlers that the frontier was destined to become the realm of white men. However, the settlers' racism was not solely derived from a pure devotion to the white race. Their racism was also linked to the socioeconomic circumstances of the southern states.

The North Texas frontier was populated with people who had left Upper South states, such as Tennessee, because of the increasing encroachment of white planters. Once members of the planter class moved into a region, they typically assumed control of the social, economic, and political institutions of the area. Understandably, small farmers living on the Texas frontier disassociated themselves from this elite class and sought self-governance and economic autonomy. As a result of this class conflict, small farmers also developed a degree of resentment toward slaves who represented the most visible sign of the planters' wealth. Throckmorton's life and career provide valuable insights into the political, social, and economic views of this frontier society.

Though twentieth-century scholars have afforded limited attention to Throckmorton, they have not completely abandoned him as a subject of study.[7] The most-cited examination of Throckmorton remains Claude Elliott's biography, *Leathercoat: The Life of James W. Throckmorton.* Elliott's study covered many of the major events of Throckmorton's political career, but, like many biographers, Elliott emphasized the Texas politician's accomplishments and ignored his failures. In his preface, Elliott stated that "it is true that no one service of James W. Throckmorton to his State and nation has great magnitude but it appears to me that the myriad of services which he performed should place him among the greater Texas statesmen of his time."[8] In an effort to prove his thesis, Elliott examined Throckmorton's career with blinders on, focusing more on the accomplishments of Throckmorton than on his personal and political frustrations. However, Elliott stated that he has "attempted to set forth the factual statements, and [has] made little attempt to interpret either the man or his times. It is a factual study and not an interpretation."[9]

While Elliott's approach to biography may have been acceptable in the 1930s when his book was published, it leaves readers with an incomplete understanding of Throckmorton and his times. Even though Elliott's work introduces the major events of Throckmorton's life, readers are still left wondering *why* this nineteenth-century politician is important to the history of Texas, as well as to the history of the South and the United States. One of the greatest shortcomings of this work is its failure to discuss the roles that race and class played in Throckmorton's political career. Nevertheless, despite these evident flaws, Elliott's work remains an important source of information and offers valuable insights into how the frontier shaped Throckmorton's political views.

In the 1840s, Throckmorton moved to the Texas frontier with his family. As an adolescent, he was immersed in a world where whites saw nothing wrong with pushing west onto Native American lands and claiming the land as their own. When the Indian tribes attempted to protect their lands, the whites engaged in a brutal war of extermination against Native Americans living on the fringes of Anglo society. Young Throckmorton witnessed firsthand the warfare waged between Anglos and Native Americans, and the resulting violence etched a permanent image in his mind of the hazards of settling a virgin land and instilled within him an early racial hatred of non-Anglos.

Attempting to reconstruct and explain the evolution of Throckmorton's racial biases is difficult, especially during his early life. The main obstacle is the limited number of primary sources that directly address his views of African Americans and Native Americans. Nevertheless, scholars can gain an understanding of Throckmorton's racial views by examining social influences of his early life. For example, despite befriending some of the Native Americans in the region, Throckmorton supported the complete removal of Indians to areas beyond white settlements. In his mind, Native Americans were an obstacle to Anglo domination of the western frontier. The society that Throckmorton and other white migrants attempted to create did not include a place for Texas Indians.

Throckmorton's views of the slave-owning class also helped shape his early concept of race. Between 1850 and 1861, he opposed the encroachment of planters on the North Texas frontier. This is not to say that Throckmorton did not believe in the legitimacy of the South's "peculiar institution." According to 1860 census records, he owned one slave.[10] Nevertheless, while he accepted the idea of living in a society with slaves, he did not want to live in a slave society. Ira Berlin's *Many Thousands Gone: The First Two Centuries of Slavery in North America* explains the subtle but distinct differences between these two concepts. Societies with slaves were distinguished by the fact that "slaves were marginal to the central productive processes; slavery was just one form of labor among many." Conversely, in slave societies, "slavery stood at the center of economic production, and the master-slave relationship provided the model for all social relations." Berlin continues, stating that "from the most intimate connections between men and women to the most public ones between ruler and ruled, all relationships mimicked those of slavery."[11] Throckmorton as well as other North Texans who migrated from the Upper South did not want to be politically or socially dominated by the slaveholding class.

The disdain that Throckmorton felt toward the planters was transferred to their slaves. In the minds of the small farmers and nonslaveholding professionals, such as doctors and lawyers, the slaves represented the most visible sign of the planters' wealth and were the vehicle that allowed planters to invade and dominate regions throughout the South. The people of North Texas, including Throckmorton, were willing to accept the presence of domestic slaves and even the presence of a limited number of planters as long as the planter class remained a controllable minority.

Party politics were equally important to the people living on the North Texas frontier. Generally speaking, these settlers gravitated toward the Whig Party during the late 1840s and early 1850s because it offered them an alternative to the southern Democratic Party dominated by the planter class. The Whig Party also supported many of the issues that were essential to the continued existence of their societies. For example, the Whigs tended to support government-subsidized internal improvements, a proposition that promised to connect frontier areas removed from navigable rivers with distant markets. Because North Texas was void of navigable rivers, its settlers knew that railroad development was paramount to their future economic prosperity. Additionally, Whigs tended to be strong advocates of the Union. This was particularly important to the people of the frontier who tended to be more nationalistic than many of their slaveholding counterparts. For frontiersmen, the Union represented a safe harbor from planter dominance. Even after the Whig Party ceased to exist in the 1850s, the settlers continued to exhibit an affinity for the Union. For example, during the secession crisis in 1861, many voters in North Texas cast ballots against secession. For them secession promised to ensure planter dominance in both the state and national governments of the Confederacy, a proposition they had struggled against since moving to Texas.

To test the continuity of major issues and themes in Texas' past, I examine a broad spectrum of Texas history. This study traverses three major periods in the state's past: the antebellum, Civil War, and Reconstruction eras. Because race is an integral part of Throckmorton's life, it is discussed in detail here. However, the discussion of race in this study differs from the revisionist scholarship that has tended to focus on the problems confronting minority groups in southern society. I do not directly focus on how racism affected the lives of African Americans or Native Americans; rather, I attempt to explain how whites living in North Texas constructed their concept of race.[12] Studying the problems that minorities faced is important to the understanding of racial relations, but it is also necessary to understand how whites formed their opinions of race and why they embraced the concept of white supremacy. As this study reveals, racism on the frontier stemmed from white settlers' fears of losing control of their social, economic, and political institutions.

## CHAPTER ONE

# *The Foundations of a Frontier Politician, 1825–50*

James Webb Throckmorton and his family crossed the Red River into Texas in April of 1841. James was sixteen years old at the time, and like most young men his age, he anticipated what life would be like on the rugged Texas frontier. As the Throckmorton family entered Fannin County, James's mind surely raced with thoughts of bloody encounters with Indian warriors, the thrill of hunting and exploring in virgin woods, the pleasure of fishing in gently flowing streams full of large fish, and perhaps even the endless possibilities afforded to young men living in a republic where unbridled economic opportunities abounded. Regardless of what young Throckmorton pondered as he crossed the border, he could not have envisioned the path that his life would take over the course of the next fifty years. He was destined to become a veteran of two major wars, a frontier ranger involved in Indian battles, a successful doctor and lawyer, a prominent state politician, and a member of the United States Congress.[1]

James's father, William E. Throckmorton, began his westward journey from Virginia after graduating from medical school in 1817. Having briefly practiced medicine in his home state, William migrated to Kentucky where he married Susan Jane Rotan on December 10, 1818. Three years later, the couple moved from Kentucky to Sparta, Tennessee, where they lived for several years before moving twice more, first to Illinois and then to Fayetteville, Arkansas.[2] The historical record does not reveal why the Throckmortons moved westward, but their journey was likely sparked by the same motivating factors that caused other settlers to make similar treks across the Midwest and Upper South. The majority of these early pioneers went west seeking opportunities to settle and own virgin farmlands. Others moved to escape areas heavily populated with slaves. A minority of migrants, especially doctors and lawyers, hoped to profit by providing professional services to the people living along the frontier. Given that William was a practicing physician, he likely believed the western states were ideal for establishing his medical practice.[3]

While Dr. Throckmorton probably left the Upper South for economic reasons, it was just as likely that he continued to migrate westward to escape the political and social dominance of slaveholding planters. His move from Tennessee seems to correspond with the growth of slavery in the Upper South between 1820 and 1840. During this period, slavery became increasingly important to the economy of Tennessee, especially in the middle and western portions of the state. With the growth of slavery, farmers and nonslaveholding professionals, such as lawyers and physicians, believed that the planters would soon transform Tennessee from a society with slaves into a slave society. The difference was significant for the nonslaveholding population. Though most Tennesseans believed in white supremacy and accepted the practice of slavery as a result of black inferiority, they were not willing to give up political and social control of their society to the planters who owned slaves. As a result, many of the nonslaveholding elite and farmers left the state and continued to move westward seeking a place where they could forge a society free of planters' domination.[4]

Dr. Throckmorton and his wife had a total of eight children, five of whom survived to adulthood. The three children who did not survive punctuated the difficulties and harsh realities associated with childbearing in the nineteenth century. The couple's fourth child, James Webb, was born on February 1, 1825, in Sparta, a small town located along the Calf Killer River.[5]

William and Susan Jane moved their family to Illinois for a brief time and then relocated to Arkansas sometime after the birth of the their fifth child, Robert Middleton, in 1836. Unfortunately, the move to Arkansas ended in tragedy for the family. Susan died on December 28, 1838, just a little over a year after giving birth to her eighth child, Nancy Hampton. While the frontier doctor and his children were no strangers to the loss of loved ones, Susan's death proved to have dire consequences for William's family, especially young James.[6]

Following his wife's death, Dr. Throckmorton concluded that he could not properly care for his three youngest children and sent them to live with friends of the family in Carthage, Tennessee. Between 1836 and 1841, James, his brother Robert, and his sister Nancy lived with William Bowman Campbell and his wife, Francis, who raised the children as if they were their own. In fact, William and Francis offered to adopt the children, but the Arkansas doctor was unwilling to give up his sons and daughter and called for his children to rejoin him in 1841 as he prepared to move to Texas.[7] Though the Throckmorton children stayed with the Campbells for only a brief time, the experience would forever change young James's life.

William Campbell was a noted Tennessee politician by the time the Throckmorton children came to live with him. His path to prominence was similar to that of other political leaders in the Upper South. Like many of his Tennessee colleagues, Campbell began his professional career as a lawyer. For nearly two years after being admitted to the state bar in 1829, he had maintained a thriving law practice in Carthage, Smith County. Beginning in 1831, the Tennessean also served as a state district attorney until the people of Smith County elected him to the state legislature in 1835. Campbell remained a member of that body until 1836. His constituents must have been impressed with his record at the state level because in 1837 they sent him to the U.S. Congress, where he served as a representative for the next six years.[8] Evidence of their relationship is limited, but it seems certain that the Tennessee sage introduced James Webb Throckmorton to the Whig Party and provided the youth with a political foundation that remained with him for the rest of his life.

The Whig Party was still in its developmental stages at the time that Throckmorton fell under its influence. The party could trace its beginnings to the early 1830s when the opponents of Pres. Andrew Jackson created a strong political alliance to challenge Jacksonian Democrats in local, state, and national elections. In conjunction with their initial organizing efforts, members of this opposition party began to call themselves Whigs, a moniker associated with the antimonarchists in eighteenth-century English politics. The name was well suited for the party, considering that the Whigs often referred to President Jackson as "King Andrew" because of his alleged usurpation of power in the federal government. According to the Whigs, the threats posed by the Jackson administration were personified in the president's declared war on the Bank of the United States, his apparent disregard for Supreme Court decisions and the Constitution, his frequent use of the veto, and his aggressive stance toward South Carolina during the nullification crisis of 1832–33. Thus, the Whigs believed they were guardians of traditional American liberties and believed they were duty bound to save the Founding Fathers' ideal of republican self-government.[9]

However noble their cause, the Whigs often found it difficult to convince the American public of the merits of their ideology. As a national phenomenon, the Whigs remained relatively weak until the late 1830s, at which time party members were successful in blaming the depression following the Panic of 1837 on their Democratic adversaries. The 1840s proved to be the heyday of the Whig Party. While remaining committed to the principles of republicanism, Whigs began to challenge the Democrats over controversial partisan issues, such as economic policies, territorial expansion, the Mexican War, and the extension of slavery into the western territories. When events in the 1850s, such as the Compromise of 1850, reduced or even ended partisan conflict over these issues, the Whigs returned to their ideological roots and positioned themselves once again as the defenders of the republican form of government and American liberties. However, Whigs were no longer concerned with executive tyranny as they had been when Andrew Jackson and his handpicked successor, Martin Van Buren, occupied the White House. The new threats they confronted were multifaceted but primarily grew out of the division in the country over slavery and its expansion westward.[10]

Beginning in the early 1850s, slavery not only divided party membership along the Mason-Dixon Line, but it also drove a wedge between southern Whigs as well. Southern Whigs included prosperous slave owners, merchants, and professional men. Though most Whigs in the South agreed that slavery was a legitimate labor system, the faction of professional men who did not own slaves believed that slave owners would eventually dominate the political and social institutions of their section if left unchallenged: nonslaveholding southerners feared becoming "white slaves" of the planters. In other words, they feared that the planter class would control the political affairs of the southern states and would pass legislation favorable to slaveholders and injurious to those individuals who did not own slaves. This was unacceptable to Whigs, who embraced the traditional concept of republicanism. As a result of the divisions caused by the slavery issue, the Whig Party slowly withered until it ultimately died in the mid-1850s.[11]

Nevertheless, during the time when James Throckmorton lived in the Campbell household, the Whig Party enjoyed a large measure of success in the Upper South, especially in Tennessee and Kentucky. Whig politicians and voters in the region seemed to embrace the principles that Henry Clay espoused in his American System. Like Clay, party members contended that commercial progress and economic interdependence between the various sections of the country benefited the country as a whole. Generally speaking, Upper South Whigs were businessmen and professionals who supported economic growth through the nationally chartered banks, federal funding of internal improvements (especially railroad development), and the congressional tariffs that Whigs deemed necessary for raising sufficient capital and generating industrial growth. Because they supported Clay's American System and because of their devotion to the republican form of government, Whigs tended to be staunch conservatives and steadfast advocates of the Union. As a result, Upper South Whig supporters frowned on radical political movements that threatened to divide the United States along sectional lines. Therefore, Upper South Whigs were often critical of the abolitionists in the North as well as proslavery extremists in the South.[12] William Campbell was a Whig of the Upper South stripe, and young James Throckmorton followed closely in his mentor's footsteps.

William Throckmorton, who remained in Arkansas after sending his children to Tennessee, recovered from the death of his first wife and began to court Malinda Clements. Though Malinda was twenty-eight years younger than her suitor, the couple married on January 24, 1841.[13] Now more secure in his ability to take care of a family, William sent for his children. With his family reunited, Throckmorton decided to relocate once again, moving this time to the Republic of Texas. Texans had won their independence from Mexico in 1836 and now held economic opportunities for men who were willing to brave the elements of a wild frontier. William immediately recognized the potential riches that could be made by migrating to Texas: First, he knew that doctors would be in great demand in frontier settlements. Second, he knew that early pioneers could make substantial financial gains from land speculation, especially buying and selling town lots.

The Throckmorton family crossed the Red River and entered the northern part of Fannin County in April of 1841. They stayed in the small community of Warren for several months while waiting to secure headright grants for lands farther into the interior of the Republic. Once these grants were secured, William and eight other men moved in a southwestern direction to an unsettled area along the eastern bank of the Trinity River. Throckmorton proposed creating a settlement near the present-day town of McKinney, but his companions disagreed and decided that they should settle a section of land along Rowlett Creek.

Dissatisfied with the group's plan, William returned to Warren where his family was waiting for him. In December of 1841 he secured a conditional headright certificate for lands on the banks of the Trinity River from the board of land commissioners of Fannin County. With his new grant in hand, William and another small group of settlers, including the families of

Throckmorton Creek. William E. Throckmorton settled his family along the banks of Throckmorton Creek in the early 1840s. The Throckmorton home was located northwest of the present-day town of McKinney, Texas. *Courtesy of Kenneth W. Howell.*

Thomas Rattan, Hogan Witt, and John M. Kincade, set out to settle their new claims. However, after arriving, they discovered that other pioneers had already settled on their lands. Pleasant Wilson, who was serving as a guide to Throckmorton and the others, suggested that the group retreat to the eastern fork of the Trinity River and build their homes near its banks. Following Wilson's advice, the families decided to settle an area northeast of the present-day town of McKinney along a creek that they named Throckmorton Creek in honor of their leader. Their settlement constituted one of the earliest Anglo communities in present-day Collin County.[14]

The families who moved into North Texas faced many hardships in their new frontier surroundings. They had to overcome the daunting task of preparing their lands for cultivation, building new homes, and defending themselves from Indian raids. The first two tasks were made easier by the fact that the soil was fertile and well suited for agriculture.[15] The land also provided the settlers with an ample supply of timbers for building new homes and barns. Additionally, the surrounding forests were teeming with an abundance of wild game, which offered an endless source of sustenance for the pioneers.[16] However, the threats of raiding Indians proved most troubling for the new settlers.

One of the most devastating Indian attacks in the region occurred in 1842. The families of Wesley Clements and Peg Whistler built a small settlement near Honey Creek, approximately eight miles north of William Throckmorton's home, which became known as Fort Throckmorton because surrounding settlers tended to congregate there when threats of Indian raids seemed imminent. As Clements and his companions were cutting logs to finish work on their cabins, an unidentified group of Indians attacked and killed them. The wives and children watched the brutal attack from the Clementses' cabin. One of the women had attempted to take a gun to her husband, but the attackers forced her to retreat into the safety of her home. The natives moved toward the settlers' house but were turned away when the women fired several shots in their direction. The female defenders remained in the cabin until nightfall, and then they went to the side of their fallen men. After assessing their circumstances, the women decided that Catherine Clements and her children would remain with the slain bodies during the night to keep them from being devoured by wild animals while Mrs. Whistler walked to Fort Throckmorton to seek help from other white inhabitants in the area. The following day, Dr. Throckmorton with the aid of other settlers rescued Mrs. Clements and recovered the bodies of Wesley and Peg. The families interred the slain men in a cemetery near the Throckmortons' home.[17]

The Indian raid undoubtedly was etched into James Throckmorton's mind, especially considering that Wesley Clements was his stepmother's brother. The attack served to strengthen young Throckmorton's resolve to protect the settlers from future raids. Between 1842 and 1843, he served as a member of Capt. Jesse Stiff's ranger company, which patrolled the North Texas region, guarding against future Indian depredations. Despite his age, James eventually became a sergeant of a company of sixteen men from Fannin County. Perhaps because of his family's personal loss, or as a result of his experiences as a frontier ranger, J. W. Throckmorton dedicated the remainder of his life to protecting the frontier settlers.[18]

Within a year of the attack on Wesley Clements's home, Throckmorton suffered another personal loss that would eventually lead the young frontiersman to leave the wilds of Texas for the more civilized streets of Princeton, Kentucky. His father died on October 2, 1843, and was buried near the bodies of Wesley Clements and Peg Whistler. For a brief time the responsibility of taking care of his family fell on young Throckmorton's shoulders, but he was soon relieved of this obligation when his stepmother remarried in 1844.

Free of his obligations, the youthful adventurer left the harsh environment of North Texas and went to Kentucky to study medicine with his uncle, Dr. James E. Throckmorton. He stayed with his father's elder brother for approximately two years, during which time he studied medicine at Cumberland College in Princeton. Throckmorton's decision to become a physician was not a result of a personal affinity for the profession, but rather from the great admiration he had for his father and from the constant prodding of his uncle.

Throckmorton's experiences in the Bluegrass State continued to reinforce the conservative political, social, and economic views that he first learned from William Campbell.[19] Until his return to Texas in 1846, the young frontiersman had spent all his life in the Upper South states of Tennessee or Kentucky, with the exception of the two years that he had lived in North Texas.[20] He was a man of the Upper South.

While Throckmorton was studying medicine in Kentucky, Texas came to a diplomatic crossroads. Immediately after winning their independence from Mexico in 1836, a majority of Texans called for the annexation of their newly formed republic to the United States. They realized the economic potential and safety that annexation held for their fledgling country: the United States would provide them with military protection from the threats of an invading Mexican army on their southern border and marauding Indian tribes along the western frontier. Annexation also held the promise of greater economic security and development, which would ultimately result from increased migration into Texas from the United States.[21]

While the majority of white Texans agreed that annexation was in the best interests of their homeland, American sentiments were divided over the issue. Generally speaking, the divisions in the United States followed sectional lines. Southern slaveholders and land speculators hoped to profit from the fertile lands of East Texas, especially along the navigable rivers inside the borders of the Republic. Southern planters welcomed the idea that Texas could potentially increase the South's influence in the federal government, thus aiding in their efforts to secure slavery where it already existed and to extend the peculiar institution into the western territories where its propagation was in question. John C. Calhoun, senator from South Carolina and a prominent spokesman of the South, clearly defined the motivations of most southern planters in his public pronouncement that the annexation of Texas was necessary for the continued expansion of slavery.[22]

In the North, annexation of Texas provoked staunch resistance, primarily from three groups: abolitionists, Free Soilers, and northern Whigs. Countering the arguments of men like Calhoun, both the abolitionists and the Free Soilers strongly opposed adding the Republic to the Union. They could not countenance the extension of slavery or its long-term existence in their nation. In this regard the abolitionists and Free Soilers seem to have been socially and politically in step with antislavery movements outside the United States, especially in the British Empire, where slaves were emancipated in the early 1830s. Thus, the annexation of Texas reopened debate over the institution of slavery, an issue that had plagued the country from its inception.[23]

Politicians in the Upper South, especially members of the Whig Party, tended to be more temperate in their opposition to the annexation of Texas. Attempting to avoid the controversial sectional issue of slavery, the Whigs and some moderate Democrats opposed annexation because they feared such action would ultimately lead to war with Mexico, which still had not formally recognized the independence of Texas. Whigs, including Throckmorton, understood that a rift between their southern and northern party members would develop if slavery became an issue in future elections and that such divisions could potentially destroy their party.[24]

Even though the opponents of annexation were successful in defeating an annexation treaty in the U.S. Senate in April of 1844, they failed to prevent the Republic from joining the Union the following year. Democrat James K. Polk's presidential victory on an expansionist platform in November of 1844 placed the question of annexation before Congress once again. Riding the tide of expansionism, John Tyler, the lame duck president, proposed that annexation of Texas should be placed before Congress as a joint resolution, thus requiring only a majority vote in both houses of Congress rather than the two-thirds vote needed in the Senate for approval of a treaty that annexationists had failed to win in previous attempts. The joint resolution quickly gained a favorable vote in both houses, and President Tyler signed the bill on March 1, 1845.[25] The spirit of manifest destiny proved too strong for its opponents to overcome, and the United States moved to officially annex the Lone Star Republic.[26]

Just as Whig politicians had warned, Mexican officials became enraged that the United States had annexed territory that the Mexicans believed still belonged to their country. While diplomatic relations between the two countries deteriorated, President Polk continued to pressure Mexico to recognize the Rio Grande River as the southern border of Texas. Polk ordered American soldiers under the command of Gen. Zachary Taylor to assume a defensive position near the Rio Grande; but, because northern politicians did not favor a war, the president attempted one final effort to reach a diplomatic solution with Mexican authorities.

The primary conflict between the two countries was over the disputed territory between the Nueces and Rio Grande rivers. The Mexican government considered the Nueces River as the southernmost boundary of Texas, while the United States argued that the Treaty of Velasco established the Rio Grande as the legitimate border between Mexico and Texas. In an effort to resolve the issue diplomatically and to gain additional territory in northern Mexico, President Polk sent John Slidell to Mexico City with authorization to offer the Mexican government $30 million for the New Mexico and California territories and to push for formal recognition of the Rio Grande as the official border between the two countries. Mexico promptly rejected the offer, and Slidell returned to the United States in March 1846.[27]

With many northerners opposed to war with Mexico, Polk's hands seemed to be tied; however, on May 9, 1846, the president received word from Texas which proved to be politically advantageous to his cause. A Mexican cavalry unit in late April engaged General Taylor's men in a brief skirmish along the Rio Grande border. Although the skirmish took place in disputed territory, Polk addressed the U.S. Congress and asked them for a formal declaration of war. The president in dramatic fashion stated, "Mexico has passed the boundary of the United States, has invaded our territory, and shed American blood on American soil. She has proclaimed that hostilities exist and that the two nations are now at war."[28] After a few days of deliberation, Congress agreed with Polk's assessment and issued a war resolution against Mexico.[29]

James W. Throckmorton had returned to Texas by the time the Mexican War erupted. Possessing the same adventurous spirit that had prompted his father to move westward, he joined a company of volunteers from Collin County on February 2, 1847. The company mustered into Capt. Robert H. Taylor's Company B, Texas Mounted Volunteers, at San Antonio later the same month. Along with two other companies of Texas Rangers, Captain Taylor's command remained in San Antonio until Antonio Canales, a Mexican rancher turned freedom fighter, declared all-out guerilla war against American troops stationed in northern Mexico on April 4, 1847. Following Canales's pronouncement, Texas Ranger Mike Chevallie, a close friend of Capt. Jack Hays, gathered up the Ranger companies stationed at San Antonio with the intention of moving south to engage the enemy. As was customary with the volunteer units, an election was held, and the men chose Chevallie as their commander. Chevallie and his men rode to the garrison at Camargo, Mexico, reaching their destination on April 23. Two days later the group proceeded to Monterey where the men were officially designated as Chevallie's Battalion and placed under the command of Gen. John Wool at Saltillo. During these early months the men saw only sporadic action primarily defending themselves from Mexican bandits and Indians along their way to join Wool's command.[30]

The trip from San Antonio to Mexico proved difficult for many of Captain Taylor's troops. A number of the men became too sick and too tired to continue the march to Mexico and were left behind in the desert to fend for themselves. Relying on his medical skills, Throckmorton requested to stay behind with these men in an effort to keep them alive. Captain Taylor agreed.

The volunteers' condition slowly deteriorated as they ran out of water and food. Just when all seemed lost, George Wilson, another volunteer from Collin County, ran across the ragged group. Many years after the incident, Wilson recalled finding these men in the desert. He stated, "I carried a large can of water in my wagon. It was a great ten-gallon can. Well, sir, one day I was driving across the sandy waste, southwest of San Antonio, when I came across a lot of sick men." Wilson continued, "As soon as I yelled I saw Jim Throckmorton coming toward me. Throckmorton carried the water to the men, never touching a drop for himself until all the others had gotten enough." Wilson also recalled that "the men told me that Throckmorton had given every drop of water out of his can to the sick . . . and had gone days without any food."[31] Throckmorton had treated his fellow soldiers honorably, but this incident took a toll on the young physician's health. While evidence is thin, it appears that Throckmorton never rejoined his battalion, as failing health forced him to accept a medical discharge at Camargo on June 8, on a surgeon's certificate of disability.[32] After just five months of military service, Throckmorton began the long journey home.

The North Texan returned to Collin County after receiving his discharge.[33] He established a medical practice near the town of McKinney and soon after began to court Ann Rattan, the daughter of Thomas and

Gilean Rattan of Carrollton, Illinois. The Rattan and Throckmorton families moved to the Texas frontier at about the same time, and it is probable that James became smitten with Annie before moving to Kentucky to study medicine with his uncle. Regardless of when they met, the couple, along with other members of the Rattan family, traveled to Greene County, Illinois, where the two exchanged wedding vows on January 20, 1848. Following their wedding, the newlyweds returned to Collin County where Throckmorton continued his medical practice.[34]

Annie Throckmorton epitomized the frontier woman. One twentieth-century journalist stated that her "disposition was even and lovely—if anything, too utterly unselfish and self-sacrificing. She was religious without being fanatical, living rather than talking her religion."[35] The early years of her life on the frontier must have been difficult for Ann; she not only gave birth to ten children in the isolation of North Texas wilderness, but her husband was one of the only doctors in the Collin County area, and so was often away from home for several days at a time on professional calls. Not only did Mrs. Throckmorton have to take care of her family during her husband's absence, but she had to cope with unanticipated dangers commonly experienced on the frontier.

One incident in Annie's life reveals both her personal courage and the unusual circumstances of life on the periphery of Anglo civilization. Early one morning as dawn broke, Annie noticed in the distance an approaching group of unidentified Native Americans. While she knew that her husband had developed friendly relationships with nearby tribes, she was chilled to the bone when the chief of the tribe bent over and lifted her baby from the cradle and gently held him in his arms. Years afterward Ann was reported to have said of the episode, "I thought I should die of fear and loathing, yet for peace's sake it must be endured."[36]

Annie also helped her husband care for his patients. If one of the patients required long-term treatment, he brought the individual home, using his place as a makeshift hospital, especially when great distances made it impossible for him to care for the patient on a daily basis. Mrs. Throckmorton recalled one case that involved a little girl who was almost blind. The young patient came to the doctor's home for treatment. Because light seemed to irritate her eyes, the doctor confined the little girl to a bed in a dark room for more than a month. The entire time, Annie nursed and cared for the girl's every need. After about two months, her husband decided that the child was well enough to go back home, but when her parents arrived to pick her up, she grabbed Mrs. Throckmorton by the neck and began screaming that she did not want to leave. Despite her heartfelt pleas, the parents took their daughter home with them. However, the girl continued to grieve and cry so much that she once again developed problems with her vision. As a result, her parents brought their daughter back to the Throckmorton residence where she remained for almost a year before Annie could persuade her to return home.[37] This was the life of a frontier doctor's wife.

Throckmorton continued to work as a physician for more than a year, but the strain of taking care of patients began to take its toll on his health. Also, he did not possess his father's ardor for the medical profession. Thus, the young frontier doctor made a fateful decision to pursue a career in politics. While many men changed their occupations in the fluid society of nineteenth-century America, this decision must have been extremely difficult for him, because it meant abandoning the path that his father and uncle had prepared for him. Not only did Throckmorton have to overcome emotional ties to the profession, but he also worried about whether he could take care of his family on a politician's salary. As a result, he decided to engage in an occupation that was typically seen as a steppingstone to a viable political career: he became a lawyer. While continuing to practice medicine on a limited scale, Throckmorton studied law in 1849 and was admitted to the Texas bar the following year. During this time, he also became involved in local politics.[38]

One of the most controversial political issues affecting Collin County in the late 1840s and early 1850s involved conflicting land claims between settlers and the colonizing company of the ill-fated Peters Colony. The history of the Peters Colony began when Texas was still a republic. About the same time that the Throckmorton family arrived in Texas in 1841, the Fifth Congress of the Republic of Texas began rethinking their nation's land policies. Just as in previous congressional meetings, the Fifth Congress realized that land donations were necessary to entice settlers to migrate to their country. These settlers were deemed vital to the future stability and prosperity of the Republic. However, unlike earlier congresses, the Texas government believed that granting headrights to settlers was not sufficient to bring new immigrants into the country. Therefore, the Fifth Congress turned to the old Mexican empresario system in an effort to promote greater migration to Texas. The congressmen considered three immigration bills in 1841: the Franco-Texienne bill, the Ben Fort Smith bill, and the Peters Colony bill. Of the bills proposed, only the Peters Colony bill passed both houses of the Texas Congress on February 4, 1841.[39]

The promoters of the Peters Colony consisted of twenty men, eleven from England and nine from Louisville, Kentucky. None of them had been to Texas or were qualified to fulfill the state's directives for settling the colony. The primary leader of the colonizing effort was William S. Peters, a music teacher who had migrated to Louisville from England. Peters, along with his three sons, who were also musicians, and a group of friends in England proposed the colonizing venture on a whim. It was the plan of idle dreamers unsuited for the task of settling the frontier.[40]

The Peters Colony bill authorized the administrators of the colony to settle six hundred families in an area between the Trinity and Red rivers. Each family moving into the colony was to receive a free grant of 640 acres of land. As payment for its administrative duties, the company received sixty sections of premium land for each family that moved into the colony.[41] The Kentuckians eventually organized themselves into the Texas Agricultural, Commercial and Manufacturing Company and sold a few shares of stock, but they failed to attract any measurable number of settlers during their first year of operation.

Despite the company's uneventful beginnings, W. S. Peters and his business partners eventually brought some ten thousand to twelve thousand people into North Texas before 1850. Many of these settlers came from states of the Ohio Valley, the northeastern part of the United States, and the Upper South.[42] Unfortunately for the Peters Colony, the administrators never effectively lived up to their responsibilities, and the colony continued to be plagued with controversy until the time it was dissolved in 1852.

In May 1849, James W. Throckmorton became actively involved with a movement to protect the rights of settlers against the owners of the Peters Colony grant. Primarily due to its inept leadership, the company had failed to provide the settlers with free and clear titles to their lands. The people of Collin County chose Throckmorton as one of their delegates to a meeting in Dallas, which was called by the people living in the Peters and the Mercer colonies for the express purpose of writing a memorial to the state legislature.[43] The settlers hoped that their memorial would convince the legislators to recognize the legitimacy of their claims, something that the companies' agents were unable or unwilling to do.[44]

Two aspects of this meeting were important to Throckmorton's future political career: First, the North Texan had the opportunity to associate with men who were quickly rising to political prominence in the state, such as the noted lawyer and politician from Henderson County, John H. Reagan. Second, this meeting was one of the first times that the Collin County doctor had an opportunity to formulate and express his political views, marking the beginning of James Webb Throckmorton's political career.

Once the convention settled, the delegates elected officers, selecting Throckmorton as secretary. In addition, he was appointed to a committee charged with the duty of writing a memorial that expressed the objectives and wishes of those assembled at Dallas. The committee members called on the state legislators to give the settlers full title to the lands they claimed, explaining that they were "fully satisfied in our own minds that both of the colonial contracts have been forfeited," and therefore there was no other way for them to obtain their lands except through legislative action. Furthermore, the delegates emphasized that "numbers of citizens [had] been justly entitled to patents to their lands for three and four years, and the withholding of which . . . [had paralyzed] the energies of our citizens." Finally, the committee argued that "it [was] the bounden duty of all good governments to foster the interests of her citizens."[45]

Throckmorton barely made it home from the Dallas convention when he was afforded another opportunity to serve the people of Collin County. On June 12, 1849, the leading citizens of the county held a meeting at the courthouse in McKinney for the purpose of electing delegates to a convention that was to convene on July 4 in Palestine, Anderson County, Texas. The Palestine convention was scheduled to consider the selection of a suitable place to locate the state capital. According to the 1845 state constitution, the state had to designate a permanent location for its capital, opening the way for its possible relocation.[46]

Throckmorton was once again appointed to a committee charged with the task of drafting a preamble and resolution that would be read at the Palestine meeting. Also, he had the opportunity to become further acquainted with Reagan, who had earlier attended the gathering in McKinney to give a speech concerning the importance of relocating the capital closer to the densely populated areas of East Texas. It seems likely that Reagan privately began to seek support for relocating the capital in Palestine, especially considering that the Henderson County lawyer was making plans to move there himself.[47] Though East Texans failed in their bid to move the capital, Throckmorton gained new political allies by supporting Reagan's relocation plan.[48]

At the same time that Throckmorton was becoming more actively involved in local politics, Collin County was going through economic, social, and political changes. Economically, the county was still heavily populated with yeoman farmers. These small farmers primarily grew wheat, corn, and a variety of vegetables. They also raised domesticated animals, especially pigs, which were the mainstay of the southern diet. Additionally, farmers supplemented their diet with the plentiful supply of wild animals and fowls from the surrounding forests. Despite the region's rural conditions, several of the frontier hamlets were beginning to evolve into fledgling towns, including Buckner, McKinney, Farmersville, Plano, Millwood, Rock Hill, Roseland, Mantua, Lone Tree, Highland, Rowlett Creek, and Weston.[49]

As the county became more populated, these budding towns began to establish small general stores and grist mills; some of the larger communities even had livery stables and saloons. As trade became increasingly important in the late 1840s and early 1850s, the people of Collin County became more interested in internal improvements. Goods such as tea, sugar, coffee, and finished cloth were often freighted into the county by wagon. For example, Collin County residents carried on an extensive trade with merchants in the town of Jefferson in Marion County, which was approximately 140 miles to the east of the North Texas county.[50]

Throckmorton took note of the economic circumstances facing the inhabitants of North Texas and realized that conditions would not improve unless a viable mode of transportation could be found. Mass transportation in the mid-nineteenth century was itself going through evolutionary changes. In the first half of the century improvements in transportation were primarily limited to the construction of roads and canals. However, by the 1850s, railroads were spreading across the American landscape and were seen as the most practical method of transportation. Thus, at an early stage in his political career, the North Texas politician supported the idea of constructing railroads in North Texas as a viable means of improving the economy of all the Red River counties.

Throckmorton was not the only one who understood the importance of railroad development. Following the Mexican War, Americans began to contemplate building a transcontinental railroad that would connect California and the growing industrial centers on the East Coast. Texans took great interest in the idea of connecting East with West by rail, and their representatives pressed the national government to build the road west through their state. During the late 1840s, Texas legislators offered the federal government vast tracts of public lands in exchange for the railroad. However, Congress did not see the immediate potential in the undeveloped lands of Texas and declined the state's offer.[51]

Despite early setbacks, railroad development remained on the minds of Texans throughout the 1850s because they realized that a rail line through their state would provide them access to new markets, would increase migration into the state, and would potentially inflate the price of land. Many East Texas cotton producers also understood that railroad development held political and economic advantages. East Texans had a substantial investment in slaves and were eager to advance their peculiar institution farther west. Potentially, railroads would make it profitable for North Texas planters to grow cotton instead of wheat, considering that the rails would afford North Texas planters a cheaper way to ship their goods to established trading centers such as Jefferson, Texas, and New Orleans, Louisiana.

Irrespective of the dreams of East Texas planters, many people already living in the northern part of the state cared little about cotton production. North Texas in the late 1840s and 1850s primarily was made up of wheat farmers and stock raisers. For these individuals, the rails promised to provide a feasible way to sell their wheat and livestock to outside markets. Throckmorton sympathized with this group of settlers during the 1850s, and consequently, their needs shaped his political views. Nevertheless, the young politician was astute enough to realize that if North Texas was to benefit from railroad construction, he would have to work with proslavery advocates, who were primarily members of the Democratic Party.[52]

Throckmorton entered state politics in the early 1850s as a die-hard member of the Whig Party, following the political philosophies that he had learned from William Campbell in Tennessee and James E. Throckmorton in Kentucky. If presidential elections are an indication, he was not alone in his support of the Whig Party in North Texas. In the elections of 1848, 1852, and 1856, Whig presidential candidates garnered more than 30 percent of the vote in North Texas. For example, Gen. Zachary Taylor received favorable support in the northern part of the state during his 1848 bid for the presidency even though the Whig candidate had made unsavory comments about the character of Texas volunteers in the Mexican War and despite the fact that his party had been divided over the issue of annexation and support for the Mexican War. In 1852 Gen. Winfield Scott, who reportedly had ties with northern abolitionists and was unpopular in many parts of the state, still received a sizable vote in North Texas, especially in Collin County. If the Whigs had put forth candidates friendlier to the state in these elections, they likely would have received an even larger proportion of votes.[53] Throckmorton's election to state office in 1851 proved that favorable Whig candidates could win elections in North Texas.

As the young Throckmorton left Collin County for Austin, he undoubtedly reflected on his frontier experiences that had influenced his view of the world. Recalling the numerous emotional and physical obstacles on his way to Texas, none more tragic than witnessing the deaths of his parents and three siblings, Throckmorton could take solace in the fact that each loss brought new opportunities. The loss of his mother forced him to move in with the Campbell family, where he was introduced to Whig political ideology, and where he learned core values and principles that later would shape his own career as a frontier politician. The death of his father caused him to move in with his uncle in Kentucky, where he learned the medical profession, one that earned him a living once he moved back to Texas. His professional endeavors gave him a measure of respectability within his North Texas community and explained in part why the people of Collin County trusted him to represent their interests in the state legislature. The medical profession also endeared Throckmorton to the people of his region. While treating his patients, he was able to develop close personal relationships with many of the people of Collin County. It seems certain that Throckmorton's compassion for his fellow citizens led him to protect their interests in the halls of the state legislature throughout the 1850s. Having married and settled along the South's westernmost frontier, Throckmorton probably thought his life would eventually become more settled and tranquil. Little did he realize, his adventures were only beginning.

## CHAPTER TWO

# *Guardian of the Frontier, 1851–57*

The 1850s promised to be years of hope and optimism for many Texans. During the previous decade, the United States had annexed the Lone Star Republic, and the state's citizens were consumed by the spirit of manifest destiny that was pervasive among most southern Anglos. In 1848, shortly after the United States annexed Texas, miners found gold in California, further expediting America's push westward. For American expansionists all seemed to be progressing well; however, the gold rush in California held grave political consequences for the United States.[1]

California's population exploded following the gold strikes of 1848, and it soon became eligible to apply for statehood. As a result, debate over the expansion of slavery in the territories reached a feverish pitch. Many northern politicians, especially members of the Free Soil Party, argued that the South's undemocratic practice of slavery would spread westward. Conversely, southerners believed that they had a constitutional right to carry their "human property" into the territories. Thus, the primary question confronting both northern and southern politicians was whether California would enter the Union as a free or slave state.[2]

Before tensions erupted into open warfare, Congress passed the Compromise of 1850. Originally proposed in January of 1850 by the Great Compromiser, Henry Clay, and then later maneuvered through Congress in September of the same year by Sen. Stephen A. Douglas, the Compromise of 1850 was a multifaceted plan that made concessions to both northern and southern states. It called for an end to the slave trade in Washington, D.C.; for a more stringent fugitive slave law; for popular sovereignty to determine the status of slavery in the Utah and New Mexico territories; and for California to enter the Union as a free state. Additionally, the compromise provided a settlement of the Texas and New Mexico boundary dispute, which had festered since the end of the Mexican War. This dispute centered on the legitimate boundary between Texas and New Mexico. Texas claimed the Rio Grande to its source as its western boundary, which included a large segment of present-day eastern New Mexico. The compromise stipulated that Texas would relinquish its claims to lands in New Mexico and established the present-day boundary between the two states. In an effort to compensate Texas for its territorial losses, Congress offered the Lone Star State a ten-million-dollar indemnity payment.[3]

While Texans bristled at the enormous loss of land on their western border, they understood the value of the indemnity clause. The money allowed the state to pay off the public debt it had incurred during the period of the republic and early statehood. Thus, after Congress passed the bill and Pres. Millard Fillmore signed it into law in November 1850, Texans voted overwhelmingly to accept the Compromise of 1850.[4]

The Compromise of 1850 had temporarily settled the sectional divide over slavery, and therefore, Throckmorton entered politics during a period of relative political calm. Unfortunately, there is no record of his views regarding the compromise. Though he may have been concerned about the aspects that favored the planter class, he later supported using the indemnity payment to fund railroad development in the state.

In 1851 Throckmorton campaigned for a seat in the Fourth Texas Legislature as a representative for the Twenty-fifth District, which included both Collin and Denton counties. Running as a Whig candidate, Throckmorton easily defeated his opponents, A. Johnson and Jacob Baccus. In his home county, Throckmorton received 157 votes; Johnson garnered 132 and Baccus gathered 25. Baccus fared better in Denton County, receiving 63 votes to his opponents' combined total of 44. The total vote count in the district was 421, with 221 ballots going to Throckmorton, sending the former frontier doctor to Austin.[5]

Once he arrived in Austin, Throckmorton devoted his attention to three primary local issues: the settlement of land claims in the Peters Colony, the development of railroads in North Texas, and the defense of the northern frontier against Indian depredations. These issues were paramount to preserving the yeoman farmers' political and social control of their communities. Conflicting land claims in the Peters Colony produced violent reactions and threatened public safety in the region. By 1850 settlers in the colony turned to the state legislature for relief from the unscrupulous activities of the Texas Land and Emigration Company. North Texans also viewed internal improvements vital to their economic existence; they readily supported Throckmorton's promotion of railroad development. Finally, North Texans pushed the legislature to provide them with adequate protection from Indian raids. White settlers had continually encroached on the Native Americans' lands since the earliest Anglo settlements in Texas, and the tribes struck back with fury. Once Texas was annexed to the United States in 1846, the federal government attempted to defend the frontier regions of the state, but according to frontiersmen, the soldiers posted on the fringes of civilization had offered little protection. Consequently, at the wishes of his constituents, Throckmorton called on the state to provide ranger companies to protect the people of North Texas.[6]

In January 1852, legislators sought to resolve the Peters Colony controversy. Leaders appointed a joint committee to investigate charges that the settlers had made against the promoters of the Peters Colony. Rep. R. P. Crump and Sen. G. W. Hill, who served as chairmen of the committee, reviewed the arguments presented by the settlers' hired counselor, John H. Reagan. The colonists primarily complained that the agents of the Texas Land and Emigration Company had not properly surveyed their property and had failed to provide them with clear titles to their lands. The settlers further claimed that the company had told them to settle any sections within the colony that they found convenient but that later the company's officials forced those individuals who had settled on even-numbered sections to move off their lands, stating that those sections legally belonged to the company. Also, the company had not lived up to its contractual agreement to build cabins for the settlers and to provide them with guns and ammunition. After carefully considering the colonists' claims and investigating records from the secretary of state and commissioner of the General Land Office, the joint committee reported that the promoters had made every effort possible to comply with the terms of their contractual agreements.[7] The committee's findings did little to alleviate the problems between the settlers and the promoters, and as a result, Representative Throckmorton and Sen. James H. Armstrong proposed a compromise measure in the legislature that was designed to provide relief to the settlers.[8] Fearing that the legislature would side with the settlers, the company sued the state land office.

The Throckmorton compromise, as it was known, stipulated that if the promoters withdrew their suit against the General Land Office and relinquished their rights within twenty days, the state would dismiss any legal actions the government was considering against their company.[9] The compromise measure required the settlers to claim their land before August 4, 1852. Because the company would potentially lose its best lands to the settlers' claims, Throckmorton proposed that the state grant the promoters an additional two thousand sections of land. After being formally submitted to the legislature in the form of a bill, the compromise passed both houses on February 3, 1852, and Gov. Peter H. Bell signed it into law seven days later.[10]

The settlers found little to celebrate in the compromise. They believed that the new law favored the Texas Emigration and Land Company, and they objected to the reinstatement of H. O. Hedgcoxe as the company's agent in Texas. The colonists had earlier forced Hedgcoxe from his office in the late 1840s, believing that he had cheated them out of their land titles. After the legislature reinstated him, the recalcitrant Hedgcoxe continued to provoke the wrath of the settlers by denying approximately four hundred of them title to their lands, stipulating that he was acting under the dictates of the 1852 legislation. Actually, Hedgcoxe's interpretation of the law was inaccurate because the legislators had specifically said that the Texas Emigration and Land Company could not act against the interest of the settlers.[11]

Discontent soon matured into rebellion. A group of settlers met in Springfield, Limestone County, on April 28, 1852, and penned a list of grievances against the company. The delegates' complaints paralleled the arguments that the settlers had earlier presented to the state legislature. However, the Springfield delegates viewed the law of 1852 as unconstitutional and in violation of an ordinance passed during the constitutional convention of 1845. The ordinance declared that the state's attorney general should institute legal proceedings against the company and that the original contracts between the Texas Emigration and Land Company were voided if the settlers' charges against the company proved valid. More important to the Springfield delegates' argument, the members of the constitutional convention stated that the legislature did not have the authority to extend further time limits for the settlement of the necessary number of families, or to relieve the company from forfeiture resulting from its noncompliance with the requirements of the contract. The Springfield convention contended that the people of Texas ratified the ordinance when they voted on the new state constitution. However, the delegates were mistaken in their assessment of the ordinance; it never was a part of the Texas Constitution, as it was not presented to the U.S. government for its approval at the time of annexation. Before adjourning, the Springfield convention agreed to petition Governor Bell to call a special session of the Texas Legislature to nullify the 1852 compromise law, and encouraged the delegates present to organize additional conferences in other areas of the colony.[12]

In response to the Springfield delegates' call for further conventions, the Peters Colony settlers organized another meeting in Dallas on July 10 with the intention of discussing possible solutions to the problems. At the meeting, delegates formed a committee to confer with Hedgcoxe at the company's office near McKinney and to invite him to submit the company's records for investigation. Through their actions, the delegates hoped to reach a compromise with the company. The members at the Dallas meeting then adjourned, agreeing to reconvene on July 15 to hear the committee's report. But when the convention resumed, the attendees discovered that the committee had failed to complete its task. The disgruntled members grew impatient and decided that more radical measures were needed to protect the settlers' claims. By resolution, they voted to censure Sam Bogart, the state senator for the Dallas district, and called for his resignation on the grounds that he had not properly represented the interest of the people living in the Peters Colony. Senator Bogart's most damning action had been his support of the 1852 compromise law.[13]

Inflamed by the spirit of the Dallas meeting, John J. Good led a group of approximately forty colonists in a raid of Hedgcoxe's office on July 16. They intended to force the company's agent to turn over the records in question. Having returned to Collin County at the conclusion of the regular session of the Fourth Legislature, Throckmorton had learned of Good's intentions. Because he was opposed to solving the colonists' problems through violent means, he notified Hedgcoxe that Good and his followers were on their way to his office and that his life may be in danger. By the time that the disgruntled settlers arrived, Hedgcoxe hid some of the company's records in a nearby cornfield and eventually sought refuge there himself. However, the mob was able to confiscate the company's files still remaining in the office as well as many of Hedgcoxe's personal papers. Assuming that Hedgcoxe was hiding within earshot, the rowdy crowd stood outside the company's office and shouted threats to his life. Once Good and his men had dispersed from the scene, the frightened agent loaded the company records that he had placed in the cornfield into a wagon and carried them to a safe location in Bonham, Fannin County. From there, Hedgcoxe forwarded the surviving records to the Texas Emigration and Land Company's headquarters in Louisville, Kentucky.[14]

The result of the mob's actions was to slow down the process of issuing land certificates to the settlers. In an effort to formulate a new strategy, representatives of the colonists agreed that delegates from each county in the Peters Colony would meet in McKinney on July 29, 1852, but before the meeting convened, a group of settlers who sought a peaceful solution to the colonists' problems met on July 20. Throckmorton was present at this meeting, but he was not an outspoken leader among the attendees. Instead, the leaders of the movement were J. C. Easton, Sam Bogart, S. R. Campbell, Alex Berry—all of Ellis County—and one Martin of Dallas County. Though Throckmorton did not assume a primary leadership role, convention delegates did acknowledge his attempt to aid the settlers. In the *Northern Standard* on August 7, delegates said that Bogart and Throckmorton's efforts in the passage of the compromise law of 1852 was "commendable" and "the best arrangement that could be made under all the circumstances, to secure [the colonists'] rights, and that the assaults upon their character and conduct in this behalf, are erroneous and unjust."[15]

On July 24, another group of disgruntled colonists met at Denton. The members of this group found no fault with the 1852 compromise law; rather, they blamed their problems on Hedgcoxe's interpretation of the law. They justified the earlier actions by stating that Hedgcoxe had attempted to force settlers from lands they had already made improvements on. The Denton delegates also demanded that Throckmorton resign his position in the legislature, not because he was the sponsor of the 1852 compromise law, but because he thwarted John Good's raid on Hedgcoxe's office, preventing the settlers from obtaining all the company's records. Thus, the Denton delegates accused Throckmorton of being sympathetic to the Texas Emigration and Land Company and siding with the company's agent in the ongoing dispute.[16]

As planned, the meeting at McKinney convened in late July. The first order of business was the organization of the conference. The attendees elected Rev. Azariah Bone of Grayson County as president of the meeting, B. P. Smith, also of Grayson County, as vice president, and J. W. Latimer of Dallas County as secretary. The president's first official act was to appoint a committee on address and resolution. Reverend Bone then adjourned the meeting until the following morning. When the meeting reconvened, the committee members suggested that the convention adopt resolutions similar to those of the earlier Denton meeting. They also suggested that the convention leaders should keep the company records that were taken from Hedgcoxe's office, unless the legislature revoked the 1852 compromise law.

Additionally, the committee called for a special session of the legislature and for the appointment of vigilance committees to keep the land company under surveillance.[17] However, it appears that the members did not call for the resignation of Bogart or Throckmorton.

The delegates voted unanimously on the resolutions, with two exceptions: Throckmorton, Bogart, and Wilcox of Collin County, and Stone of Dallas, voted against holding the stolen company records at Dallas, and Throckmorton and Bogart voted against the resolution calling for the censure of the state legislature's committee in charge of investigating the Peters Colony controversy. The McKinney convention called on Governor Bell to convene the legislature in special session in order to give relief to the settlers in the colony. In an effort to sway the legislature, the colonists' resolutions absolved those who had sponsored the 1852 compromise law and stated that the representatives and senators had passed the law with good intentions. Despite these good intentions, however, the law had caused greater confusion in the colony and had not solved the problems confronting the colonists, the delegates claimed. In response to the McKinney resolutions and other matters affecting the state, Governor Bell called the legislature into a special session on January 1853.[18]

In compliance with the Denton resolution, Representative Throckmorton resigned from the Texas House. In a letter to Governor Bell on September 15, 1852, he simply stated, "Sir, I herewithin tender you my resignation as representative of the Twenty fifth Representation District of this State."[19] Subsequently, he made plans to run for reelection in the special election that was to be held in November. This election pitted Throckmorton against S. R. Campbell, who was a leading opponent of the former representative's compromise law of 1852. Campbell campaigned for the repeal of the controversial legislation, while Throckmorton defended the compromise measure as sound but suggested that the legislative act might be amended to prevent company agents from further misinterpreting the original intent of the law. Throckmorton succeeded in his bid for reelection. Either widespread dissatisfaction in the Peters Colony was not as prevalent as agitators had suggested, or many voters believed Throckmorton had acted favorably on the behalf of the settlers.[20]

When the special session met in January 1853, the representatives were clearly divided over the issues concerning the Peters Colony. One group of legislators supported the position taken by the committee on land claims, stating that all legislation affecting the colony was contrary to an ordinance of the constitutional convention in 1845 and that all laws passed since the adoption of the Texas Constitution were unconstitutional. A second group, including Throckmorton, Bogart, and John M. Crockett, believed that the suspension of all the legislation pertaining to the colony since 1845 would only cause additional confusion in North Texas. The speaker of the house submitted the controversial issue to a special committee.

After studying all the gathered evidence, the members of the special committee proposed a bill that they thought would solve the Peters Colony controversy. Throckmorton and his political allies, however, believed that the proposed bill was unfavorable to the colonists; a sufficient number of legislators agreed with them and the bill was amended to their satisfaction. The amendments required the Texas Land and Emigration Company to temporarily surrender to the state all of its interests or claims to all sections, half sections, fractional sections, or alternate sections that it owned. Furthermore, the amendments provided that once the colonists had secured their land titles, the company could then take charge of lands that the state had originally promised it. The proposed amendments were then sent to the Judiciary Committee of which Throckmorton was a member. After careful consideration, the Judiciary Committee recommended the passage of the new bill, including the proposed amendments. Despite several motions against the new legislation, the House adopted it by a vote of thirty-six to twenty. Following Senate approval, Governor Bell signed the bill on February 4, 1853.[21]

The new law contained many of the provisions Throckmorton called for prior to the passage of the 1852 compromise law. It stated that the settlers were "confined to a country they love but cannot improve" and that the only solution was for the company to suspend its claims until the colonists' lands were registered.[22] The law attempted to solve the problem facing the settlers by placing the colonists' interest before that of the Texas Emigration and Land Company. With their land claims solidified, the settlers could now move forward with their lives on the frontier.

ANOTHER IMPORTANT ISSUE that attracted Throckmorton's attention was internal improvements, especially the development of railroads. By the 1850s, railroad construction became more pronounced in the South, especially in areas east of the Mississippi River. During this decade railroad mileage in the southern states increased fivefold, providing approximately ten thousand miles of rails by 1860. While southern rail lines were limited in comparison to those stretching across northern states, the massive growth of railroads in the South demonstrated the region's interest in improving its transportation infrastructure. The growth of railroading was directly linked to investments made by state and local governments. For example, by 1860 the state of Virginia had spent approximately $24 million and Tennessee $17 million on railroad development. While friendly to private rail lines during the antebellum period, Georgia actually operated a state-owned railroad, the Western and Atlantic line, which connected Atlanta and Chattanooga. Throughout the 1850s, southern states provided more than $81 million for the development of railroads, and local governments supplemented the states' investments with an additional $55 million. Obviously, southerners viewed railroads as essential for improving their region's economic future.[23]

Like other southerners, Texans sought to build railroads in their state. By 1861 the Lone Star State had set aside five million acres of public lands and appropriated $1.8 million in state bonds for the development of railways.[24] Texans understood that railroads would prove vital to the development of their state. A well-planned rail system held the promise of settling vacant lands, increasing taxable wealth, and building existing communities into thriving cities. A community could possibly ensure its economic greatness if it were located along the path of future rail lines. Therefore, the location of railroads became a source of heated competition among the fledgling towns of Texas.[25]

Farming communities, in particular, realized that the location of the rails would be important to their future. For East Texas planters, the iron horse represented a way to spread the cotton culture and slavery into the interior of Texas. The interior regions of the state were not accessible by navigable rivers and thus freight transportation from these areas was conducted by ox-wagons, an extremely expensive and inefficient method of carrying on commercial trade. Railroads seemed to be the only solution to opening up the fertile black lands of central and northern Texas for large-scale agriculture.[26] While some individuals in the northern part of the state in the 1850s may have envisioned reshaping their region so it more closely resembled the cotton economy of East Texas, it is more likely that North Texas farmers viewed the railways as a way to market crops that they were already producing in large quantities, especially wheat. Like the settlers in the Upper South states, North Texans understood that if they could sustain themselves economically, they might be able to thwart the migration of planters to the frontier.[27] As long as wheat crops proved profitable, small farmers could subsist on their lands and would be less inclined to sell their property to the members of the planter class. Finally, the people of North Texas understood that internal improvements would improve the overall value of their landholdings. Thus, if they did choose to sell their lands in the future, they could count on earning a substantial profit.

Regardless of the motives of railroad promoters in Texas, any extensive plans for the development of lines were not feasible as long as the Texas treasury was empty. However, in 1850 the economic fortunes of the Lone Star State had changed with the passage of the Compromise of 1850. With the $10 million indemnity bonds that Texas received in compensation for realigning its western boundaries, the state was able to retire its debts as well as set aside funding for internal improvements. The state would now seemingly have its railroads, but the questions of *where* the lines would run and *how* the roads would be constructed became topics of legislative debate.[28]

By 1852 the state legislature began issuing special grants of lands to various railroad enterprises. Two years later, legislators granted up to sixteen sections of land to railroad companies for every mile of track they completed. To ensure that the railway promoters did not fraudulently exploit the state's generous offer, the legislators required companies to build twenty-five miles of track before receiving title to their claims. In 1856 the Texas Legislature authorized loans of six thousand dollars per mile once the rail companies had laid the required twenty-five miles of track. The state incentives sparked the immediate interest of several railroad companies, almost all of which obtained charters from the state. However, most of the antebellum companies failed to produce a single mile of track, and as a result Texas remained a railroad-poor region at the end of the decade. By 1860 the Lone Star State could claim only four hundred miles of track inside its borders, a paltry number given that the state had granted thousands of acres of land and had loaned nearly $2 million to various railroad companies.[29]

Like other citizens from his region of the state, Throckmorton viewed railroad development as vital to the economic prosperity of North Texas. However, before the people could enjoy the full benefit of internal improvements, the state legislature had to settle another heated conflict over land claims in North Texas. On February 10, 1852, the legislature reserved a large portion of the northern part of the state for new settlements. The state required the settlers to obtain title to their lands before August 10, 1854. Later, on February 3, 1853, during a special session of the Fourth Legislature, legislators passed a 320-acre preemption law. To complicate matters further, in December of the same year, the Fifth Legislature created the Pacific Railroad Reserve and passed a new 160-acre preemption law that was approved on February 13, 1854. The new railroad reserve overlapped areas that legislators had earlier designated as public lands. The result was a state of confusion.[30]

Many settlers made claims to lands within the railroad reserve after the passage of the 320-acre law but before the passage of the 1854 law that limited preemption to 160 acres. These squatters met with no objection from other colonists, the Peters Company, or the state, and therefore they saw no reason why they could not improve the land and apply for title to the land after the August 1854 deadline. If the reservation had been allowed to expire as planned, the area would have remained opened for settlement, and the settlers would have won legal rights to the lands, leaving the matter problem free. However, with the creation of the Pacific Railroad Reserve, which included public lands that the squatters claimed as their own, land titles became blurred and confused. As a result, some settlers would receive 320 acres, some would receive 160 acres, and some would receive nothing depending upon when and where they claimed their lands.[31]

The issue of conflicting land claims in the railroad reserve became a major issue in the mid-1850s. In the August 1855 elections, the people of Collin, Cooke, and Denton counties reelected Throckmorton to the state legislature. He pledged to help the settlers who made land claims in the Pacific Railroad Reserve. Having been a staunch proponent of internal improvements, Throckmorton was made chairman of the internal improvement committee, which was expected to solve the problem of squatters living on the newly created railroad reserve. In November 1855, the house considered a bill that promised relief to the settlers whose land titles were in question. The bill required that the state give three hundred acres of land to the squatters regardless of when they made their claims. Additionally, the settlers would have to pay a rather substantial fee of fifty cents per acre for surveying and patenting their lands. Representative Throckmorton opposed the bill for three reasons: First, he did not believe that it provided proper relief to the squatters, especially considering that most would not be able to pay the expensive fees for obtaining title to their lands. Second, he thought that the law was too limited because it only applied to a small group of people who purchased land in the reserve and did not extend the same privilege to all citizens. Finally, he claimed that the law should apply equally to all public lands and not just those within the railroad reserve.[32]

Throckmorton proposed his own bill on the subject. Those individuals settling the region prior to the 160-acre law should receive 320 acres of land, he argued, and those who settled in the region after the 160-acre law should receive their 160 acres. Throckmorton based this conclusion on the following logic: First, many of the settlers came to the area prior to the legislative session that designated the region as part of the Pacific Railroad Reserve. As a result, the people did not move onto the land in violation of the law. Second, many settlers moved to the region during the winter that the reserve was being created and therefore had no knowledge of its existence. Finally, Throckmorton argued that the lands granted to the settlers would serve to populate the frontier regions in question, which he believed to be the original intent of the law. He feared that land speculators would soon purchase vast tracks of land, keeping the region from being settled until it became economically feasible to do so. In essence, speculators would prevent the lands from developing and consequently from increasing in value. Referring to the ordinary settlers, Throckmorton stated that "these people are industrious and comprise a most valuable class of citizens. The country where they have settled was a few years ago a vast wilderness, an uncultivated waste; but now it is covered with fine farms and is indeed one of the most flourishing parts of the state."[33] Throckmorton was also concerned that speculators would sell their holdings to members of the planter class, a proposition that the majority of small farmers in North Texas hoped to avoid. Therefore, he believed that the economic circumstances that existed in the railroad reserve would blend the interests of the railroad with the interests of the frontier agricultural communities, producing positive results for both.[34]

Throckmorton's opponents argued that the settlers were in violation of the law. They claimed that settlement within the reserve after August 1854 was illegal and that the settlers' ignorance of the law was no defense.[35] On December 5, 1855, Rep. James Hooker proposed an amendment to Throckmorton's bill that voided the land claims of those settlers who moved onto the Pacific Railroad Reserve following passage of the law that created it in December 1853. After refusing to table the amendment, the representatives moved to take an up-or-down vote on the issue, and Throckmorton again came to the settlers' defense: "Again, sir, there have never been any boundary lines run showing just where the boundary line is. How is a man who wants a home to take the exact longitude and latitude of his little claim of one hundred sixty acres of land and determine for himself whether he is in the reserve or not?"[36] Throckmorton reminded his colleagues that Texas had always maintained a liberal policy in granting land to pioneers, and to do otherwise in this case would go against well-established precedents.

Nevertheless, Throckmorton's appeal to logic and reason proved unsuccessful. The house passed the Hooker amendment and sent it to the internal improvement committee. Since Throckmorton was the chairman of this committee, he had a final opportunity to enact changes to the proposed legislation which would be more favorable to the settlers. On January 2, 1856, he offered a compromise measure to the bill, which suggested that the settlers moving into the reserve after December 21, 1853, should receive titles to their lands. Additionally, it provided that the state would not issue any further preemptions in the region. Unfortunately for the squatters, this compromise was rejected by a majority of the House members, and the bill was passed granting preemption only to those individuals who had received title to their land in the reserve before December 21, 1853. The governor signed the bill into law on January 26, 1856.[37]

This had been a fight between two opposing groups: the settlers residing in the Pacific Railroad Reserve and those individuals who wanted to advance the cause of internal improvements. Though Throckmorton was an outspoken proponent of internal improvements, he had allied himself with the settlers. He had lived among these people and could hardly refuse to defend their claims. They were his constituents, and unlike some elected officials, he felt obligated to represent their interests. Furthermore, Throckmorton believed the settlement of the reserve would aid the cause of internal improvements rather than hinder it. Determined not to accept defeat on this issue, in 1856 he renewed the fight in the state legislature.

On August 18, Throckmorton reported that the internal improvements committee was proposing a bill that "authorized the location, sale, and settlement of the Mississippi and Pacific Railroad Reserve."[38] This bill recommended that concessions be made to the colonists similar to those that Throckmorton had recommended on January 2. Throckmorton stated that "all persons who were settled upon any portion of the reserve [regardless of when they moved onto their lands] could have claim, not to exceed one hundred sixty acres, upon the payment of fifty cents per acre to the special school fund."[39] The law passed on August 26, 1856, bringing the preemption troubles to an end. Throckmorton achieved a major victory for small farmers in North Texas. As a result, his constituents deemed him a lasting friend.[40]

Even though Throckmorton had championed the rights of settlers in the Pacific Railroad Reserve, he did not turn his back on railroad development. He became consumed with the idea of establishing a transcontinental railroad route that would run through Texas—hopefully through or near his representative district. Between 1851 and 1857, Throckmorton clearly demonstrated his commitment to a Texas route by participating in various railroad conventions. The first railroad meeting that the Collin County politician attended took place in Austin on November 17, 1851. While he played only a limited role in this convention, the young North Texan became more keenly aware of the major issues confronting railroad development in Texas and was able to make the acquaintance of other railroad men in the state.[41]

On October 6, 1853, Throckmorton attended a railroad convention in Bonham, Fannin County. The meeting primarily was comprised of delegates from North Texas counties, and Throckmorton played a major role in the proceedings. The North Texans wanted a railway that would traverse the state. Speaking for the assembled delegates, Throckmorton announced that "counties should be able to take stock in Railroads under certain restrictions, by a majority of the votes of any county or counties, so expressing themselves at the ballot box."[42] Furthermore, he argued that "it would be best for the State to lay out one route to extend directly from east to west, across the State, and that such road be made the special care of the State and all her energies."[43] Finally, he proposed that the state legislature should make the Memphis, El Paso, and Pacific road the primary line through Texas, a road that would bisect the Red River counties. He argued that competing railroads in the state could connect with the Memphis, El Paso, and Pacific at various points along the road as "the want of the country demands."[44]

By 1856, however, Throckmorton changed his mind concerning the route that the transcontinental line should follow through Texas. Although he envisioned that the Memphis, El Paso, and Pacific would connect with the transcontinental road, he began to support a more centralized route for the main line through his state. As a result, he became a strong supporter of the Texas Western Railroad Company.[45] It seems obvious that Throckmorton's controversial shift in support from the Memphis, El Paso, and Pacific to the Texas Western Railroad Company resulted from his desire to compromise with other prominent railroad men living in areas outside North Texas, especially in the eastern and Gulf regions of the state.[46]

The Texas Western Railroad Company, commonly referred to as the Texas Western, promised to be a major link in a transcontinental railroad that would run through the southern part of the United States to California. On February 16, 1852, the Texas Legislature gave the company a charter to build a railroad across the state from its eastern boundary line near the

East Texas town of Waskom to the West Texas town of El Paso. The list of incorporators included notable politicians and businessmen Samuel Bogart and James Webb Throckmorton from North Texas and William T. Scott, the largest slaveholder in Harrison County. Other incorporators included James C. Hill, Rufus Doane, Lucius Clopton, Willis Stewart, E. E. Lott, L. B. Camp, and J. D. Todd. Capital stock in the company was divided into one-hundred-dollar shares, and no one was eligible to become a director unless he owned a minimum of five shares of stock. The legislature granted the company a right-of-way through state-owned lands, but it was limited to two hundred feet in width. Like other railroad charters during the era, the state promised the Texas Western eight sections of land for each mile of road it completed, but the company could not claim its land unless it laid ten miles of track during the first five years of its charter. Furthermore, if construction of the first ten miles was not complete during the allotted five-year span, or at least twenty miles of track had not been laid within six years, the state would consider the charter null and void.[47]

During the next four years, the Texas Legislature passed two new acts that promised additional benefits to the Texas Western. On January 30, 1854, new legislation provided that when railroad companies constructed twenty-five or more miles of track, they would be entitled to receive sixteen sections of land from the state for every mile completed and in operation. A little over two years later, on August 13, 1856, the Texas legislators once again passed legislation designed to speed up the construction of rail lines in the state. The new railroad act allowed companies to receive a loan of six thousand dollars from the Board of School Commissioners of Texas for every mile of track completed. Because the Texas Western planned to connect with a railroad that ran outside of the state, it was entitled by the 1856 law to receive a loan when it built as little as ten miles of track and had graded an additional ten miles. The incorporators of the Texas Western supported the various legislative changes and provided the railroad company with adequate resources with which to complete its planned line in East Texas.[48]

On August 16, 1856, the legislature officially changed the Texas Western's company name to the Southern Pacific Railroad Company. Also, a new list of incorporators was attached to the company, many of whom had been formerly associated with the Texas Western: Rufus Doane, James C. Hill, William T. Scott, Willis Stewart, Samuel Bogart, E. E. Lott, L. B. Camp, James W. Throckmorton, J. D. Todd, Joseph McDougal, Thomas H. Rogers, Adam Sullivan, Joshua Starr, C. B. Holbert, Mason Mosely, and

Jacob Fisher. Despite the change in the company's name and the slight change in the list of incorporators, the railroad still had to adhere to the time limits and obligations established by the company's original charter.[49]

In a meeting in New York on October 5, 1856, the stockholders of the Texas Western voted to accept the new company name. The stockholders also chose a board of directors that was almost evenly balanced in terms of northerners and southerners.[50] The day after the meeting, the board met for the first time and elected Horatio Allen of New York as the company's president, Edwin Post of New York as vice president, S. Jaudon as company secretary, and E. A. Blanch of Marshall, Texas, as chief engineer.[51]

The company immediately began preparations for construction of the railroad. Because of time limitations, the company had to locate its eastern terminus at the most advantageous position on the Texas and Louisiana border. The company's engineers decided on Swanson's Landing on the southern shore of Caddo Lake. The location was ideal for the construction of a new rail line: the company was able to ship necessary supplies by way of steamboats that traveled up the Red River and entered Caddo Lake at Twelve Mile Bayou.[52]

On February 11, 1858, the company completed twenty miles of track stretching from Swanson's Landing to Jonesville, a small East Texas community near Marshall. By the end of September, the company had constructed five additional miles of track toward Marshall. The company's chief engineer and C. A. Frazier, judge of the Sixth Judicial District, inspected the line, certifying that the company had fulfilled the obligation of its charter. At the end of 1858, the company could boast that its rolling stock consisted of two functional locomotives and five platform cars. In part, Throckmorton could claim credit for making it a reality.[53]

The Southern Pacific Railroad Company had accomplished what many railroads in Texas had failed to do: it fulfilled the requirements of its charter and became operational. This was no small feat considering that most of the railroad ventures west of the Mississippi River did not fare as well. In a commercial enterprise where speculation was rampant, most investors in railroad companies never saw a return on their investments. As one historian stated, "the railroads did not pay and the people found that the debts incurred were hard to meet, while railroad rates were high and prosperity did not ensue."[54] As a result, "overspeculation and overbuilding" led to a "financial depression ending in the panic of 1857, which was caused to a considerable extent by the floating of large amounts of practically worthless railroad stock and of greatly depreciated state and local bonds."[55] The trans-Mississippi railroads, including those in Texas, seemed to be ahead of their time. It was only after the western lines connected with the East in the 1860s that they began to prosper; thus, the railroads established in the 1850s in the trans-Mississippi area, including Texas, were little more than supplemental to the more vital system of river transportation.[56] Though the Southern Pacific had laid only twenty-five miles of track, Throckmorton could take some pride that he was involved in one of the few successful railroad companies west of the Mississippi River prior to the outbreak of the Civil War.

A FINAL ISSUE that captured the attention of Representative Throckmorton during the early 1850s was frontier defense. The direst problem confronting white settlers on the Texas frontier was Indian raids. This was not a new problem in the development of American frontiers. From the first arrival of Anglos in North America, conflicts existed between the two divergent groups. Just as other southerners had done during their states' formative years, Texans in the 1850s pushed Native Americans off their lands. As a result, tribes on the Texas frontier sought to defend their lands by attacking white settlements along the established frontier line.[57] These raids were of great interest to Representative Throckmorton because his home and his representative district in the Texas Legislature were located along the North Texas frontier and were vulnerable to attack.[58]

One example of the type of attacks taking place in North Texas occurred in 1850 at Farmersville, Collin County, approximately ten miles from Throckmorton's home. John Leary was working in his fields when he heard gunshots coming from the direction of his home. Leary's wife was firing at a group of Indians who were attempting to break into the Leary residence. Leary, along with his slave, ran toward his family's cabin, and upon their arrival found themselves in a precarious situation. The members of the raiding party successfully prevented them from entering the safety of the Leary cabin. Forced to confront their attackers in the open, the two men prepared to defend themselves with the only weapons in their possession at the time—the farming tools in their hands. As they struggled with the raiders, Mrs. Leary continued to fire shots from her position inside the home. Apparently her aim proved effective because the hostiles eventually retreated for cover, allowing the Leary men to gain entrance to the home. With the men safely inside the cabin, their assailants apparently decided it would be too costly to overrun the settlers' position and abandoned the fight.[59]

Reacting to such incidents, Throckmorton wrote a letter to Governor Bell asking for greater state assistance in protecting the people of the frontier. "You have doubtless before this time heard of the Indian difficulties on our immediate frontier," he noted. "Accounts that can be relied upon are coming in every day of the manifestations of the hostile interactions of some of the wild tribes."[60] After he reported on condition at Fort Phantom Hill and Fort Belknap, Throckmorton encouraged Governor Bell to "order out a sufficient force for the protection of the frontier, and to be held in readiness to aid, if necessary, in sustaining the U.S. troops at the different stations [on the frontier]."[61]

Throckmorton told the governor that his constituents believed the U.S. military had failed to protect the frontier adequately and that it was necessary for them to assume the task of ensuring their own safety. He wrote, "I have been requested by my fellow citizens to request of you, in case you should order out a volunteer force, to authorize Maj. George W. Barnett of this [Collin] county to raise a company."[62] Throckmorton continued, "In mentioning the name of Maj. Barnett I need only say to you that he has the entire confidence of the entire community. . . . I have been looking for a demonstration by the Indians upon the northern frontier—I was this spring above the Belknap—I was there satisfied of their intentions."[63] After reporting the conditions in the Belknap area, Throckmorton concluded his letter by giving his opinion of the effectiveness of U.S. troops on the Texas frontier: "it is absolutely necessary that a sufficient force should be raised and a campaign made upon the sources of Brazos and Upper Red River—the U.S. Government have willfully neglected to properly protect us, and I see no other alternative than to do it ourselves."[64]

Throckmorton's assertion that the U.S. Army had not effectively protected the frontier settlements was partly based on solid evidence. Despite the army's best efforts, the troop strength along the Texas frontier proved inadequate for the purposes of protection. Most of the frontier garrisons maintained only one company of soldiers and often these men were too sick to perform their duties. Consequently, the garrisons frequently had only twelve or fifteen men fit for duty each day. In addition, many of the frontier soldiers were infantrymen who had little experience riding horses, and even those individuals who had minimal knowledge with draft animals proved to be no match for the mounted warriors they confronted. Morale among the soldiers was dismal. Because of these circumstances, many Texans, including Throckmorton, began to demand that a better system of defense be initiated on the frontier. Most Texans encouraged the use of state ranger forces to aid the federal government's efforts. While the United States inaugurated a variety of defense programs, the results remained limited throughout the 1850s, and by the 1860s, most Texans living on the frontier believed that they could protect themselves more effectively than the U.S. Army.[65]

Governor Bell apparently agreed with Throckmorton's assessment of frontier conditions and the need for additional defense. In an address to the extra session of the Fourth Texas Legislature on January 13, 1853, Bell appealed for state funding of frontier defense. After recounting the hostile conditions on the frontier, the governor stated that he had repeatedly asked the federal government for additional aid for defense. According to Bell, the secretary of war had notified him that Pres. Millard Fillmore had asked Congress for additional men on the Texas frontier, but Congress had adjourned without taking any action. Governor Bell stated that the secretary's statement represented "an unqualified admission . . . that the United States had failed to give adequate protection to the frontier."[66]

Frontier defense remained a concern for Throckmorton throughout the 1850s. In March 1853, he made a speech favoring an appropriations bill to cover the expenses of volunteer companies on the frontier. The bill passed. Legislators also passed additional acts designed to provide greater protection on the frontier between 1855 and 1857, and in every case Throckmorton voted in favor of the defense bills.[67]

During the years that Throckmorton served in the Texas House of Representatives, he remained dedicated to issues that directly affected his constituency. He had devoted much of his attention to settling land claims in the Peters Colony, developing railroads that would benefit North Texas, and attempting to provide more efficient and adequate frontier defense to guard against the numerous raids on the Texas settlements. His actions revealed his commitment to goals that earlier settlers established upon arriving on the North Texas frontier.

Like his constituents, Throckmorton harbored certain suspicions of the planter class. These suspicions undoubtedly influenced the North Texan's view of slaves. Identifying slaves as the most visible sign of the wealth and power of the planters, Throckmorton developed an irrational hatred of them. Ironically, his hatred of the planters' slaves did not cause him to question the validity of slavery. Like most white Southerners, he did not have a problem with the institution of slavery as a legitimate labor system. Rather, he harbored animosity toward the planters who used slave labor to amass wealth and dominance in the southern states. In this regard, the accumulation of political, social, and economic power seemed to be his primary concern. Like the people he represented, Throckmorton aspired to create a society that allowed him and his constituents to retain political, economic, and social control of their lives.

However, Throckmorton's disdain for the slaves did not purely stem from his distrust of the planter class. Like other North Texans, he also strongly supported the traditional southern views of white supremacy. Evidence of his racist views was first demonstrated in his desire to remove the Native Americans from their ancestral lands. Tenaciously, Throckmorton called on state government to protect his constituents from Indian raids along the northern frontier, believing that the Native Americans had no place in white society.

As the sectional conflict over slavery in the late 1850s and early 1860s created a widening rift between the northern and southern states, Throckmorton found it increasingly difficult to protect North Texas from planter influence and from Indian raids. As Texas embraced the fanaticism of secession in 1861, Collin County's guardian of the frontier had to make difficult political decisions that eventually led him down paths he would have otherwise avoided.

# CHAPTER THREE

# *The Storm of Passion and Sectional Hatred, 1857–61*

Between 1857 and 1861 James Throckmorton continued to protect the interests of the small farmers in North Texas by focusing his attention on railroad development and frontier defense. He found it increasingly difficult, however, to concentrate his efforts on these political objectives because sectional debates about slavery began to force Texas politics in new directions. All U.S. citizens realized that the period of calm that followed the Compromise of 1850 was coming to an abrupt end.[1] In response to national events during the 1850s, southern politicians, even those on the southern frontier, were forced to choose between remaining loyal to the United States or joining the radical movement for secession. As Texans pondered the legitimacy of secession, Unionists in the state attempted to ward off the efforts of the secessionists. The Unionists' undertakings proved to be in vain as the secession movement grew too powerful to be averted.[2]

Throckmorton's experience on the frontier and his early affiliation with the Whig Party led him to oppose the fanaticism of secession. In part, his Unionism, or nationalism, can be explained by his adherence to a conservative Whig ideology, which called for political stability, economic growth, and an enduring attachment to traditional American and Protestant values. These Whiggish views led Throckmorton to champion two local issues—frontier defense and railroad development. There was little doubt in Throckmorton's mind that these two issues could only be achieved within the Union.[3] He realized that the development of a transcontinental railroad running through Texas depended on northern investment capital, and he knew that northern and western markets would prove vital to the future prosperity of North Texas.

Throckmorton also understood that the protection of the Texas frontier depended on the continued presence of the United States military. Even though settlers, including Throckmorton himself, were critical of the U.S. Army's tactics on the frontier, the soldiers did provide adequate defense against Indian raids occurring within close proximity of their assigned posts. Furthermore, the frontier units served as a potential market for North Texas crops, especially wheat and corn. The absence of the military would leave North Texans exposed to the increasing threats of Indian raids and a shrinking economy.[4]

Throckmorton's commitment to Whig political philosophy also contributed to his stance against secession. Throughout the late 1840s and early 1850s, Whigs generally supported the idea of creating a strong central government that could protect the political and economic rights of U.S. citizens. Party members' devotion to the Union often led them to resist many of the tenets that were part of the South's states' rights doctrine. Throckmorton, similar to Whigs in the Upper South, believed that the federal government could protect nonslaveholding southerners from the political, economic, and social domination of the planter class. Unfortunately for Texas Whigs, party members witnessed the decline of their political influence in the mid-1850s as their party became the first victim of the sectional debates over the Kansas-Nebraska Act.[5]

The passage of the Kansas-Nebraska Act brought the issue of slave expansion to the national stage once again. In essence, this act threatened to void the Missouri Compromise of 1820 that prohibited the extension of slavery in the Louisiana Territory above 36°30′ latitude, replacing the former restriction with the ideological concept of "popular sovereignty." According to its provision, the new law called on the first legislatures elected in the Kansas and Nebraska territories to decide whether or not slavery would exist within their borders. It was understandable that antislavery supporters in the North were outraged, viewing the measure as a triumph for proslavery advocates. Likewise, southern slaveholders were pleased with the new legislation, believing the act would afford them an opportunity to spread their peculiar institution westward.[6]

Sen. Sam Houston voted against the Kansas-Nebraska Act, arguing that the U.S. Constitution did not allow territories to govern themselves and that treaties between the United States and the Native Americans living in the lands west of the Missouri River had already dictated that the region in question belonged to the native inhabitants.[7] Additionally, Houston tried to appeal to the common sense of southern slave owners by stating that "no event of the future is more visible to my perception than that, if the Missouri Compromise is repealed, at some future day the South will be overwhelmed."[8] Houston correctly pointed out that sectional differences would boil over in the fight to gain dominance in the territories.

Loyal Unionists in Texas, such as Throckmorton, approved of Sam Houston's vote against the act, but proslavery Democrats ardently opposed his stance, viewing it as a direct challenge to the future of the South's peculiar institution. This single issue served as the point of origin for divisions in Texas between Unionists and secessionists. Furthermore, the act proved to be the death knell of the Whig Party. Beginning in the late 1840s, national debates over slavery threatened to divide the Whigs into northern and southern contingents. The Kansas-Nebraska Act dealt the final blow to the party's national unity and prominence as the members divided along sectional lines. Even though Whigs hoped that their party unity could be revitalized in time for the 1856 presidential election, many Whigs understood that their party was essentially dead. As a result, Texas Whigs, including Throckmorton, began to seek new ways to express and achieve their political objectives. A significant number of nationalists, like Sam Houston, entertained the idea of joining the newly formed American Party, also known as the Know-Nothing Party. Others, including Throckmorton, eventually decided to join the well-entrenched Democratic Party, believing that they could wrestle control of the party away from its more radical slaveholding members.[9]

The divisions caused by the Kansas-Nebraska Act continued as the state prepared for the 1857 gubernatorial election. After Houston's vote against the act, many Texas Democrats pressured him to resign his Senate seat, but rather than cowering to their demands, Houston decided openly to confront his Texas critics by becoming a candidate in the state's gubernatorial election of 1857. At the same time, Democrats held a nominating convention in Waco. It was clear that proslavery Democrats controlled the convention when Louis T. Wigfall and Thomas P. Ochiltree, both secessionists, assumed leadership roles. Under their direction, the platform committee endorsed the Virginia and Kentucky Resolutions of 1798 and 1799 in which James Madison and Thomas Jefferson explained the states' rights doctrine of interposition. The committee argued that states had the power to annul federal laws if those laws were deemed unconstitutional, an argument that Sen. John C. Calhoun of South Carolina had advocated since the 1830s. Wigfall and other radical proslavery delegates also supported reopening the African slave trade, stating that every white man in the South should own at

Sen. Sam Houston, a staunch Unionist during the 1850s. Despite being a slaveholder, he challenged Texas secessionists on numerous occasions during the latter half of the 1850s and early 1860s. *American Treasures at the Library of Congress Exhibition, Library of Congress.*

Gov. Hardin Runnels, a devout secessionist. His victory over Sam Houston in the 1857 gubernatorial election moved Texas closer to seceding from the Union and represented the only time that Houston lost a popular election. *Texas State Library and Archives Commission.*

least one slave. Nevertheless, the final draft of the platform did not address this more radical position. Even though the delegates were unwilling to support the reopening of the African slave trade, they did endorsed Hardin Runnels, an ardent secessionist, as their gubernatorial candidate.[10]

Throckmorton represented Collin County at the Waco Convention, but evidence suggests that he played a limited role in the conclave's final decisions. The printed proceedings reveal that Throckmorton voted with the majority of the delegates regarding the acceptance of the party's platform resolution and endorsement of Runnels. In doing so, it appears that Throckmorton willingly embraced a position within the party that ran counter to his core political principles. It is probably that the North Texas politician used his endorsement as a way to ingratiate himself with the Democratic leadership. In other words, Throckmorton felt compelled to give at least limited support to the pro-southern platform formalized in the convention because he was a new convert to the party.[11] Regardless of

Louis T. Wigfall, a noted Texas politician and supporter of Hardin Runnels's campaign in the 1857 gubernatorial election. Throughout the 1857 campaign, Wigfall reminded Texas voters that Senator Houston had voted against the Kansas-Nebraska Act and therefore had betrayed the interests of all southerners. *Civil War Glass Negative Collection, Library of Congress.*

his motives, he was able to maintain political viability and power by fully supporting his new party.

Within two weeks after the Waco Convention, Houston announced his intentions of running against Runnels as an independent candidate for governor. With their candidacies solidified, Houston and Runnels began their gubernatorial campaigns. Crisscrossing Texas in a crimson buggy, the hero of San Jacinto made speeches throughout the summer attacking the policies of his opponents and heralding his own record. In an attempt to stall Houston's momentum, Louis T. Wigfall and W. S. Oldham, both staunch supporters of Runnels, followed the Texas legend, claiming that the senator had betrayed the rights of southerners because of his own selfish desire to gain northern antislavery support for a possible presidential nomination. Houston countered the remarks of his detractors with his own stinging indictments. Alexander W. Terrell, a member of the anti-Houston faction, recalled that "Old Sam" closed one of his East Texas speeches by stating that "he understood a man named Whiggletail [Wigfall] would follow him—that he was an assassin, nullifier and a common liar, and that those who were fond of lies might remain and hear him."[12]

Houston's attempt to deflect the negative pronouncements of his opponents proved to be an impossible task. Wigfall and Oldham's comments resonated with many Texas voters. Perhaps more voters might have ignored the claims of anti-Houston Democrats, but Houston unwittingly gave his opponents' arguments validity as he vigorously defended his congressional record, including his negative vote on the Kansas-Nebraska bill. Additionally, it is likely that his lukewarm support of the anti-immigrant American Party candidates in 1855 turned many German and Tejano voters against him. As a result, Runnels defeated Houston for the governorship by a vote of 36,527 to 23,628. The election proved historic for Houston; it was the first and last time that he lost a political contest. More importantly, the election represented a solid defeat for the Unionist movement in Texas.[13]

Throckmorton fared better than Houston in the 1857 elections. North Texas voters sent their favorite son to the Texas Senate, believing he would continue to represent their interests within the Democratic Party. Their faith in him was well founded. Between 1857 and 1859, Throckmorton continued to work on railroad development and frontier defense in the state senate, and he became increasingly critical of the fanatical secessionist position of the Runnels administration.[14]

While evidence does not directly reveal the extent of Throckmorton's concern over the ultra-southern position in Texas between 1857 and 1859, his actions after the gubernatorial election of 1859 suggest that he agreed with the views espoused by fellow Unionist John H. Reagan, who was elected to the U.S. House of Representatives in 1857.[15] Following his election victory, Reagan outlined his stand against the radical southern perspective, stating that he was "in favor of the preservation of the Union under the Constitution" and "opposed to the Abolitionists of the North and to the Secessionists of the South." In regard to filibustering activities, such as the actions of the infamous William Walker in Nicaragua, Representative Reagan further stated that he "was opposed to filibustering because we would not be justified in morals or in law in making war on and murdering and robbing people who had done us no harm, as a matter of political policy." Commenting on the call to reopen the African slave trade, Reagan stated

John H. Reagan. This photograph was taken shortly after Reagan was appointed the postmaster general of the Confederate States of America in 1861. Despite his appointment, Reagan was a staunch prewar Unionist. Throckmorton tried but failed to get Reagan to support his idea of creating a new Unionist party in Texas in the late 1850s. *Selected Civil War Photographs Collection, Library of Congress.*

that he was "opposed to [it], independently of any question of morality, because the United States had treaty engagements with a number of great nations, prohibiting that trade . . . and because a majority of the people of the United States were opposed to it . . . and because it was impracticable, unreasonable, unjust, and unstatesmanlike."[16] Throckmorton later echoed these same sentiments prior to the state elections of 1859 in Texas. Because the Runnels administration embraced the revival of the African slave trade, favored filibustering activities in Latin America, and supported the idea of secession, Throckmorton increasingly sought to distance himself from pro-Runnels Democrats.[17]

Throckmorton also found himself at odds with the Runnels administration over political issues that directly affected the development of North

Texas. In a message to the Eighth Texas Legislature, Governor Runnels made clear that he believed the Texas volunteer forces could not adequately protect the frontier and questioned whether it was appropriate for the state to place additional troops on the frontier. According to the governor, this was squarely the responsibility of the U.S. government. Runnels stated, "It is the duty of the Federal Government to afford the protection required, and that the expense is one which the State should not properly be encumbered with."[18] The governor's position did not please men like Throckmorton, who believed strongly in the protection of the frontier regardless of the financial burden to the state.

Furthermore, Runnels proved to be an obstacle to the development of railroads, which promised to aid the development of North Texas. On February 4, 1858, the governor sent a message to the legislature explaining his veto of a bill designed to give the Memphis, El Paso, and Pacific Railroad Company an additional six years to fulfill the terms of its charter, the original of which had granted the company four years to grade one hundred miles of road; the proposed amendment allowed the company an additional six years to grade half the original distance. In a rare moment of clarity, Runnels stated that "there is, and can be to my mind, no good reason existing for such extraordinary delay. By it, not only the hopes of those who have been induced to embark their means in the enterprise, are unnecessarily deferred and disappointed, but the object, which may be presumed to have controlled the State, in granting the charter is defeated, and its consideration is forfeited."[19]

The governor also vetoed a bill to reinstate the Texas Western Railroad Company. According to Runnels, the company had "never made any report, under the general railroad law; and there is no official information that any stock has ever been subscribed, or that a dollar in money has been paid," despite the fact that the company's original charter had been granted six years earlier.[20] Runnels further stated that "the Memphis, El Paso and Pacific, and the Southern Pacific, all have the right to run on the same line. This charter is believed to have been once sold to the Pacific Railroad Company, and if that contract has ever been annulled there is no stipulation in the present bill against a repetition of the abuse hereafter."[21]

The politically astute Throckmorton viewed Runnels's political actions as an obstacle to the local issues that mattered most to his North Texas constituents. Protection from Indian depredations was a critical issue to voters who lived along the Texas frontier, and the economic prosperity of North Texas depended on the development of the railroad companies that

Runnels opposed. Throckmorton's commitment to these local issues helps to explain his strong support of the Union in the latter part of the 1850s.

On April 9, 1859, local Democrats held a meeting in Collin County and elected Throckmorton to represent their county at the state's Democratic convention that was slated to convene in Houston on May 2. Members of the local meeting also announced their support for two politicians in the upcoming state elections. They called for the reelection of John H. Reagan to U.S. Congress and for the election of Samuel Bogart as the party's nominee for lieutenant governor. Throckmorton agreed with the endorsements, respecting the political views and accomplishments of both men. At the state convention, Throckmorton quickly realized that his influence in the party was just as restricted as it was two years earlier in Waco. Nonetheless, he managed to work behind the scenes to garner limited support for the nominations of Bogart and Reagan.[22]

The political division between Unionists and proslavery Democrats became more evident in the 1859 gubernatorial election. Factions within the Democratic Party began to emerge at the state convention in Houston. Once delegates had organized the meeting, they voted to adopt the Waco platform of 1857 as the basis for their 1859 platform. Additionally, the members of the convention declared the *Dred Scott* decision to be a valid exposition of the U.S. Constitution and claimed that territorial legislatures had no right to prevent the extension of slavery into the western territories. They also insisted that Cuba should be made part of the United States as quickly as possible. However, just as they had two years earlier in Waco, the delegates defeated a resolution calling for the reopening of the African slave trade. Finally, the majority of the members at the convention nominated Governor Runnels for reelection.[23]

The Democratic platform and the nomination of Runnels caused concern among Texas Unionists, especially Throckmorton and his frontier constituents.[24] As a member of the Texas Legislature between 1851 and 1859, Throckmorton was able to avoid taking a decisive position on secession. However, in the 1859 gubernatorial election, he was faced with choosing sides in the sectional debates that threatened to rip the country apart. His choices were evident: he had to either join radical Democrats in support of Runnels or join the Unionists in their support of Houston. He chose to stand with Houston.[25]

Throckmorton supported Houston for varied reasons, but none was more important that Senator Houston's position on railroad development. In a broadside published before the gubernatorial election, Houston supporters defended their candidate's railroad policy. They stated that "Gen. Houston is not only in favor of the present bonus of 16 sections per mile to Railroads, but originally advocated the granting of 20 instead of 16 sections." Houston's supporters continued, "Thanks to the action and influential exertions of Generals Houston and [Thomas] Rusk, we are mainly indebted for the magnificent arrangement by which we sold a part of the Santa Fe territory to the General Government, and thereby enabled Texas . . . to leave a large surplus to aid in building our Railroads." Printed on this same broadside was a letter that Houston penned himself. The senator expressed that "other subjects than those of a local nature have engrossed my attention, but should I be elected Governor, I will not fail to give my especial attention to the subject of railroads, as well as to other subjects, connected with the general interest and prosperity of the country."[26] Throckmorton undoubtedly saw Houston's candidacy as beneficial to the economic well-being of the northern counties of the state.[27]

Furthermore, conditions on the frontier were becoming increasingly volatile. In late May 1859, the citizens of Collin County held a public meeting at McKinney to discuss Indian depredations on the northern frontier. With Throckmorton presiding over the meeting, those present expressed their determination to aid settlers living in frontier counties. They proclaimed that the citizens of Collin County would give settlers living on the western fringe of the Texas frontier "all the aid in our power towards removing the Indians North of the Red River." Additionally, they vowed to assist the frontier settlers in "the protection of their homes, their firesides and their families, from depredations of the savages." Finally, the leaders of Collin County called on the state government to remove the Indians living on reservations in western Texas, warning that if the officials failed to do so, Native Americans would force the settlers to abandon their homes.[28] Many Texans, including Throckmorton, believed that Houston would be more effective in eliciting federal funding and troops for frontier defense. Thus, Throckmorton found another reason for supporting the Houston camp.[29] He even toured his North Texas district in support of the aging Texas hero.[30]

With the 1859 gubernatorial race hinging on Runnels's inability to provide adequate frontier protection and his ultra-southern stance, Houston won the election by a vote of 36,227 to 27,500.[31] Edward Clark became lieutenant governor with 31,458 votes to Francis Lubbock's 30,325.[32] Conservative Unionists seemingly had won a major victory. On August 17, Throckmorton reported in a letter to John H. Reagan that "the battle is fought and won. The enemy are routed horse, foot, and dragoons. The slave trade faction must go under."[33] The defeat of those politicians supporting the radical position of reopening the slave trade was important to Throckmorton and his constituents. If the advocates of renewing the slave trade had been successful, Texas could have been inundated with new slaves. Thereby, the planter class could have solidified its control of the state, including the North Texas frontier. This was a proposition that nonslaveholding Texans could not accept.

According to Senator Throckmorton, the conservative Unionists' victory was not a rebuke of the Democratic Party, but rather it was the righting of wrongs that had been committed at the Houston Convention earlier that year. Throckmorton believed that delegates at the state Democratic convention had nominated unfit men for office and made an effort to lug in new issues, pledging Texas Democrats to them.[34] On August 17, 1859, Throckmorton wrote John H. Reagan informing him of his plan to organize a new Unionist Party and to persuade him to lead it. In trying to win Reagan to his side, Throckmorton argued that the Runnels faction blamed him [Reagan] for their defeat. He suggested that the leaders of the Democratic Party had supported Reagan's senatorial bid out of fear, not because of their friendship. The North Texas senator told Reagan that he was in political danger and that he should head the new political party to ensure his own political future. "If such a plan of Union is not pursued and carried out energetically, every living Union man may see the state ruled by the secessionist and slave trade men. Whenever they have the strength they will make the attack on you."[35]

Even with Sam Houston's victory at the polls, Throckmorton realized that Unionists lacked the organization of an effective political faction. As a result, he set out to create a new Unionist Party that would give meaning to the 1859 gubernatorial election. In an attempt to achieve his goal, Throckmorton sought the aid of other prominent Texas Unionists, including Benjamin H. Epperson, a wealthy businessman in North Texas and steadfast promoter of railroad development in the northern part of the state. On the day after writing Reagan, Throckmorton wrote Epperson a letter that laid out his plan for organizing his new political party.[36] Senator Throckmorton asked the rhetorical question, "How can old line Whigs and conservative men best subserve their own interests?" Then the senator proceeded to answer his own query, "Why, I say by taking that material that approaches nearest our own notions of what is right. But I wish to do more. I am for taking Reagan, and with him for a leader, build up a Conservative Union

Benjamin H. Epperson, a close and loyal confidant of James Webb Throckmorton throughout his political career. *Texas State Library and Archives Commission.*

Party in Texas. This can be done by showing him his true position—and the estimation in which he is held by the Runnels faction. They curse him in their heart of hearts. Necessarily he must fall with us." Throckmorton continued, "But we must manage so as to stretch out the arms of [leading antisecessionist Democrats] to catch him when he falls, and we poor devils who have always been for the Union and the Constitution without any other mixtures must stand somewhat in the background to sustain these gentlemen."[37]

After receiving Throckmorton's letter, Reagan wrote back to the North Texan, cautioning him against the idea of creating a new political party, especially since the members of the Whig and American parties had failed in their earlier attempts to challenge the Democratic authority in the state. Instead, Reagan suggested that Throckmorton should try to achieve his political objectives by reforming the Democratic Party from within. On September 9, 1859, a disappointed Throckmorton wrote to Reagan again. He stated that "I have canvassed in my mind . . . and cannot say but [that] the suggestion you make [is] correct." Throckmorton clarified his position by stating that "in my judgement much depends upon the course that will be adopted by those who have heretofore and who still assume to speak for the Democratic party." He continued by declaring that he could only support Reagan's position "if those gentlemen who have advocated the slave trade doctrine, and who . . . have attempted to foster it upon the party as a part of its creed will back down entirely from that position." Throckmorton conceded that "if they will in the next Democratic convention express the will of the people of Texas in opposition to the slave trade—and if they will cease their proscription of Union conservative Democrats . . . then it may be best that there should be no effort to organize the Democratic party anew."[38]

In the same letter, Throckmorton once again reminded Reagan of the difficulty that confronted Union men within the Democratic Party: "if the proper spirit is pursued by these men [secessionist Democrats], it would be well to heal the differences that have arisen during the late canvass, which have been brewing since the Democratic convention of '56 . . . but I wish to impress upon you that your position is a delicate one and not entirely free from danger, and it depends upon the course which you pursue whether or not you can sustain your position." Throckmorton continued, "I merely allude to these things to show you that from the African slave trade men, filibusters, secessionists, etc., and the friends of Governor Runnels you have nothing to expect." Then the North Texan voiced his strongest warning to his Democratic colleague: "a temporizing course with them on your part will injure you with the strong conservative element, and will not do you any good with these men because they have determined to hunt you down." As a solution, Throckmorton advised Reagan to "remain firm, and instead of receiving advice from them, dictate to them yourself. Show them that you do not regard their threats or machinations."[39] Despite the senator's plea, Reagan still refused Throckmorton's overture to make a break from the Democratic ranks.

With his efforts to found a new Unionist party in Texas dead, Throckmorton followed Reagan's advice and attempted to reform the Democratic Party from within. He began by suggesting changes to the Democratic platform, declaring that "Congress should have the power to protect slave property in the territories; . . . the slave trade should not be reopened; . . . the states should have the right of local self-government; . . . filibustering should not be tolerated; and . . . Federal aid to the construction of the Pacific Railroad should be encouraged." Throckmorton believed his positions to be the basis of a "good, strong, old-fashion Democratic platform."[40] It is perhaps more accurate to view this platform as a mixture of old-fashioned democracy and traditional Whig principles. Furthermore, he believed that an independent organization at the next Democratic convention should attempt to force his party to adopt a conservative platform. Such was the state of the Texas Democratic Party at the time of the 1860 presidential election.[41]

While attempting to reorganize the Democratic Party, a series of unfortunate events occurring between October 1859 and the end of 1860 undermined the conservative Unionists' political agenda. During this brief period two critical events occurred that fueled the flames of secession in Texas—John Brown's raid at Harper's Ferry, Virginia, and an insurrection-arson panic that swept through East Texas. Both incidents caused fear in the hearts of Texas citizens and gave credibility to secessionist propaganda that claimed that abolitionists were making plans to kill white southerners and free the South's slave population.[42]

The first of these two incidents occurred in October 1859 when the noted abolitionist John Brown attempted to seize the federal arsenal at Harper's Ferry and to free and arm the nearby slave population. According to his plan, Brown contrived to march his newly formed army southward, freeing all the slaves that he came across and killing white southerners who stood in his way. In this manner, the army of freed slaves would grow as it marched across the South. The result would be a revolution wherein the slaves would essentially win their own freedom. Unfortunately for Brown and his fellow conspirators, his invasion never materialized; the U.S. Army captured Brown after a brief skirmish at Harper's Ferry and turned him over to the civil authorities in Virginia. Following a speedy trial, a Virginia court found Brown guilty of treason and sentenced him to death. He met the hangman on December 2, 1859.

John Brown proved more effective as a martyr than a revolutionary. Northern abolitionists strengthened their resolve against the South's peculiar institution, which in turn promoted greater fears of future attacks throughout the slaveholding states. Texans were not immune from such fears, and the citizens of the Lone Star State often blamed any accident or deviant behavior in the state on abolitionist plots designed to kill white southerners and to free the slaves. Logic and reason were lacking during the period following Brown's raid, a point made clear during the summer of 1860.[43]

On July 8, in Dallas, Denton, and Pilot Point, several unexplained fires broke out, burning buildings in each of these North Texas towns. Immediately Texans in the northern and eastern regions of the state blamed the fires on covert abolitionist activities. Panic swept through the Lone

Star State as reports of similar incidents, some real and some false, began to circulate among the citizenry.[44] During an exceptionally hot summer, local men in every corner of the state armed themselves and patrolled the immediate areas surrounding their communities. In the frenzy, whites beat and killed blacks as well as whites suspected of inciting slave insurrections.[45] However, as the summer came to a close, the panic subsided almost as quickly as it had begun. Closer investigations of the fires revealed that many of the reported burnings in East Texas were exaggerated or even false and that new unstable phosphorus matches were probably the cause of the few fires that actually had occurred. Apparently the matches had spontaneously ignited on the shelves of mercantile stores as a result of the intense heat of the Texas summer.[46] Despite this scientific explanation of the fires, many Texans remained unconvinced and continued to place blame on a coordinated abolitionist plot to incite slave rebellions.[47] Before Texans had time to erase the fires from their memories, the outcome of the presidential election of 1860 seemed to suggest that more trouble was on the horizon.

The presidential election of 1860 perhaps more than any other national event influenced the direction that Texas politics would take immediately prior to the Civil War. Abraham Lincoln's victory in the election strengthened the secessionist position throughout the South, especially considering that Lincoln did not carry a single southern state. In Texas, Throckmorton's failure to organize conservative Unionists allowed the secessionists to seize control of the Democratic Party and to enjoy the advantage of commanding the strongest political machine in the state. Additionally, Lincoln's sectional triumph led many Texans to believe that his electoral victory represented the first step in making white southerners the "slaves" of northern politicians. In other words, they believed that they would soon be at the mercy of northern political whims. Secessionists were quickly able to capitalize on events occurring outside the state and to turn their political momentum into a popular movement that eventually swept Texas from the Union.[48]

Lincoln's election to the presidency moved the secessionists in South Carolina toward action. In less than a week after the election, the South Carolina legislature called for a convention to be held on December 17 to determine if the state should remain in the Union or if it would secede. At the same time, many Texans planned their own secession convention. On December 3, 1860, a group of Texas secession leaders asked Governor Houston to call a special session of the legislature to consider the possibility

Gov. Sam Houston, pictured here with his famous leopard-skin vest. Houston defeated incumbent Hardin Runnels in the 1859 gubernatorial election. However, his Unionist views would force Texas secessionists to remove him from office because he would not pledge loyalty to the newly created Confederate government. *Texas State Library and Archives Commission.*

of seceding from the Union, but Houston refused. Shortly following the rejection of their proposal, the secessionists drafted and issued an address to the people of Texas urging them to send delegates to a popularly called secession convention.[49] They suggested that each representative district should hold local meetings on January 8 and should elect a slate of delegates who would represent the district in a popularly called assembly scheduled to convene in Austin on January 28, 1861. Governor Houston immediately realized that the secessionists were determined to meet, either in the legislature or outside it. Thus, he called for a special session of the legislature to convene on January 21, just one week prior to the secessionists' called convention. Three days after Houston called for the special session of the legislature, South Carolina seceded from the Union.[50]

Speaking at various public meetings, Throckmorton espoused his opposition to secession. At a meeting in Plano on December 13, he attempted to stall the growing influence of leading secessionists in Collin County. Rev. T. J. Malone, who presided over the meeting, called for the formation of a committee to draw up resolutions expressing the county's support for secession. Once completed, the members planned to forward their resolutions to the state legislature. Though many of the attendees favored a break with the Union, they still invited Throckmorton to express his views. In his address, he offered an alternative to secession. He suggested that the southern states should hold a general convention for the purpose of formulating a cooperative plan of action that would force the federal government to address the South's concerns. In this way, the southern states could avoid the radical step of secession and the inevitable widespread carnage that prominent Unionists like Sam Houston were predicting would follow. The attendees at the Plano meeting voted on the question of including Throckmorton's proposal in their resolutions—they flatly rejected his ideas. The final draft of the members' memorial was predictable: Texas must secede. Representing a lone voice of reason at the Plano meeting, Throckmorton cast the only vote against joining the southern confederacy.[51]

Though the secessionists carried the day at Plano, divisions among the citizens of Collin County prevented them from electing delegates to the popularly called secession convention. The county was divided between two political factions, a pro-secessionist party led by George W. Barnett and a pro-Union party led by Throckmorton. Brutal disputes between the two sides were inevitable. Although little is known about Barnett, he evidently moved to Plano in 1843 and established himself as a prosperous farmer, slave owner, and businessman.[52] Less is known about his political views, but the editor of the *Dallas Herald* stated that he was "a candidate on the secession ticket [and that he should] put the question fairly to the people—will they go with the North or with the South?"[53] In the days following the Plano meeting, Barnett charged that Throckmorton was a traitor to the South and that he was willing to submit to the whims of northern abolitionists. Throckmorton, however, was not a submissionist. He never questioned the South's grievances against the federal government, but he simply did not believe that secession was the answer to the problems confronting the southern states.[54]

Critics also accused Throckmorton of plotting to divide Texas. The editor of the *Southern Intelligencer* on January 30, 1861, alleged that the senator was at the forefront of a plan to make a small state out of the northern counties located near the Red River, including Denton and Collin. Once this new state was created, the editor claimed that Throckmorton planned to have it admitted to the Union if Texas voted in favor of secession.[55] While this rumor would have been consistent with Throckmorton's political beliefs, no evidence exists that he actually proposed a plan to divide North Texas into a separate state prior to the mid-1860s. Therefore, it is likely that Throckmorton's detractors circulated this rumor in an effort to discredit him. Their efforts failed, especially considering that Collin County voters elected him as their representative to the Secession Convention.[56]

Ironically, Throckmorton was unaware that the voters had elected him to the forthcoming convention. He had left the county before the local election had taken place in order to attend the special session of the legislature that Governor Houston had called forth on December 17, 1860. In Austin, Throckmorton attempted to stem the tide of secession by introducing a bill calling for the election of delegates to a general convention of the people of Texas. If the bill had passed it would have required new elections to take place, affording the Unionists time to effectively organize throughout the state. Additionally, Unionists hoped that more time would temper the emotional propaganda of the secessionists. Unfortunately for the Unionists, their plans did not materialize. Throckmorton's bill was read twice before it was buried in the Committee on State Affairs, effectively stopping the senator in his tracks.[57]

Though opposed to secession, Throckmorton was just as much opposed to the idea of federal coercion.[58] Despite his devotion to the Union, he contended that the federal government had no constitutional right to prevent a state from seceding from the United States. He believed that such coercive actions on the part of the federal government justified the right of secession. Therefore, the senator believed in the right of secession, but not in the wisdom of it at this juncture. This position was evident in his support of the Shepard Resolution of January 26, 1861, which declared that coercion subverted the Constitution and would be fatal to the existence of the Union. The resolution also stated that Texas would join any state in resistance to such unconstitutional action by the federal government.[59]

Two days later, delegates to the Secession Convention began arriving in Austin, and members of the Texas House of Representatives voted fifty-six to twenty-four to pass a resolution that legitimized the popularly called assembly. The House sent its resolution to the state Senate where Throckmorton, Isaiah Paschal, Emory Rains, Martin Hart, and Eggleston

Townes tried to defeat it. The senators attempted to force a substitute resolution that called for a general convention of southern states. Sen. George Quinan, a secessionist, moved to table the substitution, and Throckmorton countered with a call for an immediate vote on the substitution. However, Quinan's motion was sustained. The substitution was tabled with a vote of twenty to ten. At this point, Senator Townes proposed several amendments to the pending resolution: that the action of the convention should be voted on in a referendum; that the people should send delegates to a general convention for the purpose of amending the state constitution to conform to the relations of the state to the Union; and that in case a new convention was not called forth and the popular convention whose members were elected on January 8 proceeded to convene, there should be an election of new delegates in those districts where the current attendees were elected by less than a majority of the registered voters so that the minority's interests would be represented in the convention. Unfortunately for the Unionist faction, the pro-secession senators managed to table the Townes resolutions by a vote of twenty to ten. The Senate then read the original house resolution and passed it by a vote of twenty-five to five. The Unionist senators had failed to stall the secession movement.[60]

According to plan, the Secession Convention met in Austin on January 28 with 177 delegates in attendance. At the close of the first day the organization of the convention was complete, and Oran M. Roberts, an ardent secessionist, was elected to preside over the meeting. Delegates quickly drafted an ordinance that called on the state to sever its ties to the Union. The ordinance of secession was put before the convention on January 30, and debate over the issue revealed that the delegates were divided as to whether the ordinance should take effect after a vote in the convention or whether the issue of secession should be decided in a statewide referendum. During the evening of the following day, the delegates agreed that the issue should be put before the people. They also decided that the convention would vote on the issue at noon on February 1.[61] Despite Throckmorton's outspoken opposition to secession, the fate of the state was virtually sealed when convention delegates overwhelmingly supported the ordinance of secession by a vote of 166 to 8.[62]

Now that the delegates had voted to approve secession, they deemed it necessary to draft a document that would explain their actions and hopefully persuade voters in the state to follow their lead. On February 2, the committee charged with penning the declaration of causes completed its task. The committee's justifications for secession simply mirrored those circulating throughout the other southern states, especially in the Lower South. The committee's draft stated that the federal government had failed to protect slavery in the western territories following the passage of the Kansas-Nebraska Act. Furthermore, committee members stipulated that federal officials had not enforced the 1850 fugitive slave laws. In addition, they declared that southerners no longer had a voice in the national government. Though this argument was an exaggeration of the actual circumstances in Washington, D.C., the logic of the members was based on the fact that Lincoln had won the presidency without carrying a single southern state, including Texas. The committee also stated that the federal government had failed to adequately protect settlers in their state from bands of hostile Indian who frequently attacked citizens living along the western frontier and from marauding groups of outlaws who invaded South Texas from Mexico.[63] After approving the committee's declaration of causes, the members of the secession convention voted to adjourn on February 4, planning to reconvene on March 2 after the referendum.[64] It was ironic that the delegates chose this date to reconvene their meeting—it marked the twenty-fifth anniversary of Texas independence from Mexico. Apparently, secessionists hoped to use the "Spirit of 1836" to gain popular support for their ordinance of secession.

Once the convention adjourned, Unionists believed that they had one more chance to prevent their state from leaving the Union. They planned to conduct a major campaign against the ordinance of secession, which was scheduled for a referendum on February 23.[65] Before leaving for their home districts, Throckmorton, three fellow senators, fourteen representatives, and six additional members of the Secession Convention drew up an address to the people in which they presented their arguments against the act of secession.[66] It is difficult to determine what role Throckmorton played in drafting this document, but given his rigid opposition to secession, it is likely that he was one of the principal authors.

In their address to the people, the Unionists acknowledged that the North seemed hostile toward the South's institution of slavery, especially considering that many northern states passed personal liberty laws to prevent the enforcement of the fugitive slave law. The Unionists also accepted the premise that Lincoln's presidential victory made further provisions for the protection of slavery necessary. However, they were not willing to accept that secession was justified solely on the basis of the 1860 presidential election results. Clearly, Throckmorton and his fellow Unionists believed that there was still room for compromise between the northern and southern states and that prudent action on both sides could still save the Union.[67]

Additionally, the authors argued that secessionists had deceived the citizens of Texas. They stated that those who favored a break with the Union believed secession was the only way to protect the rights and prosperity of the southern people. According to the Unionists, a break from the United States would only serve to end slavery even faster than the abolitionists could hope for. The authors predicted a grim future for "a confederacy [formed from] cotton states alone." They stated that "it is already apparent that in such a confederacy slavery will be recognized as the principal interest to be fostered by the government," and therefore "the legislation of such a Government would almost necessarily proceed upon an invidious distinction between those who owned slaves, and those who did not." Continuing, the authors stated that "this would tend to make the confederacy a confederacy of slaveholders." As such, the interests of slaveholders would dominate the country. Ultimately, the Confederacy would evolve into a military state that would protect the welfare of slaveholders and would work against the interests of nonslaveholding citizens. The authors rhetorically asked, "How long, in such a confederacy, would liberty and free institutions survive the formation of a powerful military force?"[68] The Unionists ended their address with an alternative plan of action:

> We would have you remain true to every constitutional obligation although your northern brethren, in some respects, proved recreant to theirs. We would have you put forth your best efforts in aid of such of the slave holding states as may make the attempt to reconstruct the Union. In the meantime, through the agency of your state government or what may perhaps be better through a convention called for that purpose, and clothed with full powers, we would make preparation for the worst that can come. And having done that, if you cannot by the help of others, restore the Union, with every abuse corrected and all your rights fully secured, then change your form of government as you may think best.[69]

On February 9, three days after the publication of the Unionists' address, Throckmorton and several other leading Unionists spoke publicly at Buass Hall in Austin. According to a report in the *Austin Southern Intelligencer,* the speeches "were able and eloquent . . . denunciations of the [Secession] Convention for its usurpation of powers—its establishment of a Committee of espionage, styled Safety—its *secret sessions,* its midnight plottings,

James Webb Throckmorton. Despite his Herculean effort, Throckmorton was unable to prevent the secession of Texas in 1861.
*Texas State Library and Archives Commission.*

its attempting to establish in our midst and to carry out the Reign of Terror, inaugurated in parts of Texas by Vigilance Committees."[70] Afterward, Throckmorton went to McKinney where he tirelessly campaigned against secession.[71] His efforts seemed to bear fruit; Collin County rejected secession by an overwhelming vote of 710 to 215. However, despite the senator's success at home, the secessionists won statewide. Texans voted to leave the Union by a vote of 44,317 to 13,020.[72] The voters of Texas had sealed their fate.

After the voters decided to secede from the Union, Throckmorton traveled back to Austin to attend the Secession Convention as it reconvened. Arriving when the conclave was already in session, the senator found the delegates in the middle of a vote. When the roll was completed, Mr. Matthew Locke, a member of the convention from Upshur County, proposed that every member of the convention should cast a vote unless properly excused from doing so. Throckmorton inquired about the issue at hand and was informed that a vote was being taken on the adoption of the provisional constitution of the Confederate States. Throckmorton addressed the president of the convention:

> Mr. President, only a moment since I returned from my home where I had been to persuade the people of my district to vote against the ordinance of secession. I have the satisfaction to know that my constituency agree with me on that grave and momentous question. When I entered the chamber the vote was being taken upon a question unknown to me. When my name was called I did not vote. But since the gentleman from Upshur has called the attention of the chair, I have inquired and ascertained that the vote is upon the adoption of the provisional constitution of the confederate states. Not knowing its provisions if required to vote I shall vote against it. But Mr. President, while I am up if the convention will indulge me I beg to say a word. Sir, I had thought that I had satisfied every member of this body that I was not afraid to vote or express my opinion on any subject . . . my position has been well understood. But sir, I desire to go a little further, and announce a determination known to my friends, but perhaps not generally known to members of this body. I believe we are on the verge of a long and bloody war, the consequences of which none can foresee. While my judgement dictates to me that we are not justified by the surroundings or occasion, a majority of the people of Texas have declared in favor of secession; the die is cast; the step has been taken, and regardless of consequences I expect and intend to share the fortunes of my friends and neighbors. I wish to say especially for the benefit of those who doubt my devotion to my country that I have no doubt that the time will soon be upon us when the clash of arms will be heard and the blood of my countrymen will be shed in a great civil war. When it comes I will be in its midst, and I doubt not will be there long before the gentleman from Upshur.[73]

Following Throckmorton's comments, Ochiltree made a motion and it was seconded that Throckmorton be excused from the vote.

While the convention was still in session, Throckmorton's loyalty to the Confederacy was put to the test. Houston had attempted to have Gen. David E. Twiggs, who was in command of the Union troops at San Antonio, surrender his arms directly to the state government rather than to the convention's Committee on Public Safety. This fact adds credibility to a story that A. W. Terrell told in later years. According to Terrell, President Lincoln sent a dispatch to Sam Houston by way of George Giddings informing the Texas governor that the federal government would send fifty thousand soldiers to Texas to keep the state in the Union. After Houston received the letter, he called a select group of Union sympathizers to his home. Among those present at the meeting were Throckmorton, Benjamin Epperson, and David Culberson. Houston apparently read Lincoln's letter to the men and asked for their counsel. To a man, Houston's guests cautioned against accepting Lincoln's offer. They suggested that if the governor accepted the offer, a violent civil war would erupt in their state. Houston heeded their advice and cast Lincoln's letter into the fireplace. On April 1, the Secession Convention adjourned, and the state government assumed the position of power that it had held prior to being supplanted by the convention.[74]

Unionism in Texas had been solidly defeated, and now nationalists were left with difficult choices: they could continue to support the federal government and run the risk of being persecuted by Confederate authorities; they could remain neutral in the approaching conflict; or they could bow to the will of the Texas voters and join the Confederate cause. Following the logic and reason of Sam Houston, Throckmorton chose the latter. Even though Houston was removed from the governor's office because he refused to take an oath of loyalty to the Confederacy, he respected the will of the majority of Texas voters in the referendum on secession.[75] On October 18, 1861, Houston clearly stated his position on Texas joining the Confederacy in an article appearing in the *McKinney Messenger:* he claimed to support the decision made by the majority of voters even if he did not personally feel that it was the best course of action. He stated, "Had I been disposed to involve Texas in [a] civil war I had it in my power, for I was tendered the aid of seventy thousand men and means to sustain myself in Texas by adhering to the Union; but I rejected, and . . . I gave my advice to the Federal Government."[76] Houston suggested that Lincoln should "evacuate Fort Pickens and Sumter [and] recall all the Federal troops from Texas."[77]

Houston also believed that the Lincoln administration was operating outside the executive branch's constitutional authority. "Mr. Lincoln and his cabinet have usurped the powers of Congress and have waged war against the Sovereign States," Houston declared, "and have thereby not only absolved the States, but all the people of the several States from their allegiance to his government, the Federal Government having ceased to exist by his act of usurpation."[78] Defining the coercive actions of the president, Houston added that "[Lincoln] proclaimed martial law in Missouri and assumed the civil administration of the affairs of that State, thereby ignoring the Constitution and setting at nought the sovereignty of the people, and he has in fact, with more than Vandalic malignity and Gothic hate sought to incite a servile insurrection in that State."[79]

Several years after the Civil War, Throckmorton echoed the same conclusions reached by Houston earlier. In front of a crowd at the International Fair Association at San Antonio, Throckmorton reflected on the causes of the Civil War. He stated, "My friends, on a recent occasion I heard it announced by one of the most eloquent men of Texas that slavery was the cause of the Civil War. Unquestionably it was one of the leading causes, and undoubtedly it was the great lever used, both North and South, that precipitated it, but there were other causes, some apparent, and others latent, that gradually led up to, and together with the institution of slavery, brought about the unhappy contest."[80]

Throckmorton traced the causes of the war to the formation of the federal government at the Constitutional Convention of 1787 in Philadelphia. He stated that "there were two sets of statesmen who differed radically as to how the Constitution should be construed, and the policy upon which the government should be conducted." Throckmorton explained that "one party, in which there were many eminent men who had rendered the country great service, believed the Constitution should be construed liberally, that the powers of government should operate directly upon the citizens and [their] affairs, and that it should become practically a parental government." In contrast, according to Throckmorton, "the other party, in which there were equally as eminent and patriotic men, believed that the constitution should be construed strictly, and that no power should be exercised unless it was clearly defined, or made plain by the implication from the letter and spirit of that sacred instrument."[81]

Throckmorton commented that the two factions engaged in bitter disputes concerning the "questions of free speech and liberty of the press; how taxes, internal and external, might be levied; whether industries of certain kinds should be protected and encouraged; and for what purposes appropriations from the common treasury should be made." These questions, he explained, were the foundation of the "causes that led up to sectional strife that brought about the Civil War." He reminded his audience that "nullification first reared its front in New England, and afterwards took root in South Carolina." During this time, the North Texas politician contended, "there was a strong conservative element in the country that did not go to the extremes of either of the great parties that strove for the mastery; the representatives of that element contended for moderation and forbearance, and on different occasions exercised a salutary influence for peace and fraternity."[82]

Throckmorton also believed that "in a number of the Northern States, and, as our people believed, in violation of the Constitution and laws passed in pursuance of it, the fugitive slave laws were enacted." Echoing Sam Houston's argument against coercion, he claimed that the fugitive slave laws as well as the question of the status of slavery in the territories "culminated in the election of Mr. Lincoln to the Presidency, but not by a majority of the votes of the American people." Like many people in the South, Throckmorton concluded that Lincoln's "election was regarded by many as a sectional triumph and as a menace to the institution of slavery."[83]

Throckmorton then commented on the secessionists and their motives. He felt that the secessionists "urged the untoward condition of affairs to influence the public mind, and [brought] about a dissolution of the Union, not the overthrow and destruction of the government, but the erection of a new government out of States that had belonged to the old." Offering further justification of the secessionist cause, the North Texan continued by declaring, "We, of the South, were willing that our Northern brothers should retain the old government, enjoy their convictions of right and duty, and manage their own affairs. We claimed the same privilege, and asked, to be let alone with our institutions, that had grown up with us, and were as old as the colonies, from which all the States had sprung."[84]

Throckmorton contended that "there was a strong element of conservatism in both sections [North and South], led by great and good men, who tried to allay the storm." He then spoke of the virtues of the political conservatives, stating that "this class of men in the South did not believe the election of Mr. Lincoln sufficient cause for a dissolution of the States, or that the institution of slavery in the States was seriously threatened." He further observed that the conservative perspective was shared by "many in the North, and while those who entertained such views appreciated the serious gravity of the situation, they believed an honorable adjustment of differences could be made, and that no peaceful remedy should be left untried to attain an end so priceless."[85]

Commenting on southern conservatives, Throckmorton claimed that they acknowledged "the Constitution and laws had been infracted, yet we did not believe secession the remedy, or that we could maintain our cause by a resort to arms." Like Governor Houston, he stated that conservatives "further believed the constitution conferred no power upon the federal government to coerce a State by an invasion with its armies, nor did we believe the constitution would have been ratified by the requisite number of States had such power been expressed in it." Throckmorton concluded that "when the efforts of the peace party failed and the storm of passion and sectional hatred . . . swept over the country, and civil war . . . became a certainty, there was but one course, in the judgment of a very great majority of the South to be pursued—and that was to fight it out to the bitter end."[86]

Earlier, Throckmorton proved a loyal advocate of the Union aligned against the forces that were pushing the state toward secession. Between 1854 and 1861, several factors shaped the senator's Unionism, including his commitment to traditional Whig political ideology, his desire to promote economic prosperity through railroad development, his devotion to protecting small farmers from the political, social, and economic domination of the planter class, and his desire to preserve white supremacy on the frontier of North Texas by removing Native Americans. Furthermore, the senator was concerned with what he perceived as the coercive nature of the federal government. In this regard, Throckmorton was closely aligned with his constituency. A large segment of the population in North Texas had migrated from the Upper South states of Tennessee, Kentucky, and Virginia. As with the Upper South, North Texas did not have a strong commitment to slavery, and therefore its people were more reluctant to embrace the rhetoric of southern fire-eaters. Despite the results of the referendum vote, Unionists still hoped to work out a compromise between the northern and southern states. However, their plans for saving the Union came to an end when news reached Texas of the hostilities at Fort Sumter and President Lincoln's proclamation calling for seventy-five thousand state militia volunteers to crush the southern rebellion. Many Unionists perceived Lincoln's move as an act of coercion and as a result abandoned their efforts to preserve the Union. Following Lincoln's proclamation, Throckmorton made the fateful decision to join the Confederacy.[87]

## CHAPTER FOUR

# *The Civil War*

### "HE THAT IS NOT FOR US IS AGAINST US," 1861–65

Senator Throckmorton along with other North Texas Unionists worked diligently to keep Texas in the Union and thereby prevent the planter class from gaining political control of the state, but their efforts ultimately failed. Thus, people living on the frontier had to come to terms with the fact that their worst fears had become a reality. Their hopes of creating a society isolated from the control of the planter class had vanished and they now found themselves residing in a country where planters completely controlled the social, economic, and political institutions of the nation. Thus, Throckmorton and his constituents were confronted with several difficult choices: they could either flee the state northward and live under the protection of the federal government; they could remain in Texas and continue to oppose the Confederacy; or they could accept and defend their state's decision to leave the Union.

Throckmorton chose to remain in his home state and to pledge loyalty to the Confederate government. There can be little doubt that political expediency and a desire to defend the frontier in the northwestern part of the state influenced the senator's decision to take an oath of allegiance to the Confederacy.[1] Writing to his friend Benjamin H. Epperson on January 19, 1862, Throckmorton explained his decision: "reason had become dethroned in the North and was not very stable in the South—success with the Bl'k Republicans would make us hewers of wood and drawers of water—and whilst I had as ardent an attachment for the old Gov't as any man living . . . I would not consent to reunite with the north." Throckmorton continued, saying that "the struggle is over with me—we had better be separate—our interests, pursuits & habits are too diversified ever to be made to harmonize."[2] Throckmorton understood the necessity in convincing state authorities of the northern counties' willingness to support the Confederacy. If he failed, North Texas would have become the scene of civil war between Unionists and secessionists in the state. More personally, Throckmorton knew that by supporting the Confederacy, he could still wield political power.

After the secession convention and the state legislature adjourned, Throckmorton returned to his home district and resumed his law practice. His decision to support a government founded upon on the false pretenses of secessionists could not have been an easy one, especially considering that the frontier society of North Texas had functioned as a place of refuge from the control of the planter class.[3] Nevertheless, the senator now believed that the safety of the frontier hinged upon remaining loyal to the Confederacy.

As a settler in a region accustomed to Indian raids, Throckmorton undoubtedly worried about frontier defense. He knew that the federal troops stationed at fortifications in western Texas would soon withdraw from their post, leaving the region in danger of future Indian depredations. Therefore, Throckmorton supported the Confederate government's attempt to occupy the abandoned frontier posts. However, he did not become a diehard proponent of the Confederacy until April 1861, when national events provided him with what he considered more valid reasons for siding with the newly formed southern government.

While President Lincoln declared secession illegal, he took a temporizing position regarding the South's break from the Union. The president said that he would not attempt to reclaim federal property that Confederate authorities seized in the states of the Lower South. However, two military institutions in the South remained under federal control, Fort Sumter in Charleston harbor, South Carolina, and Fort Pickens at Pensacola, Florida. After weeks of indecision and pressure from his own party to ignore the Confederacy's demands that the forts be surrendered, Lincoln sent a naval expedition to resupply Fort Sumter, the primary cargo being food. Unwilling to allow the fort to remain in Union hands, the Confederates bombarded it on April 12 before the Union navy vessels arrived. Following more than thirty hours of continual bombardment, the commander of the fort, Maj. Robert Anderson, surrendered to his attackers.[4]

The attack on Fort Sumter immediately elicited an outcry of patriotic indignation in the northern states, and Lincoln was forced to take stronger measures in dealing with the southern rebels. He issued a call for seventy-five thousand volunteers to put down the rebellion. Southerners considered the president's call for troops an open act of aggression. Throckmorton later commented that "I had hoped that the evil hour was not upon us—and that our whole country as it was could be preserved, but when the alarm was sounded at Fort Sumter I gave up that hope."[5] While ignoring their own arguably treasonous behavior, southerners claimed that Lincoln had abandoned the principles of democracy by refusing to allow Dixie to leave the Union when a majority of the citizens in the southern states clearly wished to do so. At this point, many of these self-proclaimed, constitutionally minded Confederates, including Throckmorton, professed that the Union was attempting to coerce the southern states back into the Union.[6] Despite the evident flaws in the Confederates' argument against coercion, the South's perception of the federal government's actions caused Virginia, North Carolina, Arkansas, and Tennessee to follow the Lower South in secession.[7]

After the fall of Fort Sumter and Lincoln's call for volunteers, Throckmorton attended a convention in Collin County organized by local secessionists. The convention opened at the courthouse in McKinney on April 27, 1861. Fearing that Unionists in the county might engage in espionage, Confederate supporters refused to let them attend the meeting. In protest, David C. Dickson, the former American Party candidate in the 1855 Texas gubernatorial election, led a group of Union men to the Methodist church and held an independent meeting. Aware that such a move would invoke the suspicion of the Confederates, Throckmorton refused to join them and decided that it would be better to remain at the courthouse, even though the gathering would not officially recognize him.[8]

The intent of the Confederate meeting was to elect delegates for a forthcoming meeting in Dallas that was scheduled to discuss matters concerning the Confederacy. However, the event turned into a political rally for politicians seeking to win office in the upcoming state elections. Nevertheless, the attendees endorsed the Confederate constitution and elected twenty delegates for the Dallas convention. Among the delegates was George W. Barnett, Throckmorton's earlier adversary during the secession crisis.[9]

Even though the members of the McKinney convention doubted Throckmorton's allegiance to the Confederacy, they gave him the opportunity to address the delegates of the meeting once they had officially adjourned. The senator reaffirmed his newfound devotion to the Confederacy, and he suggested that southerners should form a united front against the coercive federal government. He called on Texans to wash away the political dissension present since the beginning of the secession crisis. To accomplish greater unity, he argued that future political meetings should be suspended until the end of the war. Throckmorton concluded his address by explaining that he would be the first to sign up for the Confederate cause. True to his word, when the delegates created a list of volunteers for service in the military, Throckmorton's name was one of the first recorded.[10]

While embracing southern rhetoric regarding the coercive nature of the federal government, Throckmorton had other, more pragmatic motivations for becoming a crusader for the Confederacy. In a letter written after the war, he declared that his decision to embrace the southern cause was based on a desire to prevent a civil war in his region of the state. Throckmorton wrote to Hamilton Bee:

> The war came, I saw that unless I did something to prevent it, that neighbors and friends of my own immediate section of the state would be embroiled with each other in a deadly conflict. I at once consulted with [Benjamin] Eppearson and [D. C.] Dickson and told them this must not be. The only way to prevent it was for ourselves to set the example. Our friends were calling on us to head the opposition. They agreed with me as to the course and I immediately called for men. . . . Our course saved the enactment of the scenes of Missouri.[11]

Additionally, Throckmorton realized that the federal government would eventually attack the southern economy by waging a war against the institution of slavery, an action that would forever change southern society.[12] Whites on the frontier feared that emancipated slaves would move to areas in the western regions of the Lone Star State where slavery had not been a significant part of the economy, effectively challenging white dominance in the region. In this regard, whites in North Texas were not much different than their northern counterparts who were concerned that emancipated slaves would migrate to northern states, thereby competing with northern laborers for jobs. Thus, Throckmorton and other like-minded individuals in North Texas concluded that the society Anglos created on the Texas frontier might potentially be threatened on two fronts if the Confederacy lost the war: Native Americans would try to push the frontier line eastward and reclaim the lands that they had lost to white settlers during the previous three decades, and former slaves would push into the frontier from eastern counties in Texas that had been the scene of their bondage.

Throckmorton's immediate concern, however, was the physical safety of individuals living on the northern frontier of Texas. Settlers in this region were exposed to two different threats. First, Confederate authorities believed that federal troops who were previously stationed in the Indian Territory might reorganize and invade the state from the north. Second, Indians still posed a real threat to the safety of North Texas settlements. With federal troops withdrawing from forts along the frontier line in Texas and in the Indian Territory, nothing stood between the Native Americans and the citizens of north-central Texas. Motivated by a desire to protect settlers from these potential threats, Throckmorton became actively involved in the military defense of the Red River counties.[13]

The first task of the newly mustered Confederate forces in states contiguous with the Indian Territory was to move against the U.S. troops stationed at Fort Washita, Fort Arbuckle, and Fort Cobb.[14] Because federal troops had abandoned these forts before the arrival of Confederates, the rebels' objectives were effectively completed by the end of May 1861.[15] In essence, the engagements between federal and Confederate forces were minimal, and Throckmorton's initial period of service in the volunteer unit lasted less than a month. Throughout the month of May, Throckmorton's company served in a frontier regiment under the command of Col. William C. Young, who was appointed by Gov. Edward Clark to defend the northwest frontier. The men in the regiment elected Throckmorton as their lieutenant colonel, which was more a testament to his standing with the citizens of his region than to his military abilities.[16]

After Confederate forces occupied the forts, Throckmorton returned home and resumed his legal practice. Apparently, he was temporarily satisfied that the immediate threat to the southern frontier had passed.[17] However, while attending district court at Sherman, Grayson County, Throckmorton learned of new threats to North Texas. Earlier in May, Colonel Young had warned that "if war continues we shall have forays from Kansas, and this northern frontier must be well prepared." Young continued, "we [North Texans] cannot afford to send troops to the South. Any where on the Gulf coast, or in the railroad region, troops can be rapidly conveyed to any assailed point. But up here a foray could be made, immense damage done, and the parties away, before we could have a defensive force to repel them." The colonel's solution was simple: "we must maintain Washita, as a permanent post, and should have spies out northward, on all traveled routes, constantly, regularly relieved and reporting."[18]

Additionally, Colonel Young feared that the Kickapoos and Caddoes would soon pose a threat to Fort Cobb and probably North Texas, too. According to one account, these Native American tribes were "about [Fort] Cobb in small squads, painted and taking whatever they wanted. The force in garrison was too weak to control them."[19] Colonel Young also made it known to the citizens of North Texas that he planned to organize a volunteer cavalry regiment for service in the Indian Territory, even though he did not have authority to receive any volunteers at that time.[20]

There is no record of Throckmorton meeting Colonel Young in Sherman in late May or early June, but it seems certain that the colonel's assessment of perceived threats to North Texas prompted the lawyer to action. Throckmorton concluded his legal duties at Sherman and returned to McKinney, where he soon initiated efforts to raise another voluntary cavalry company for active duty. He quickly completed his task. At a public meeting held on June 8, 1861, in Lebanon, Collin County, local men mustered into military service. They gave straightforward reasons for joining the newly formed company, stating that "whereas our country is threatened with war, our homes and firesides with devastation; it therefore becomes necessary for each and every man to define his position, for he that is not for us is against us." Additionally, the volunteers stressed that they were forming a "military company for the protection of our homes and our rights." Finally, the men claimed that they had forsaken their earlier Unionism: "We now of our own accord lay aside all party issues and unite upon one common platform that is in the defense of our rights to repel [an] invasion."[21]

On June 19, the editor of the *Dallas Herald* reported, "We are indebted to Hon. J. W. Throckmorton for [sending us a] list of officers of two companies of troops just organized in Collin County." Continuing, the editor stated that the "100 men rank and file [were] ready for any service that they can get. Capt. Throckmorton visited [Dallas] in order to get his men into the regiment of Col. Greer. That regiment, however, was already full, and could not receive them." The editor then revealed in a postscript that "Capt. Throckmorton's company [was] received into service, under Col. Young's call, and will go into immediate service in the Indian Nation."[22]

Young and Throckmorton proceeded to Ben McCulloch's headquarters at Fort Smith where they requested that the brigadier general receive their regiment. McCulloch denied their request, stating that he did not have the authority to receive additional troops. However, the general requested that Colonel Young carry a message back to the people of North

Texas informing them that troops would soon be needed to defend Arkansas and Texas from a Union force then present in Missouri. Young agreed to the general's request. The Clarksville *Northern Standard* reported that Throckmorton's "mission to Fort Smith, undertaken for the purpose of having his company received into Gen. McCulloch's command, was not successful. . . . The company will be stationed temporarily at Fort Cobb, at which place Capt. Throckmorton will join them in a few days. We understand from him that Col. Young will soon start to Austin and will go thence to Richmond, on important business connected with his regiment."[23]

After his interview with McCulloch, Young ordered Throckmorton's company to join troops already stationed at Fort Cobb.[24] However, Throckmorton did not immediately join his men at the frontier garrison. Instead, Young requested that the former senator accompany him to Texas and help inform the frontier settlers of the current circumstances north of the Red River. The two men brought news that Union troops under the command of Jim Lane were planning to attack Arkansas and, if successful, would then carry their attack forward to North Texas. Throckmorton and Young also informed their fellow citizens that McCulloch thought a general call to arms might soon be necessary to raise additional troops to counter Lane's forces. McCulloch stated that "the State of Missouri is almost subjugated; the small force she has yet in the field is being driven back upon Arkansas. We march today to help and aid them!" McCulloch attempted to incite patriotic fervor by subtly equating the approaching Union forces with past ethnic enemies: "Texans remember your former victories and prepare to march to others. You won your independence from Mexico and will again do it from a more tyrannical foe. The South will never be subjugated, NEVER, NEVER!"[25]

On July 9, Throckmorton wrote to Gov. Edward Clark informing him of General McCulloch's assessment of the battlefront in Missouri and Arkansas and requesting that the governor arrange for his regiment to join McCulloch's command.[26] "I have just returned from a trip with Genl Young to see Ben McCulloch at Fort Smith," Throckmorton explained. "He had no authority to [receive] our regiment, but expected out of necessity to have to call for troops from Texas soon." Throckmorton continued, "I see it stated in the papers that two regiments will be [received] from Texas. Now my Dr Sir, don't overlook our section. Our regt is all ready complete and stationed in the forts north of [the] Red River." Throckmorton revealed that he planned to leave the following morning to join his command at Fort Cobb.[27]

Throckmorton waited before answering McCulloch's general call to arms. During this delay, his volunteer company remained at Fort Cobb until the end of August, when it returned to Sherman for winter provisions.[28] While in the North Texas town, Throckmorton and his men resigned from state service and joined the regular Confederate Army. Throckmorton wrote to Governor Clark regarding the company's resignation: "the company which I command, in the Regiment of Col Wm C Young, when they ascertained that they were not in the Service of the Confederate States . . . disbanded—which was on the 31st day of August 1861."[29] Throckmorton and many of the men under his former company of volunteers went to Camp Bartow, near Dallas, and officially mustered into the Sixth Texas Cavalry on September 12, 1861.[30] Throckmorton was commissioned as captain of Company K, in the Second Regiment of Texas Cavalry Volunteers, commanded by Col. B. Warren Stone.[31] After mustering into the Confederate service, Stone's regiment marched forward to join McCulloch's army at Camp Jackson, near Van Buren, Arkansas. They arrived on October 16.[32]

Stone's regiment faced its first major test in combat on December 26, 1861, at the Battle of Chustenahlah in the Cherokee Nation. At Chustenahlah, Stone's regiment confronted a group of Creek Indians who remained loyal to the Union and who were traveling north to seek the protection of federal troops stationed in Kansas.[33] Douglas John Carter, who served in the Third Texas Cavalry, recalled the battle:

> It was Christmas day, 1861 when we came upon the enemy some ten or twelve miles from where we had spent the night. Their pickets fired a few shots at our advance column and retreated to their main army which occupied a very strong position, fortified by nature on a hill, a real breast work of rocks and standing trees, and behind these they were waiting to receive our attack. We formed a line of battle in front of them. Bullets and arrows were coming pretty fast. A feathered arrow passed in front of my face just before we were ordered to dismount, and produced a strange sensation in me. After dismounting we were ordered to leave every fifth man to hold our horses. Henry Miller of our company was crying when the order came to charge because he had been detailed to hold horses. We made the charge in "double quick" and climbed over the breast works. They fired volley after volley of rifles and arrows as we charged and climbed over those rocks. Seeing they could not stop us, they commenced running. We were then ordered to go back for our horses and get over those rocks with them as best

> we could and form in line and continue the charge. Some of those Indians were very brave and daring and would not leave, but continued to shoot. Of course, they were killed. One big feathered cap fellow stood out from the trees and continued shooting until he fell. I had shot both barrels of my gun and one of my holster pistols at him before he fell. I don't know who killed him. I thought I had, but some others of our company said they shot at that feathered cap Indian. We continued this running fire about seven miles and until there were no warriors in sight.[34]

According to the battle report of Lt. Col. John S. Griffith, Sixth Regiment, Texas Cavalry, Throckmorton led his men with grit and valor. Griffith stated, "To the brave and gallant Captains Ross, Hardin, Wharton, and Throckmorton . . . I am much indebted for the success we had by their fearless charges in the front of their respective commands, which so signally routed the enemy from every point." Griffith concluded his report with "I must return my sincere thanks to Captains Ross, Wharton, and Throckmorton, and Adjunct Gurley for timely assistance when I was in imminent personal peril, and my gratitude to Providence for crowning our arms with victory."[35] The Creeks suffered more than three hundred casualties and the Confederate forces captured all their provisions, wives, children, and slaves.[36] Following the battle, Throckmorton returned to his home in McKinney, escorting the remains of his friend Gabriel S. Fitzhugh, who lost his life in the battle.[37] He rejoined Company K in winter quarters near Fayetteville, Arkansas, in mid-February 1862.

Following his arrival in Fayetteville, Throckmorton's company received orders to ride north toward Bentonville, Arkansas. After several skirmishes along the route to their destination, he and his men were involved in the Battle of Elkhorn Tavern, more commonly known as the Battle of Pea Ridge. Even though Pea Ridge proved to be a Confederate blunder that ended any hopes of bringing Missouri into the Confederacy, Throckmorton and his men were once again cited for bravery under fire. In a report submitted on April 14 to Maj. Gen. Earl Van Dorn, commander of the Trans-Mississippi Department, Colonel Stone stated that his "regiment gallantly led [a] brilliant charge, which was but momentarily withstood by the enemy, who left his guns in the most precipitous flight." The colonel continued by stating that "the first three companies, under Captains Wharton, Throckmorton, and Bridges, poured a most destructive fire upon the enemy near his guns, killing more than 80 of his number. Thanks to these gallant officers for their promptness, valor, and success."[38]

During the course of the Battle of Pea Ridge, a Union bullet took the life of General McCulloch. As a result, Colonel Stone's cavalry unit transferred to General Van Dorn's command. On March 19, Gen. Pierre G. T. Beauregard ordered Van Dorn to move his forces to Corinth, Mississippi, to protect the Memphis and Charleston Railroad from the approaching Union army under the command of Brig. Gen. Ulysses S. Grant. Despite the importance of this assignment, Colonel Stone resigned his command and returned to Texas to raise another regiment; it seems evident that the colonel no longer had confidence in Van Dorn's leadership abilities. Even though he respected the colonel's decision to return to Texas, Throckmorton decided to make the trip to Corinth with his men.[39] However, upon arriving in Mississippi, he fell seriously ill and was forced to accept an honorable discharge on May 25, 1862, after which he returned home to recover.[40] Throckmorton's ailment was not recorded, but it possible that he suffered from some form of kidney ailment just as he had during the Mexican War.

On account of his earlier stance against secession, Throckmorton made several bitter enemies who would not forgive him for his earlier Unionist sentiments. Upon returning home, he discovered that his political adversaries had circulated a report stating that he had left the service at Corinth because he had not been offered a rank higher than captain, and thus he had returned home in hopes of obtaining a higher command with a new volunteer regiment.[41] While other Confederate military leaders, especially commanders of volunteer companies, might have used such tactics as a way to improve their rank within the military, the accusations regarding Throckmorton were unfounded.

In another effort to further impugn Throckmorton's character, his political enemies widely circulated the rumor that President Lincoln had earlier appointed him as a commissioner for the collection of taxes in the rebel district of Texas. Thus, his enemies claimed that Throckmorton was consorting with other Unionists and was in essence a traitor to the Confederacy.[42] Throckmorton answered these charges in a letter published in the *McKinney Messenger* on August 20, 1862:

> I have by no word, act, or deed countenanced in any manner whatsoever, or been privy to this or any other appointment. So far as I am concerned it is wholly unwarranted. Nor have I had any connection or correspondence with any person whatever since the war began who is in the confidence of,

> or friendly with, the government of the United States. . . . Because I and thousands of others in our state believed that our southern leaders were too rash and precipitate and that other remedies should be resorted to before secession, is no reason why I should look on approvingly and see the mad hand of fanaticism kindle the flames that are to consume every city, town, and hamlet throughout the South.[43]

This public pronouncement addressed the charges of his enemies, but Throckmorton also acknowledged for the first time in writing why he—and undoubtedly other North Texans—was fighting in the war. He stated that "the best and unscrupulous conduct of the Lincoln administration upon the slave question, its utter disregard of the Constitution, . . . too clearly show that this is a war, not only against our institutions and property but a war of entire and utter subjugation." The former senator continued by stating that "it is the determination of the Federal Government to make slaves the equals of white men, to rob us of our property, and to make Southern freedmen hewers of wood and drawers of water, none can doubt."[44] In part, Throckmorton's pronouncement clearly indicated that he entered the war to thwart federal coercion and to preserve white supremacy.

Adding to Throckmorton's problem was the discovery of a secret peace party conspiracy in North Texas, especially in the counties of Grayson, Wise, and Cooke. The peace party, also known as the Loyal League, was made up of Unionists and others who entertained the idea of bringing the war to an end through negotiations. Furthermore, the members of the peace party movement opposed the Confederate conscription law of April 1862, which threatened to force Unionists into Confederate military service.[45] The members of the peace party met in secret and created an organized hierarchy, with those closest to the top being the strongest advocates of negotiating peace with the federal government. Apparently, the group's plan was to increase its numbers until it was strong enough to mount a revolt against Confederate authority in the state, reclaiming Texas for the Union. The plot went according to plan until Newton Chance, a loyal Confederate from Wise County, was approached to join the movement. Chance immediately reported the incident to William J. Hudson, a Confederate officer at Gainesville. The result was that Confederate authorities detained some fifty-five men and hanged more than forty of them for treason. Although some of the members of the organization were of questionable character, many of the men were forthright citizens who were misled about the true nature of the secret society. They were simply told that the society was created to promote peace between the North and the South.[46]

Throckmorton was the friend of several of the Union men involved with the Loyal League, and he felt personally responsible for their plight. Many of the accused Unionists had supported him during the secession movement, and their loyalty to the Union was strengthened as a result of his influence. Throckmorton also agreed with the peace party's position on the Confederate conscription law of 1862. In October 1862, he learned that local authorities had arrested several Unionists in the nearby town of Sherman and were preparing to lynch them. Fearing another incident like that which unfolded in Gainesville, Throckmorton traveled to Sherman with the state district judge Robert W. Waddell and defended the men's right to be fairly represented in court. While their specific arguments were not recorded for posterity, the two men's plea for due process of the law persuaded local authorities to send their prisoners to the Confederate district court at Tyler, where all were eventually released.[47]

Despite giving aid to some of the accused Unionists, Throckmorton did justify the lynching of others in the Red River counties by stating that a "great good to society" had been accomplished because a group of dissenters had been eliminated. Apparently, he made these comments after learning that some of the dissenters hanged at Gainesville had murdered his former commander and friend Col. William C. Young. Furthermore, he believed that the accused individuals posed a threat to settlers on the frontier especially considering that they were found guilty of aiding a federal invasion of North Texas.[48] Thus, while he could appreciate their Unionist stance, Throckmorton could not accept the idea of destroying the community that he helped to create on the frontier, and as a result the former senator justified the executions of North Texans who did not wholeheartedly pledge to protect the interest of the people living on the frontier.[49]

The peace party movement in North Texas forced Throckmorton once again to think about the vulnerability of white settlers on the frontier. On October 25, 1862, he sent a letter to Governor Lubbock expressing his concerns and offering to raise and to command a new frontier regiment. In the communication to the governor, he stated that "the fact that the multiplied thousands of our gallant men are beyond the Mississippi & beyond the limits of this state, and the threatened invasion of our soil from the north, as well as the federal landing on the coast, our own internal commotions [peace party movement], and defenseless condition has filled me with serious apprehension."[50] Throckmorton believed that if the federal army moved into the Indian Territory, "the reserve Indians . . . will be turned loose on our border—and our grain section here will be an inviting field for federal raids—perhaps invasion."[51] Throckmorton concluded his letter by suggesting that he was willing to assume command of any troops that the governor would authorize for service in his region of the state.[52] Lubbock, however, was in the process of transferring state troops to Confederate service and did not plan on organizing additional forces for service on the frontier.

Frustrated that Lubbock failed to see the validity of his request, Throckmorton rejoined the Confederate Army.[53] He joined Colonel Stone in February 1863 in organizing a new company for service in Col. Isham Chisum's regiment of Texas Cavalry, also known as the Second Partisan Rangers.[54] Throckmorton was commissioned a major in the regiment. The men gathered near the town of Fairfield in Freestone County and remained there until March.[55] Confederate leaders then ordered the regiment to Navasota in Grimes County, where they spent much of their time engaged in military drills, gathering supplies, and mustering men into their regiment. Colonel Stone was able to raise and equip two regiments before receiving orders in late April to report to Louisiana.[56] Between May and August of 1863, Colonel Stone's regiments engaged federal troops in Louisiana at Cheneyville, Brashear, and Fort Butler. During this time Throckmorton's health failed him once again; apparently he suffered a renewed bout with kidney disease and was eventually forced from the field to a hospital in Vermillionville, Louisiana. While in Vermillionville, he learned that his friends back home had elected him to represent Collin and Grayson counties in the state senate. As a result of his failed health, the army discharged Throckmorton on September 12, 1863, and he started the long journey back home to resume his political career.[57]

When Throckmorton arrived in Texas in late September, he found North Texas in turmoil. The region still remained unsettled by the conscription issue. Concerned about frontier defense, a majority of North Texans refused to serve in the eastern theater of the war. As a result, Confederate authorities considered the northern region of the state a haven for deserters, common criminals, and staunch Unionists—disloyal parties who threatened the sovereignty of the Confederacy.

Believing that dissent in North Texas might lead some Unionists to ship their crops and livestock to Union soldiers, Confederate authorities sent regular troops to the region in 1863. Brig. Gen. Smith P. Bankhead, who was successful in combating German dissenters in Central Texas, took command of the newly formed Northern Subdistrict. Bankhead proved ineffective in dealing with dissent, and Lt. Gen. Edmund Kirby Smith, commander of the Trans-Mississippi Department, replaced him with Brig. Gen. Henry E. McCulloch, who also proved unsuccessful in dealing with dissent in Central Texas. Smith and McCulloch forged a new policy designed to curb dissent by offering amnesty to all deserters in the Confederate Army, providing that they agreed to reenlist. McCulloch asked prominent North Texas men, such as Throckmorton, to aid in successful implementation of the new policy.[58]

In an effort to calm the crisis that was developing in the northern counties, Throckmorton published a letter to his constituents in local newspapers in October 1863. The newly elected senator reminded them that if the Confederacy failed to win the war, the white society they had forged out of the wilderness would be utterly destroyed:

> If we fail in this struggle, we become the most degraded people on the face of earth. Our own slaves will be put on an equality with us by our masters. Nay, they will become our taskmasters. Our inheritance will be divided out with them. Our property will be confiscated and so burthened with taxes that the severest toll and most rigid economy cannot pay them. Our lands will be sold by the tax gatherer, and Yankee capital will become the purchaser; our whole country will be overrun with Northern adventurers. Your ancestral homes will be filled with new faces of Northern aspect; your sons and daughters will mingle their blood with that of the new-comers. You and your sons will become renters of your own soil, and wanderers on the face of the earth; and in a few years the race of southern chivalry in this beautiful land of ours, will have [become] extinct and numbered among the things that were.[59]

In part, Throckmorton wrote this letter to persuade the citizens of North Texas to renew their commitment to the Confederate cause and to convince deserters to return to their post, but the underlying meaning is clear: the senator wanted to remind people that white supremacy on the frontier was in danger. Apparently, Lincoln's Emancipation Proclamation convinced Throckmorton that the federal government was now waging a war to free the slaves and give them an equal status with southern whites.

Throckmorton's call for support of the Confederacy had a limited impact on many North Texans. For example, Henry Boren, the leader of a large contingent in North Texas, sent word to McCulloch that his men would join the Confederate service if they were permanently stationed near their homes and families. Brigadier General McCulloch was angered that Boren's men still refused to serve anywhere except on the North Texas frontier and issued a stern warning to them in a letter penned on October 24, 1863. McCulloch stated that the Texans would be allowed to temporarily remain in the region "with the distinct understanding that you cannot be allowed to elect officers, and that you may be ordered to meet the Yankees if they approach this section of the country from any quarter." McCulloch then issued Boren and his men another warning: "if you are not willing to fight our common enemy . . . I don't want you on the frontier or anywhere else in our service. If you are not willing to do this, you are not our friends, and properly belong to the other side."[60] Such pronouncements from McCulloch did little to stabilize conditions on the northern frontier.

In November, Senator Throckmorton traveled to Austin and assumed his duties in the Tenth Legislature. During his tenure, he debated and voted on several key issues confronting the Lone Star State, including the depreciation of Confederate currency, the Confederate government's impressment of cotton, the continued development of economic enterprise, the rising crime rate, and various other less significant matters. Throckmorton's positions on the issues were by this time predictable. He staunchly supported the economic development of North Texas and called for the protection of the settlers in the region. However, he also believed that the Confederacy had to succeed in its bid for independence.

Despite the apparent gravity of the circumstances surrounding conscription and dissent in the frontier counties, the legislators spent relatively little time debating the matter.[61] However, state leaders did not ignore the issue completely. On December 15, 1863, the legislators approved an act for protecting the frontier. It called on able-bodied men from certain counties to enroll in small frontier companies to protect the Texas frontier from Indian raids. According to the provision, the governor was to divide the frontier into three separate regions and appoint a commander over each. The commanding officer was instructed to accept only bona fide men, meaning those individuals who actually lived inside the counties that they were charged with protecting. A quarter of the men in each district was to remain on duty at all times, and the commander could call all of his men into service in an emergency. Also, the governor could order the frontier forces to any place on the frontier to prevent Indian raids or other lawless activities, providing the men were not used for more than one month at a time.[62] With this act, the legislature initiated a new policy concerning the use of Texas soldiers on the frontier. Apparently, the governor and the legislature deemed it more appropriate to use the able-bodied men of Texas to defend the state's frontier regions rather than serve in the Confederate armies in the defense of other southern states.[63]

Beginning on January 6, 1864, Gov. Pendleton Murrah began implementing the new frontier defense policy. In doing so, he had to complete two tasks: First, the governor transferred the Frontier Regiment to Confederate service on March 1, 1864. Second, he authorized the organization of a new frontier force—the Frontier Organization. The new state troops helped to fill the void that existed after the Frontier Regiment was officially transferred to the Confederate Army.[64]

Governor Murrah immediately formed the new Frontier Organization, wanting to have the regiments in place by March 1, 1864, when the existing state troops were scheduled to transfer to the Confederate Army. Following the legislature's guidelines, the governor divided the frontier counties into three districts and appointed suitable men to command the troops stationed in the new districts: William Quayle commanded the First Frontier District, headquartered in Decatur; George B. Erath commanded the Second Frontier District, headquartered in Gatesville; and James M. Hunter commanded the Third Frontier District, headquartered in Fredericksburg.[65] The appointed commanders immediately filled their ranks with new recruits and by March 1, 1864, approximately four thousand men mustered for frontier service.

By forming the Frontier Organization exclusively for use on the fringes of Anglo settlement in Texas, Governor Murrah and the legislature found themselves in direct confrontation with Confederate authorities, who claimed that all frontier units, including the newly formed Frontier Organization, were subject to service in Confederate armies outside the state. In essence, the Texas government found itself in a constitutional debate with Confederate commanders over conscription. Governor Murrah claimed that the state law that gave him the authority to form frontier forces was superior to the conscription law passed by the Confederate Congress. Commanders in the Trans-Mississippi Department disagreed, arguing that the laws passed by the Confederate Congress were superior to state law. The military's position regarding conscription became even more uncompromising after the summer of 1863 when it became apparent that the tides of war were going against the South, and Confederate recruitment began to decline.

As a result of the increasing need for men in defense of the Trans-Mississippi theater of the war, Gen. John B. Magruder, Confederate commander of the District of Texas, New Mexico, and Arizona, attempted to force conscription on all eligible men in Texas. Governor Murrah balked at Magruder's heavy-handed tactics but eventually conceded to the general's demand for troops once the U.S. Army, under the command of Gen. Nathaniel Banks, moved up the Red River in the spring of 1864 and threatened to invade northeastern Texas. However, even as his state faced possible invasion, the governor wrote to General Magruder requesting that the commander define how many troops were needed and detail where the recruits would be stationed outside the state. The governor's concession came too late to affect the outcome of the Red River campaign, but it did effectively end the controversy between state and Confederate authorities over the question of conscription.[66]

In an effort to enlist men from the Northern Subdistrict in Texas, General Magruder suggested that the Confederate authorities use influential men from the region to aid in recruitment. Knowing that approximately ten thousand men in the Northern Subdistrict were eligible for military service, Magruder stated that "of these, several thousand can be got out by influential men like Throckmorton, using his influence as a State brigadier-general, but if the general [E. Kirby Smith] would appoint Brigadier-General Throckmorton . . . to have the same rank in the Confederate Army, we could thus secure his influence and utmost exertions, and furnish a brigadier-general to the reserve brigade."[67]

While the state and Confederate authorities came to a mutual agreement over conscription, Governor Murrah and the Texas Legislature never fully conceded state control over potential draftees who resided on the Texas frontier. The governor continued to maintain the position that frontier settlers should be able to protect their homes and were not liable to Confederate conscription. The Confederate Conscription Bureau of the Trans-Mississippi Department attempted to seize control over frontier conscripts in Texas throughout the summer and fall of 1864, but the state government refused the bureau's demands. General E. Kirby Smith finally deemed the situation in Texas as hopeless and submitted the matter to the Confederate government for a final resolution, but before the matter could be settled, the war ended.[68]

Brigadier General Throckmorton became concerned with the growing division between diehard Confederates and those who questioned the viability of the southern war effort. Throughout 1864, Throckmorton began to doubt whether the Confederacy could successfully win independence from the United States. He expressed his concerns and doubts about the war in a letter to his close friend and confidant, Benjamin Epperson. In his correspondence, Throckmorton discussed his concern over a set of resolutions that radical Confederates introduced on the opening day of the second extra session of the Texas Tenth Legislature that met from October 19 to November 15, 1864.[69] The senator noted that "on the first day of the session [the legislature considered] a long set of resolutions that the power to make peace [with the federal government] was delegated to the Confederate government [and] that Texas would never reconstruct." Throckmorton was against the introduction of these resolutions because he believed that it would produce disunity among the state's leaders and the people of Texas.[70]

The primary cause for Throckmorton's alarm was the extremism of those who sought to condemn any individual who did not fully support the Confederacy. The North Texas politician openly challenged Sen. Chauncy Shepard's statement that "any man who talked of reconstruction would be hanged."[71] Throckmorton reminded his colleagues:

> Enthusiasm [for the war] was first damped by the conscript law, which had induced thousands of gallant soldiers to believe that they were serfs & slaves and not freemen—that this was a government in the opinion of these men not supported by the voluntary offering of a free people, but supported by a military despotism—that instead of being left to their chivalry & devotion to the cause of liberty to sustain the government they were hunted down like wild beasts & forced into the ranks of the army with the bayonet thrusting them along. . . . Then I reviewed our actual condition—the loss of territory—the immense destruction of property—the thousands dead & thousands maimed & diseased . . . judging by the past four years more would bring our armies to the waters of the gulf & the conscription up to the age of 100—from a million of fighting men to none—If this statement should continue—if Congress kept on centralizing the government—if the military were to continue to grind the people into the dust with the iron heel of tyranny . . . If then, in such a fearful contingency, some old gray haired minister of God's holy church who through years of weary toil & suffering prayed for our success, but . . . believed that the war should cease,

> and that reconstruction was the surest & best means to ensure it. Was he, I asked, to be swung to a limb?[72]

After venting his frustrations about the illogical position of the extremists, Throckmorton reaffirmed his personal commitment to the Confederacy. Furthermore, he told Epperson, "I asserted that I was not for reconstruction—but for separation & Independence & that I wished no one to misunderstand me in this. Now you will see from this what course I think we (you & I) [should] pursue. Let everybody else take a different course if they will. But let us be the last to yield."[73] It was clear that Throckmorton feared the violent suppression of dissent in the Lone Star State, especially in North Texas. However, he believed that a Confederate victory was the only way to protect the dominant position of whites in the state. Thus, the senator continued to give unwavering support to the Confederate military until it proved itself incapable of protecting white supremacy in Texas.

When the state legislature was not in session, Throckmorton commanded troops on the Texas frontier. As a military leader, the North Texas politician served as a brigadier general of two different frontier forces. On March 1, 1864, Governor Murrah appointed Throckmorton to command Brigadier District Number 3, one of six militia districts created for service on the frontier.[74] Throckmorton maintained this position until the governor ordered him in October 1864 to replace Maj. William Quayle as commander of the First Frontier District.[75] Therefore, Throckmorton remained in the state's frontier forces and carried out his charge of providing military protection to the citizens of the Red River counties. Additionally, Throckmorton's troops tracked down Confederate deserters and helped local officials maintain law and order within the northern region of the state.[76]

Throckmorton dutifully carried out his orders, especially after assuming command of the First Frontier District. With an increase in Indian depredations on the frontier, Throckmorton ordered settlers to build blockhouses and stockades in which to live and to protect themselves from potential attacks.[77] He urged the men of the Frontier Organization to cultivate a friendly intercourse with the Confederate forces when they were serving in the same area, and he took steps to rid the frontier forces of men who were not residents of the frontier region prior to July 1, 1863. Throckmorton also recruited new men for service in the Frontier Organization. Largely due to his efforts, the First Frontier District had twenty-six companies with a total enrollment of 1,436 men by December of 1864.[78]

To help combat Comanche and Kiowa warriors who were crossing the Red River and raiding North Texas settlements, Throckmorton suggested to the governor that some of the men under his command be used as search-and-destroy units that would primarily operate in the Indian Territory. In February 1865, the North Texas commander further recommended that the newly formed units be given leeway to openly confront hostile Indians, Jayhawkers, outlaws, and deserters. In regard to attacking tribes in the Indian Territory, Throckmorton believed that the soldiers should confiscate their enemies' property. By doing this, Throckmorton proposed that the Indians' property should be given to his men and that the total value of the confiscated items could be deducted from their pay. In this way, the units would be self-sustaining, would be active on the frontier, and would keep him informed of the enemies' movements. Despite the apparent logic of Throckmorton's plan, bad weather and logistical problems prevented the search-and-destroy units from effectively fulfilling their task.[79]

Throckmorton was also concerned that his men were not properly provisioned. This had been one of the motivating factors behind creating the self-sufficient search-and-destroy units. Circumstances apparently were bad enough that he called on the state government to organize the frontier forces into an active unit under the command of the Confederate authorities, believing that the southern government was in a better position to supply his troops with adequate provisions. Additionally, Throckmorton informed the governor that most of the soldiers serving on active duty with the frontier troops, or in reserve for emergency measures, would be willing to spend three-fourths of their paychecks for provisions and mounts. The advantages according to Throckmorton were twofold: First, this arrangement would provide frontier soldiers with some form of regular compensation, thereby improving the overall morale and discipline among his troops. Second, the provisions purchased for his command would primarily come from North Texas, allowing farmers and manufacturers in the Red River counties to survive the economic hardships caused by the war.[80] However, before the governor and Confederate authorities responded to Throckmorton's suggestions, the Confederacy reassigned him to the Department of Indian Affairs.

Throckmorton's superiors deemed his military service between January and March 1865 honorable. The Collin County politician had never shown any outward signs of disloyalty to the Confederate cause. Nevertheless, as the war continued and as casualties mounted, Throckmorton began to seriously doubt the rebels' ability to win the war. In a letter to Epperson on February 3, 1865, Throckmorton suggested that a Confederate victory hinged on the southern government's ability to secure foreign assistance. "I presume Mr. Davis all ready knows what terms we will have to subscribe to get foreign aid," he told Epperson. "The abolishment of slavery is the first sacrifice. This is the base of all other terms."[81] The North Texas senator could accept this proposition considering that he owned only one slave, and therefore, his personal economic loss would be minimal in comparison to large plantation owners who had a significant amount of money invested in slaves. Also, Throckmorton knew that abolition would cripple the political and social dominance of the slaveholding planters. Throckmorton continued by stating that he expected "to remain faithful to the Confederacy and the State until the people determine another course. But I feel if the Ship of State is compelled to founder that duty & patriotism requires every effort be made possible to save the crew." The senator concluded that "if there is no chance for foreign help, we should make terms while we are in a condition to demand living ones, and not postpone it until the chains of slavery are riveted upon a helpless people."[82] Throckmorton understood that the Confederacy was on the verge of collapse.

In March 1865, Throckmorton wrote to Epperson once again regarding the status of the Confederacy and the inevitability that foreign aid would not be forthcoming. Throckmorton stated that "if this be true, and everything now indicates that it is, nothing but diplomacy and skill [brought] to bear [on] Lincoln and the federal government can save us from irretrievable ruin, and the most appalling degradation." He continued, "I have strong hope that some of the statesmen of the Confederacy know and appreciate the condition of affairs, and are determined to make a mighty effort to save us. This can only be done, I imagine, by reconstruction." He soberly observed that "we may have to give up slavery, but even that is not hopeless if properly managed; or at least the force of the shock to the great industrial interests of the Country may be greatly paralyzed and deadened."[83] This letter indicated Throckmorton's loyalty to the white supremacy: the abolition of slavery did not necessarily mean the end of white dominance over blacks. Additionally, his willingness to secure a peaceful and quick reconstruction with the federal government reveals that he no longer believed that the Confederacy would win the war.[84]

In March and April of 1865, the Confederate government desperately sought to enlist the help of Native Americans in their failing attempt to win independence. Confederate authorities believed that the Kiowa, Arapaho, Cheyenne, Shoshone, Snake, and Blackfeet tribes were willing to make peace with the Confederacy. Capt. M. L. Bell, the assistant superintendent of Indian Affairs of the Confederate States of America, sent Maj. J. C. Vore, a Confederate Indian agent to the Creek Indians, to consult with the various tribes and to explore whether a meaningful peace treaty could be arranged between them and the Confederate government. Acting on the advice of Vore, General E. Kirby Smith, without consulting Governor Murrah, appointed Throckmorton as the Confederate commissioner to the Indians. He proved to be a good choice. The North Texan was well known and respected by many of the principal tribes living in Texas. Seeing the soundness of General Smith's decision, the governor appointed Maj. John W. Lane as a substitute to command the First Frontier District and immediately commissioned Throckmorton as an Indian agent for the State of Texas, giving him wide latitude in making peace with the frontier Indians. Throckmorton left Decatur, the First Frontier District headquarters, and traveled to Kenzos on the Washita River, near Elm Springs, for the scheduled May 15 meeting with the various tribes in the Indian Territory.[85]

Confederate authorities ordered Throckmorton, known as Leathercoat to the Native Americans, to obtain a peace agreement between the friendly tribes of the Indian Territory and to secure Native American support for a potential Confederate raid into Kansas. In essence, Throckmorton was charged with making a tripartite agreement among the Native Americans, the Lone Star State, and the Confederate government. Concerned that Native Americans might be unwilling to negotiate with an agent from Texas, General Smith decided to have an additional agent accompany the North Texan during the negotiations that were slated to take place at Council Grove, Indian Territory, in early May of 1865. General Smith first asked Albert Pike of Arkansas to join Throckmorton, but when the Arkansan declined, the Confederate commander selected Col. W. D. Reagan, a judge in the military court of the Trans-Mississippi Department. Colonel Reagan accepted the position and immediately set out to join Leathercoat, who was already in the Indian Territory.[86]

Throckmorton and Reagan set up a council meeting with a number of warriors and chiefs of the Choctaw, Cherokee, Seminole, Creek, and Osage tribes. The Confederate agents even asked some of the more warlike tribes to attend the peace talks, including the Comanches, Cheyennes, Caddoes, Arapahoes, Lipans, Kickapoos, Kiowas, and a limited number of Sioux. Official reports estimated that there were approximately twenty thousand Native Americans present at the council meeting. During the course of negotiations, Brig. Gen. D. H. Cooper, Confederate commander of the Indian Territory, sent Throckmorton a dispatch informing him that the Confederacy was in dire straits. Cooper believed that their country's circumstances would preclude Throckmorton from "undertaking anything more than to secure peaceful relations among and with the Indians."[87] Confederate commanders in the Trans-Mississippi realized that by 1865 an attack on Kansas was impractical, and therefore they abandoned their original plans to secure support for a joint Indian-Confederate raid.

Heeding the advice of General Cooper, Leathercoat once again focused on protecting the frontier by attempting to negotiate a treaty with the Indians that would forbid the tribes from traveling south of the Red River. Masking his racial motivations, he argued that frontier citizens could not tell which Native Americans were friendly and which were foes. If all the various Indians tribes agreed to stay north of the Red River, there would be less chance of accidentally killing members of friendly tribes. While the Texan's argument seemed logical, the chiefs refused to sign any agreement that required them to give up their rights to travel south of the Red River and freely hunt on lands west of Anglo settlements during the autumn months. Throckmorton, however, was able to secure a mutual agreement promising friendly relations between the frontier settlers and the various tribes represented at the council meeting. After winning the best terms possible, he returned to Texas in the early June 1865. Upon his arrival, he discovered that General E. Kirby Smith had surrendered the Trans-Mississippi Department to federal troops just two weeks prior to his return.[88] The war was over.

The Frontier Organization continued to protect the Texas frontier until the latter part of the summer of 1865, when the federal military ordered it to disband. Once the Native Americans discovered that the Texas frontier was void of defensive troops, the more hostile tribes resumed their attacks on the settlers, effectively pushing the frontier line in the Lone Star State eastward in some places by a distance of 150 to 200 miles from its prewar position.[89] It seemed that the Anglo society that had existed on the southern frontier since the 1840s was on the verge of destruction.

On June 10, Gen. Philip H. Sheridan, U.S. commander of the Military Division of the Southwest, ordered Gen. Gordon Granger to occupy the Lone Star State with a force of eighteen hundred men and to establish strategic interior posts between Galveston Island and the small town of Brenham, Washington County. General Granger entered Galveston nine days later and found the state in shambles. Despite the pleas of Governor Murrah for county authorities to protect the public property of the state, former Confederates soldiers began stealing state property, including guns, ammunition, horses, and wagons. Some soldiers even began looting local merchants and county treasuries, as well as the state treasury in Austin. The ex-Confederates justified their actions by simply stating that they had not been paid for their military service and that they were only taking what was owed them. The actions of these miscreants stimulated general mayhem in the state. Circumstances did not improve when state officials who feared prosecution at the hands of the approaching federal army fled to the safety of Mexico: Governor Murrah was one of those officials seeking asylum in a foreign land. With no official government in Austin and the county governments in disarray, lawless bands formed in the state and began a wider campaign of looting and murder. The activities of these lawless rogues promised to bring the full weight of the federal government to bear on all Texans in an effort to restore order to the state.[90]

Throckmorton recognized that the uncontrolled violence posed a threat to conservative Democrats' chances of controlling the state government. As an able politician, he apparently understood that Unionists would capitalize on the violence in an effort to secure political office. Throckmorton believed that these Unionists would side with Radical Republicans in Washington, D.C., and as a result, they would impose their political views on the citizens of Texas. On June 13, Throckmorton wrote to Epperson that he feared "Radicalism will prevail in the federal councils. If so, none of our sort will be elected [to political office], for the simple reason that the people will be easily persuaded that such things are done through the advice of our friends." The North Texan continued that "there must be another thing guarded against by us. We must prevent, if possible, too many men who were opposed to Secession to run for office. Whenever a man of an opposite policy can be found who is conservative & sensible offers[, w]e should show a willingness to sustain him." Thus, Throckmorton revealed his early views about the reconstruction of his state: conservatives must triumph over the Radical Republicans in statewide elections. In essence, he and other North Texans believed that the defeat of the Confederacy was a golden opportunity to reconstruct the state's social and economic systems in such a way as to protect the white supremacy on the frontier. To successfully achieve this goal, prominent frontier politicians wanted to replace the antebellum plantation system with an economic alternative that would encourage former slaves, now known as freedmen, to remain in the same geographical location where their former masters had held them in bondage. Additionally, these frontier politicians had to convince the state and national government to continue their relentless extermination of the Native American tribes that threatened to stall the westward advancement of Anglo cultural and society. Throckmorton unequivocally supported the ideology of white supremacy and was willing to sacrifice his future political career to ensure white dominance in the state.

## CHAPTER FIVE

# *Tainted Blood*

## EARLY RECONSTRUCTION IN TEXAS, 1865–66

The end of the Civil War brought drastic changes to the people of Texas as they faced the challenges of reestablishing their state as a viable part of the Union. One of the most difficult issues for white Texans, especially ex-Confederates, was accepting the results of the war. The federal government was now in charge of setting the standards for reconstructing their state. To make matters worse, Pres. Andrew Johnson and Radical Republicans in Congress did not agree on the method of restoring the Union. Political conflict at the national level only added to the confusion and misunderstanding with the southern states. While opposing factions in the federal government worked out its differences, ex-Confederates and former secessionists sought ways to maintain the prewar status of their social, political, and economic institutions.[1]

During the early days of Reconstruction, Throckmorton sought every opportunity to create a new society where blacks were prevented from rising in social status and the former slaveholding planters were prevented from dominating the people of North Texas. The small farmers on the frontier believed that the elite planters were overrepresented in the state legislature, undertaxed, and thus essentially subsidized by the state government. Frontier farmers had grown to despise the large plantation owners as well as their slaves who, were symbols of the planters' wealth and dominance in society. It is reasonable to assume that the North Texas yeoman farmers could accept emancipation of the slaves if it worked to diminish the wealth of the planters. But frontier Texans were not willing to accept black equality. Prejudices and a strong belief in white supremacy prevented them from supporting politicians who wanted to extend full civil rights to the freedmen. Many North Texas whites believed that it was necessary to prevent African Americans from moving to the frontier regions of the state, infiltrating the society that they had created on the fringes of civilization. In their minds, they were simply protecting the frontier from another potential invader. Given these attitudes, it comes as no surprise that the yeoman farmers turned to a prominent local elite like Throckmorton to represent them in government.[2]

To ensure that the northern counties remained firmly under the control of white citizens, Throckmorton believed that two objectives had to be accomplished. First, the Texas government needed to remove Native Americans from the northern frontier to the Indian Territory. Second, the state government needed to develop policies that would keep the newly freed slaves from migrating to the frontier lands. In other words, a system would have to be created that kept the freedmen on lands in the regions of the state where they had lived in servitude. As part of this policy, legislators would have to deny freedmen the right to vote, especially considering that the former slaves would almost certainly support Republican candidates. Throckmorton believed that Radical Republicans would call for greater racial equality in Texas and would thereby thwart any plans to ensure white supremacy. His position became clear early in the process of Reconstruction.

Scholars typically divide the Reconstruction era in Texas into three different phases: Presidential Reconstruction, which began in June 1865 and ended in March 1867; Congressional Reconstruction, from March 1867 to April 1870; and Radical Rule, which ended in 1873. Presidential Reconstruction began when Gen. Gordon Granger landed at Galveston with eighteen hundred federal troops. He declared the Emancipation Proclamation in effect in the state, nullified all acts passed by the Texas government after secession, and began the process of paroling soldiers of the Confederate Army. Presidential Reconstruction ended on March 2, 1867, when Congress took control of the administration of the southern states from President Johnson. Radical Reconstruction began with the adoption of the Texas Constitution of 1869 and the election of Edmund J. Davis as governor. The military authorities officially gave control of the state to Davis's administration on April 16, 1870. Radical Republican control of the state began to deteriorate when Texas Democrats regained control of both houses of the state legislature in the 1872 general elections.[3]

Following the Union's victory over the Confederacy, President Johnson established provisional governments in each of the southern states. In Texas, he appointed Andrew Jackson Hamilton as the provisional governor

Pres. Andrew Johnson. Johnson became the chief executive after President Lincoln's assassination. He continued Lincoln's lenient policy of Reconstruction, which infuriated his Radical Republican detractors in Congress and initiated a political struggle in Washington that ultimately led to Congressional Reconstruction and Johnson's impeachment. *Brady-Handy Photograph Collection, Library of Congress.*

of the state on June 17, 1865. The new appointee arrived in Texas at the end of July. Hamilton was a reasonable choice for the position because he had served in various state offices in Texas before the war and, like Throckmorton, he was a noted Unionist during the secession crisis. However, unlike many of the Unionists in the Lone Star State, Hamilton entered the Union army in 1862 and assumed command of a Texas cavalry unit during the latter part of the war. As a result, Johnson hoped that Hamilton's past would make the provisional governor acceptable to Unionist Democrats in Texas as well as Radical Republicans in the northern states.[4]

Johnson, like Lincoln before him, sought a speedy reconstruction of the southern states. As a result, his plan of reconstruction required the southern states to renounce the right of secession and to accept the abolition of slavery. However, the president, a southerner himself, was unwilling to demand that the defeated states extend constitutional rights, especially suffrage rights, to the freedmen as a requirement for readmission into the

Union. Therefore, Johnson left the way open for southern lawmakers to obstruct the rights of freedpeople.

In late July, Throckmorton traveled to Austin where he tried to influence the political decisions of Governor Hamilton. The North Texan hoped that political strife would not stand in the way of quick readmission to the Union. Throckmorton hoped to achieve two purposes in going to the state's capital. First, he wanted Governor Hamilton to retain all county and local officials then currently holding office. Second, he wanted Hamilton to convene a state constitutional convention. Hamilton received Throckmorton and considered his proposition but ultimately disagreed with the North Texan's plan for readmission to the Union.[5]

On August 6, Throckmorton wrote a letter to his friend and confidant Benjamin Epperson in which he expressed his concern over the political developments in Texas. He argued that Hamilton should "authorize by proclamation all the county officers elect to go on and discharge their several duties with the statement that if any county officer had rendered himself obnoxious by his bad conduct, upon the proper representation he should be turned out and another put in." Throckmorton believed that the "state could be organized in one month" if these measures were enacted. He admitted, however, that Hamilton did not completely agree with his assessment of the political environment in the state. Commenting on public speeches that Hamilton had made while traveling to Austin, Throckmorton speculated that the governor "was an abolitionists & glorified in it and I fear that he is for negro suffrage & sitting on juries." Throckmorton declared that he would rather remain "under military rule always rather than yield anything but an acknowledgment that the negro has been freed by the act of the govern't & that we recognize it as an existing fact and that we have no disposition to quarrell any more about it." He denied "any desire to reestablish slavery," but he expressed optimism that "we will be enabled to adopt a coercive system of labor." Throckmorton adamantly added, "I take it that it is our policy to look out for ourselves. Certain it is I do not intend to be abolitionized nor to be the aiders or abetters in the further humiliation & degradation of our people."[6]

Throckmorton was clearly unsatisfied with the provisional governor and other Unionists who had gathered in Austin. As a result, he suggested to Epperson a contingency plan:

> One thing is well worth our serious consideration—a division of the State when the convention meets, or at least the ground work for it—Western

> Tex with the foreign element here now & that to come will unquestionably make this section purely radical. Think of this—keep it to yourself—with a new State East of the Brazos our section will have the votes—small farms & white labor can flourish—we will have a dense population—Red River Co as much so as any of our counties—but all this aside. My dear friend I feel very much like doing one of two things—either settling quietly at home & never appearing in any public capacity—or of emigrating the first chance—I am thoroughly disgusted [and] wearied & feel that I should give up all public life forever.[7]

With this statement, Throckmorton revealed his intention to preserve white supremacy in Texas, or at least white dominance in the northern counties.

A frustrated Throckmorton decided that he had done all he could in Austin and made the long journey back home in early August. However, he had not completely given up on trying to influence the Hamilton administration. Writing to the governor to inform him of the current conditions on the frontier, he stressed that the judicial districts in his region were in a state of confusion. Apparently the people of North Texas were puzzled about changes in jurisdiction and even the times when the courts should convene. Throckmorton assured the governor that "three fourths of the community & perhaps greatly more, are really desirous of testifying their loyalty to the government—at least such was the impression made upon my mind with the people whom I met & conversed with on my way from Austin." He then informed Hamilton that he had received word of increased Indian depredations on the frontier. Throckmorton reported that "the Indians seem to be worse than ever known before, and great numbers of the settlers are moving. Since [the] breaking up of the state frontier forces, & withdrawal of other troops, the Indians seem to know it, & instead of coming in and depridating as usual and then leaving, they now remain in country." Throckmorton concluded his letter by commenting on the lawlessness in the counties on the western fringes of the frontier. He suggested that "a speedy opening of the courts is the best remedy for such evils, and I will take the liberty of suggesting that instructions from you to the judicial officers of the state [ordering them] to hold the courts as soon as jurors can be qualified will do much to restore order & quiet." Throckmorton even acknowledged the breakdown of law and order in his home county, stating that "every few days there is a row & sometimes a shooting scrape and as there is no person to issue a warrant of arrest[. T]his sort of gentry have their own way. Besides [people] are refusing to pay their rents & the parties concerned are powerless to enforce payment." Throckmorton made it clear that the circumstances on the northern frontier could be improved if the Hamilton administration would enact practical solutions to the region's existing problems.[8] It was ironic that Throckmorton's personal animosity toward Governor Hamilton eventually undermined the prospects of a broader alliance of conservative Unionists.

In accordance with President Johnson's plan of Reconstruction, Governor Hamilton called on the counties in his state to elect delegates to a constitutional convention that was slated to convene at Austin in February of 1866. The election of delegates took place on January 8, 1866. Voter turnout was poor due to inclement weather, voter apathy, and the fact that only those individuals who qualified according to President Johnson's general amnesty proclamation, or had received an official pardon from the president, could vote in the elections. The increasingly embittered Throckmorton, however, claimed that the voters were muzzled and that the whole election was a farce. He argued that many North Texans believed that the elected delegates would simply travel to Austin and would confirm the edicts of their conquerors. Regardless of his personal convictions, the people of Grayson and Collin counties elected Throckmorton as their representative to the constitutional convention. He immediately left home to join other delegates as they gathered in Austin for the opening of the convention in early February.[9]

Texans in other counties also chose to send former antisecession men to the convention. Prominent Unionist delegates included Isaiah A. Paschal, Edward Degener, John Hancock, Edmund J. Davis, Xenophon B. Saunders, Albert H. Latimer, Robert H. Taylor, and James W. Flanagan. These men typically took a moderate position concerning the reconstruction of Texas. However, a strong contingent of former secessionists, many whom were elected despite the fact that they were not covered under the federal government's general amnesty policy and had not received presidential pardons, challenged the moderates at the convention. The most prominent of this group of former secessionists was Oran M. Roberts, who in 1861 had been president of the Secession Convention in Texas. Other well-known secessionists included Hardin R. Runnels, John Ireland, Dewitt C. Giddings, Reuben A. Reeves, James W. Henderson, John W. Whitfield, and Thomas N. Waul. They tried to preserve as much of the prewar status as possible, especially concerning the fate of freedmen.[10] Despite the fact that the *Dallas Herald* called the convention members "some of the

John H. Reagan, shown here in a photograph taken after the war. Reagan remained a political ally of Throckmorton throughout the postwar years. Even before Throckmorton was elected governor, Reagan warned him and other Texas Democrats to proceed with caution during Reconstruction and to fully comply with the military authorities stationed in the state. Throckmorton and his fellow Democratic leaders, however, chose to follow their own path toward redemption and led the state into near ruin. *Brady-Handy Photograph Collection, Library of Congress.*

ablest and far-seeing men in the State," the presence of ex-Confederates at the convention led many loyal Unionists to question the motives and legitimacy of the convention.[11]

On August 11, 1865, John H. Reagan, a prominent state politician during the 1850s and a cabinet member in the Confederate government during the war, sent Texans a prophetic warning from his federal prison cell at Fort Warren in Boston. Like other high-ranking officials in the Confederate government who were captured during the final days of the war, Reagan was placed in a northern prison where he learned more about northern plans for reconstructing the South. However, unlike other southern captives, Reagan took it upon himself to share his newly acquired knowledge with his fellow Texans. In a widely published letter, he attempted to persuade Texans to "adopt a course which would save them from military government and from universal negro suffrage." First, Reagan reminded his readers that they were part of a conquered nation and that they should accept the terms handed down by their victors. He noted that "a refusal to accede [to] these conditions would only result in a prolongation of the time during which you will be deprived of the civil government of your choice, and will continue [to be] subject to military rule." Next, Reagan suggested that Texans should recognize the supreme authority of the U.S. government and its right to protect itself against secession and to accept the abolition of slavery as well as to accept the rights of the freedmen. Finally, he revealed that the more radical members of Congress considered it necessary for the ex-Confederate states to extend full civil rights to the freedmen. Before any southern state could reassume its former position in the Union, its legislators would have to grant the freedmen suffrage rights and equal access to the courts. Nevertheless, the captive Texan suggested that state officials could limit black suffrage by establishing carefully constructed voting requirements, such as a literacy test, residency statutes, and taxpayer qualifications. While some politicians heeded Reagan's advice, most Texans ignored his suggestions.[12]

Throckmorton knew that Hamilton did not trust him to take part in reconstructing the state. He believed that the provisional governor's opinion of him was based on two primary issues: First, he had failed to rejoice in the defeat of the Confederacy. Second, he received support from the secessionists in his election to the convention. Hamilton had reason for concern. In a letter to Epperson, Throckmorton shared his thoughts on the major issues that the delegates would address in the constitutional convention. Challenging Hamilton's charges against him, he rhetorically asked, "What excuse have these gentry for such insinuation? None on earth, except, I did not shout hosannas to our defeat & ignominy, and because some who were secessionists have expressed themselves favorably to me."[13]

More important, Throckmorton openly discussed ways to obstruct federal Reconstruction policies. He stated that "if our people had moral courage, if our merchants were patriots instead of greedy speculators we could tame their radicalism and insolence." The North Texan continued, saying that "we could sell & buy from Europe, or not sell or buy at all. We had better do this until they [federal officials] show a disposition to treat us as countrymen & friends." Without considering that he was a rebel just a few months before, Throckmorton stated that "if I had my way not one dollar from the South or one pound of cotton or tobacco or anything else should go north, nor should one Yankee land here until we [are] treated as a Christian people should be treated." However, he added that "as a matter course when I speak of Yankees, I do mean not to include all, because of these & of the foreigners who come amongst us there are men who are an ornament to any country or people."[14]

Apparently, the number of ornamental northerners and foreigners were few in Texas, because he venomously announced that "I wish to see no yankee in my neighborhood. I desire no foreigner of any class, and so help me God, I would go home & spend all the days of my life, teach my children honest industry, and live within the earnings of our own circle than to see these cheating canting hypocrites, or foreign scum among us." Part of the reason Throckmorton held such disdain for northerners and foreigners stemmed from his belief that the New England states had been "contaminated with fashion & folly" and were "carried away by fast living" and "luxuries." Regarding northern society, he stated that "foreign immigration, greediness for gain, an inordinate desire to grow rich fast, crowded towns & cities, has enervated her people. They preserve but two distinctive elements of their original character, yes three, one puritanical psalm singing hypocrisy, chicanery, & a desire to get rich off of other people's labor." Fearing that the South would follow a similar path of decline, Throckmorton claimed that if "psalm singing, lying, swindling yankees & sour krouts & blackguard Irish" infiltrated the southern states, a few of us may grow rich, but as a "whole we become corrupted with fast times. With follies & dissipations and luxuries, our children so grow up, they catch the spirit of speculation & fine & fast living and finally they marry these d—m—d negro worshiping skunks and southern blood is tainted & spoiled forever—I want none of it."[15] While Throckmorton championed white supremacy, he also believed that some whites were superior to others.

In addition, Throckmorton discussed an issue slated for debate at the constitutional convention—the right of African Americans to testify in court cases. He declared that he had "weighed in [his] own mind all the reasons pro & con, and I am clearly of the opinion it is wrong except" in cases involving their race, which "is just because otherwise laws for their protection would be a farce." He further stated that "it is wrong because the hell hounds of radicalism demand . . . a right [that] many of their own free states do not allow, and wrong, because if we yield, [it will allow freedmen] to sit on juries, suffrage [rights], and finally to perfect social & political equality." While Throckmorton was willing to comply with the wishes of the president, he stated that "upon these questions which the Constitution gives the states the right to determine, I am for standing by them." He then concluded by announcing that "if they have a sufficient radical majority to keep us from our proper place in the Government, why, we can stay out, and they may be d—m—d." Thus, Throckmorton's biased views were apparent prior to the convening of the state's constitutional convention in Austin.[16] He clearly understood that black suffrage threatened the chances of white Democrats obtaining political power in the state.

The convention assembled on February 7, 1866, with sixty-two of the eighty-nine elected delegates present. James H. Bell took the chair on the motion of Throckmorton, called roll, and verified the credentials of the delegates. It soon became apparent that the members were divided into two main groups—Unionists and former secessionists. The Unionists were composed of Republican Unionists, commonly referred to as radicals, and conservative Unionists, referred to as conservatives. The faction of ex-Confederates and secessionists was also divided into two camps—extremists and moderates. On the second day of the convention, with James W. Henderson of Harris County presiding as president pro tem, the delegates nominated several men to preside over convention: James W. Throckmorton, Hardin R. Runnels, Robert H. Taylor, and Albert H. Latimer. Because the members considered their nomination too divisive, they removed Runnels and Taylor from consideration. When the delegates voted, Throckmorton defeated Latimer by a vote of forty-one to twenty-four. He received the support of the more moderate secessionists and conservative Unionist members. However, because the former secessionists favored him, many Republican Unionists viewed Throckmorton as unsound on the question of Reconstruction. Remembering that Throckmorton was a staunch nationalist before the Civil War, many Unionists believed that Throckmorton had betrayed his earlier principles. Nevertheless, whatever his earlier principles may have been, he was now one of the chief defenders of President Johnson's Reconstruction policies.[17]

If newspaper accounts reflected popular opinion, it appears that Texans were pleased with Throckmorton's election as president of the convention. The *Houston Telegraph* wrote, "Hon. J. W. Throckmorton, President of the Convention, stands confessedly in the front rank of public men in this State. He is a man of great judgment and thorough appreciation of human nature."[18] The *Tyler Journal* reported, "No better selection could have been made and all parties ought to be satisfied. . . . He is a fine speaker, in every respect a man of ability, and will grace any position that his State may honor him with."[19] Even outside the state, newspapers were singing his praise. The

*New Orleans Picayune* stated that "Mr. Throckmorton is one of the most talented, influential and respected citizens of North Eastern Texas. . . . As soon as the war ended, he exerted himself to calm the troubled waters and to restore harmony and peace."[20] This widespread praise of Throckmorton's reputation among the general public undoubtedly filled him with a false sense of security and fueled his political ambitions.

On February 10, Governor Hamilton spoke to the members of the convention. He stressed that "the most important questions . . . grow out of the emancipation of those who were formerly in a state of bondage, and who still remain in our midst." He informed the convention that "our former slaves are declared by the Constitution of the United States to be free. . . .[L]et us not deceive ourselves by the supposition that the nation will fail to make that declaration good, or to redeem, fully, the high obligations which it has assumed in this behalf, before the civilized world." The provisional governor concluded by stating that "there could not be devised a more successful mode of procrastinating our return to our original position in the Union, than to deny to the freedmen, in our midst, those civil rights and privileges, without which, to call them free would be only to keep the word of promise to the ear, and break it to the hope."[21]

As the presiding officer of the convention, Throckmorton addressed the assembled delegates, but his inaugural address was more focused on bringing the state back into the Union than ensuring civil rights to the freedmen. Throckmorton reminded the members that they "had passed through a period in the history of our country momentous in its character, and from which a new era will be inaugurated." He continued by stating that "as the representatives of the people of Texas we have been intrusted, at a critical moment with her most sacred interests. We should act with the purest patriotism, and, in my humble judgment, with a view to the future—uninfluenced by past predilections or opinions, and uncontaminated by passion or prejudice." Finally, the presiding officer called on the delegates to "strengthen the hands of the Executive of the nation, and by a ready and willing compliance with his suggestions, show to our Northern brethren that we are, in good faith, disposed to renew our allegiance to the general Government." In essence, Throckmorton informed the convention that he favored the speedy reconstruction of Texas, according to the policies of Presidential Reconstruction. However, he made no mention of providing civil rights to black Texans.[22]

At the conclusion of Throckmorton's address, the delegates began debating several issues. The most important of these centered on whether the delegates should take the loyalty oath and if they should declare secession null and void from its beginning; whether the state laws of Texas passed during the years of the rebellion should be claimed null and void (an issue commonly referred to as ab initio); whether the debt of Texas should be rendered invalid; and whether the legislature should pay outstanding wartime debts. Additionally, the delegates had to decide if they were going to ratify the Thirteenth Amendment, and they had to define the future status of the freedmen.[23]

On the first question, delegate Isaiah A. Paschal introduced a resolution that all members should take the "constitutional" oath. After much debate and the introduction of alternate resolutions, John Hancock of Travis County offered an amendment to Paschal's proposal that would strike out "constitutional" and substitute "amnesty." Throckmorton believed that the federal government would more likely accept Paschal's original resolution. He knew that if the convention refused to take the constitutional oath, northerners would perceive this as an act of defiance and even disloyalty. Throckmorton's view reflected the general mood of the delegates; consequently, Paschal reintroduced his resolution, which passed with a majority vote.[24]

In deciding whether the convention should declare the ordinance of secession null and void and thus to accept that the Constitution denied the right of a state to withdraw from the Union, the delegates declared the state's ordinance of secession void. However, the members did not agree on the ab initio issue. After much debate, the delegates decided that all laws not directly contradicting the U.S. Constitution would remain intact. Throckmorton supported the idea that the secession ordinance was null and void, and he agreed with the convention's decision on ab initio. One of the primary reasons he supported maintaining the state's laws centered on his support of railroad development in Texas. If ab initio had passed, it would have voided state legislation concerning railroad charters and funding, essentially delaying railroad construction in Texas.[25]

The status of the freedmen was the most controversial of the issues before the convention. The members agreed that the Thirteenth Amendment freed the former slaves and that by taking the oath in support of the Constitution, they had indirectly accepted that slavery was abolished in the United States. However, the delegates were divided on the ratification of the Thirteenth Amendment. Throckmorton was opposed to the forced ratification of the amendment, viewing it as an act of coercion by the federal government. Following his lead, the convention did not formally ratify the

Thirteenth Amendment; rather, the delegates claimed that taking the constitutional oath was sufficient. However, the delegates did suggest that the next session of the legislature should take up the matter of ratification.[26]

The delegates were divided on the question of allowing the freedmen to testify in the courts. The majority favored limiting the freedmen's testimony to civil and criminal cases involving other blacks. However, a strong faction supported giving blacks the right to testify in all cases on an equal basis with whites. Throckmorton believed that the freedmen's testimony should be limited to cases involving their own race, and he stood unswerving on allowing them anything more.[27] Throckmorton eventually compromised on this issue, offering to extend to the legislature the power to authorize testimony in all cases when it saw fit. Throckmorton suggested that the freedmen were mentally incapable of immediately participating in the political process. In addition, he objected to black testimony because he was afraid that it would eventually lead to complete social and political equality with whites, especially in regard to suffrage rights.[28]

Throckmorton was ill during the final days of the convention and had little to do with its official proceedings. In his absence, delegates elected David C. Dickson president pro tem. On the last day, the delegates passed an ordinance for a possible division of the state. It was rumored that Throckmorton was the main force behind this move to divide the state into several new states. It seems that this charge was overstated. According to a report in the *Dallas Herald,* William Jones was the originator of the resolution that called for the dissection of the state. Additionally, the newspaper stated that Throckmorton "only wanted the resolution referred to a committee."[29] However, as previously mentioned, Throckmorton had entertained the same idea prior to the convention, believing that North Texas could become an independent state. If the northern counties had become a state, whites in the region would have found it easier to regulate the affair of blacks and thereby protect white supremacy in their settlements. Considering that this was one of Throckmorton's political objectives, it is probable that he strongly favored Jones's resolution.

The stage was set to elect a new government for Texas. The delegates at the constitutional convention set June 25, 1866, as the date for state elections, and August 6 as the date when the Eleventh Texas Legislature would convene. The quick action of the convention was pleasing to most conservatives, but there were others who believed that Texas should refuse to send members to Congress as long as southerners were required to pass the test oath, or loyalty oath, in which citizens pledge their loyalty to the

U.S. government. Throckmorton was part of this group, and prior to the convention, he expressed that he was not in favor of sending men to Congress if the federal government did not receive the southern states back into the Union as equals.[30]

Throckmorton's commentary on northern immigration further revealed his bitterness toward the people in the northern states. He objected to all proposals at the constitutional convention designed to encourage northern migration. But he was in the minority. Throckmorton did not elaborate on the matter to the other delegates. Unable to reach a consensus, the delegates decided to leave the matter to the state legislature once it convened.[31]

The convention adjourned on April 2. Despite heated debate, the meeting had been more harmonious than many leading Texans expected. Nonetheless, party lines were clearly evident during the course of the convention, and there was much contempt on all sides.[32] Throckmorton found it somewhat disturbing that some of his earlier political allies seemed to favor the radical position. Of James H. Bell, he lamented, "in my heart of hearts I have grieved that one so gifted should have suffered himself to be so easily molded & controlled by one [Hamilton], who, through a long career has shown himself so unstable, and such a unrelenting enemy to the land that gave him birth." He made the same observations about Latimer, calling him a "radical."[33] Throckmorton then claimed that "these gentlemen, who denounce everybody else as unsound and disloyal, shirk the only great question before the American people. It is plain why they do so: They are themselves for [Thaddeus] Stevens & [Charles] Sumner's policy. They hate the President, & every now & then some of them in the bitterness of their hearts leak it out." Generally speaking, Throckmorton characterized the radicals as individuals who "drew their swords against their country; who led armies to sack & pillage their own state; who rejoiced in the ruin of their native & adopted land; who shed no tears of sympathy over the utter degradation of their fallen Countryman; who rejoiced in the deaths of thousands of their fellow citizens; [and] who laugh at the broken hearts & of the orphans & daughters & mothers of their own land."[34] The Civil War left Throckmorton bitter. In his resentment of the circumstances confronting Texas in the postwar period, he blamed the extremists in both the North and South for starting the war.

While Throckmorton showed complete disdain for the radicals, he noted with surprise that the secessionists had been willing to work so closely with the conservative delegates. He explained that before the convention he "did not foresee that the Secession party would lay down their prejudice and act with so much discretion, and I am glad to say, disinterestedness & patriotism." He further declared that "the secession men said they desired to support conservative men both to convince the Government of their earnest desire for an early restoration as well as loyalty, and to show the masses at home that we should forget, forgive, harmonize and work like brothers together for the general good."[35] Believing that ex-Confederates were now willing to accept the consequences of the South's defeat and that Radical Republicans wanted to punish the southern states for their rebellious actions, Throckmorton aligned himself, not surprisingly, against those who supported the radicals' agenda. The factional differences noted by Throckmorton would ultimately pervade the political landscape in the upcoming state elections.

During the closing days of the constitutional convention, members met in various caucuses to nominate candidates for the forthcoming gubernatorial election. Two weeks prior to adjournment, a caucus of radicals nominated A. J. Hamilton for governor. However, Hamilton, who was worn down by the war and his efforts as provisional governor, declined the radicals' offer. After Hamilton refused to run, the radicals nominated Elisha M. Pease for governor, and they chose Benjamin Epperson as their candidate for lieutenant governor. Meanwhile, a conservative caucus chose Throckmorton as its candidate for governor and George W. Jones of Bastrop County for lieutenant governor. Both men supported Presidential Reconstruction and opposed black suffrage. Though reluctant at first, Throckmorton agreed to accept the nomination, but he realized that the conservative movement was in danger of breaking apart if Epperson, a noted conservative, remained on the Pease ticket. The two men corresponded with each other regarding the matter, and Throckmorton eventually persuaded Epperson to withdraw his name from the Pease ticket. For his friend's loyalty, Throckmorton promised that if he won the upcoming gubernatorial election, he would use his influence to assure Epperson's election to the U.S. Senate. Radicals quickly replaced Epperson with Livingston Lindsay.[36]

The campaign for governor was characterized by strong rhetoric on both sides. Radicals denounced the work of the Constitutional Convention, claiming that the secessionists and conservatives had conspired to preserve their prewar status. They suggested that if Throckmorton were elected governor, he would immediately forget his Union principles just as he had done in 1861 after the state had seceded. Additionally, radicals correctly charged that Throckmorton would be an impediment to restoring the state to the Union because he opposed congressional Republicans' suggestion that the southern states give the freedmen the right to vote. However, the radicals could not make the most of this issue because E. M. Pease also opposed universal suffrage for black Texans. At best, Pease was only willing to concede the vote to freedmen who could read and write.[37]

Throckmorton and his supporters countered the radicals' arguments by reaffirming that he supported President Johnson's plan of Reconstruction and that he would work diligently for the speedy restoration of the state to the Union. The strong show of support for Presidential Reconstruction resulted primarily from the fact that President Johnson opposed giving suffrage to the freedmen. Throckmorton reinforced wild rumors and speculation circulating throughout the state about Radical politicians by telling voters that northern radicals and their supporters in Texas favored the social and political equality of blacks with whites and that they called for an amendment to the U.S. Constitution to disenfranchise white southerners and enfranchise the freedmen. Throckmorton claimed that the radicals wanted to centralize the federal government's power over the states, leaving the South at the mercy of politicians in Washington, D.C. Throckmorton's rhetoric resonated with the majority of white Texans who were opposed to granting blacks anything more than their freedom, and as a result, Throckmorton won the governorship by a landslide, receiving 48,631 out of 60,682 ballots cast. The North Texas politician now prepared to fulfill his agenda of protecting the frontier and preserving white dominance in the state.[38]

On August 6, the Eleventh Legislature of Texas assembled at Austin and declared Throckmorton and Jones the duly elected governor and lieutenant governor of the state. While no instructions had been received from Washington concerning the new government, the state legislature made arrangements for the inauguration of the newly elected administration. On August 9, in front of both houses of the Texas Legislature and a large crowd of citizens, U.S. district court judge Thomas H. Duval administered the oath of office to the new governor.[39]

Throckmorton's inaugural address presented the legislature with a guideline for rebuilding the state and for solidifying its restoration in the Union. The governor's speech painted a somewhat biased portrait of the current conditions in the state:

> At a time like the present, when we have just emerged from the most terrible conflict known to modern times, with homes made dreary and desolate by the heavy hand of war; the people impoverished, and groaning under public and private debts; the great industrial energies of the country sadly depressed; occupying in some respects the position of a State of the Federal Union, and in others, the condition of a conquered province, exercising only such privileges as the conqueror in his wisdom and mercy may allow; the loyalty of the people to the General Government doubted; their integrity questioned; their holiest aspirations for peace and restoration disbelieved, maligned and traduced, with a constant misapprehension of their most innocent actions and intentions; with a frontier many hundred miles extent, being desolated by a murderous and powerful enemy, our devoted frontiersmen filling bloody graves, their property given to the flames, or carried off as booty, their little ones murdered, and their wives and daughters carried into a captivity more terrible than death, . . . unprotected by the government we support, with troops quartered in the interior, where there is peace and quiet; unwilling to send armed citizens to defend the suffering border, for fear of arousing unjust suspicious as to the motive . . . under such circumstances, with such surroundings, when so much depends upon prudence, and so great an amount of patriotism and intelligence is required, I feel sadly oppressed with difficulties which lie before me.[40]

After noting that the state had renewed its relations with the federal government and had recognized the end of slavery, Throckmorton pledged his support to help the freedmen. The governor stated that he "would endeavor to recommend and aid in carrying out such measures as [would] insure exact justice to all classes of men, of every political faith, religious creed, race and color." The governor announced that the freedmen would receive the protection "of all the rights of person and property guaranteed them by our Amended Constitution." Throckmorton promised that black Texans would soon be convinced that white Texans were their "truest friends." Obviously, this was a claim that proved more rhetoric than reality.[41]

Throckmorton reflected on a variety of other issues confronting the state, including conditions on the frontier, crime, taxes, internal improvements, the public school system, establishment of a state university, and charitable care of the "afflicted and unfortunate portion" of the population, referring in particular to the mentally ill. At no point did Throckmorton clarify that African Americans would be included in these improvements.[42] In many ways, the governor's speech foreshadowed his future failure to provide equitable treatment to the freedmen and their white allies, a circumstance that would continually cause him problems throughout his tenure as governor.

Two days after Throckmorton's inauguration, President Johnson sent a letter that officially recognized the North Texan as the governor of Texas. The same day, A. J. Hamilton received a dispatch relieving him of his duties as provisional governor. Throckmorton's administration immediately took possession of the state's official papers and property and assumed the duties of governance. On August 20, President Johnson issued a proclamation declaring the insurrection in Texas finished. Throckmorton interpreted the president's proclamation to mean that civil authority was once again superior to military rule in the state and that Texas had been readmitted to the Union.[43]

On August 21, the legislature convened in joint session to elect U.S. senators. Their actions were encumbered by a problem that would plague the state until the end of Reconstruction: Unionists and ex-Confederates found it difficult to put their past behind them and to work together for the common good of the state. While the legislature considered eight or ten individuals for the senate position, four men were clearly frontrunners for the position—Oran M. Roberts, David G. Burnet, Benjamin Epperson, and John Hancock. In accordance with an agreement among the legislators, one of the new senators would be chosen from eastern Texas and the other from the west. The candidates from the western district included Burnet, Hancock, and former governor E. M. Pease. Burnet was easily elected on the first ballot. Roberts and Epperson along with five other candidates attempted to secure the eastern district seat. Despite Governor Throckmorton's promised support for his friend Epperson, the ex-Confederates were successful in securing the election of Roberts after thirteen ballots. Thus, the Texas Legislature chose to send two former secessionists to Washington, a decision that later led Radical Republicans to refuse the elected Texans their seats in the Senate. Additionally, Congress prohibited the elected representatives from Texas, George W. Chilton, Epperson, and A. M. Branch, to take their seats in the House of Representatives. The Texas delegates remained in Washington for a short time before deciding to return to Texas. Only Epperson stayed in Washington, keeping Throckmorton abreast of events in the nation's capital.[44]

The state legislature took other actions that created distrust among northern Republicans and proved detrimental to Throckmorton's administration. Believing that military defeat and universal emancipation of the slaves had already caused Texans enough humiliation, the legislators refused to ratify the Thirteenth and Fourteenth amendments to the U.S. Constitution. If this were not enough, in November 1866, the legislators passed a series of laws known as Black Codes, which were designed to restrict the rights of the freedmen in areas such as interracial marriage, apprenticeships, and contract labor. The codes also called for segregation in public schools and on railroads. Furthermore, the legislature reinforced the idea that the homestead laws only applied to whites and passed laws that regulated vagrancy and convict leasing. Additionally, they denied freedmen the right to vote, to hold political office, to serve on juries, or to give testimony in court except in cases involving other blacks. The only civil rights afforded blacks were the rights to enter into binding contracts, to sue and be sued in the courts, to hold personal and real property, to make wills, and to have personal security. In essence, the Black Codes reduced black Texans to a position of semislavery.[45]

Throckmorton's approval of the legislature's actions placed him at odds both with radical members of the U.S. Congress and federal military authorities in charge of reconstructing the state. Two issues were especially problematic—the rejection of the Fourteenth Amendment and the passage of the Black Codes.[46] While the Black Codes were consistent with the governor's recommendation that the legislature pass "laws to secure the protection of [the freedmen's] person and property," he found it difficult to convince military authorities of the state's good intentions toward black Texans, and therefore, Texas' chief executive failed to achieve the removal of "all military forces and the Freedmen's Bureau" from the "interior of the state."[47] General Sheridan rightly considered the Black Codes as "oppressive legislation" that developed a "policy of gross injustice toward the colored people on the part of the courts."[48] In regard to the rejection of the Fourteenth Amendment, the legislators simply followed the governor's recommendation. On August 20, Throckmorton recommended the "rejection of the proposed fourteenth article of the United States Constitution, that was passed by the late Radical Congress," calling the amendment "impolitic, unwise and unjust."[49] This statement reinforced southerners' commonly held idea that the freedmen were socially and politically inferior to whites. Under these circumstances, the military authorities felt that the state's freedmen faced serious danger with Throckmorton in power.

Gen. Philip Sheridan, commander of the Fifth Military District, which included the states of Texas and Louisiana. Before being relieved from command, Sheridan removed Governor Throckmorton from office, finding him to be an "impediment to Reconstruction." *Brady-Handy Photograph Collection, Library of Congress.*

Even though the legislature did little to help strengthen the relationship between the state and the federal government, Governor Throckmorton's dealings with federal troops stationed in Texas between August 1866 and April 1867 provide better insights into the lack of cooperation that prevailed between the state and national authorities. The governor's personal confrontation with individual military commanders resulted from two major problems. First, the state confronted an increasing wave of lawlessness caused by the refusal of white Texans to accept the emancipation of the slaves. Second, Throckmorton, though a Unionist prior to the war, had no intention of implementing political, social, or economic reforms that were slowly gaining support in the U.S. Congress between early 1866 and mid-1867.[50] The governor made his views of Reconstruction clear in a letter to James J. Diamond, a prominent secessionist in Grayson County. He wrote:

> I hold that it is the duty of every patriot to contribute his best exertions in behalf of the country. Heretofore at different periods of the country's history, the purest devotion to principle have been largely in demand to save American institutions and Republican Government from destruction. But at no former period has the danger been so imminent or menacing. . . . The stars and bars have gone down, and will perhaps only live in history. But that which was failed to be accomplished by war, will be fought for at the ballot box. Although many seem not to realize the magnitude of the great contest now going on, yet no great length of time, in my judgement, will elapse before it is determined by the American people whether their government shall be perpetuated as it was intended to be by its founders, or shall become a consolidated and centralized despotism, more terrible and oppressive than the most absolute monarchy. . . . The experience of the past will arouse statesmen and patriots to renewed exertions, and the ship of state will be headed again on the old Republican track, and the respective land marks of National authority and States rights will be remarked and more permanently established. To accomplish this victory the South is powerless, except so far as she may contribute, by prudence and wisdom. . . . [W]hen I speak of prudence, I do not mean to guard against useless expressions that can avail nothing, or acts that are calculated to pull down those who are storming the beach that we may be saved. . . . Such are the objects which our Northern friends are now battling to achieve. Shall we aid them by reasonable conduct, or weaken them by folly?[51]

The governor apparently felt secure under Johnson's tutelage to effect minimal reforms and to oppose the military's role in enacting the adjustments demanded by Congress. Perhaps if Throckmorton had followed the advice that he wrote to Diamond, he would have served out his term as governor. Unfortunately for him, he chose a different path, which placed him on a collision course with federal authorities.

# CHAPTER SIX

## *"Every Exertion within My Reach"*

### CHALLENGING PRESIDENTIAL RECONSTRUCTION IN TEXAS, 1866

Throckmorton's governorship was characterized by three key issues: frontier defense, his belief that civil authority triumphed over military rule, and the governor's removal from office. The North Texan's attempt to preserve white supremacy was the basis for the position he took in each of these issues. Regarding the defense of the frontier, the governor wanted to remove the Indians from the state's western lands, making that part of the state safe for Anglo settlements. Also, if whites effectively were going to keep blacks from enjoying full citizenship, it was clear that the civil government would have to be able to work independently of the military authorities who were charged with the duty of protecting the freedmen and their white allies. Thus, the governor sought to eliminate the necessity of military courts, particularly those of the Freedmen's Bureau, and to induce military authorities to yield to the jurisdiction of state and local courts. Finally, Throckmorton was removed from the governor's office because he refused to accept Congressional Reconstruction, which promised to give the former slaves an equal footing with white Texans.[1]

By the time of Throckmorton's inauguration on August 9, 1866, white settlers on the Texas frontier were suffering from repeated Indian raids. While the conditions in which the settlers lived were deplorable, the new state government carefully approached the issue of frontier defense. Some legislators believed that the federal authorities opposed the idea of sending state troops to the frontier counties. According to them, the federal government believed that the Texas forces might later be used against the U.S. troops in the interior of the state.

Though the legislature was initially timid about protecting the western region of the state, Throckmorton was not. He had lived on the frontier most of his life and had witnessed Indian raids on white settlements. His sympathies clearly were with the settlers. Before his inauguration, Throckmorton wrote to a group of citizens living on the frontier to assure them that adequate protection would soon be forthcoming: "every exertion within my reach shall be exhausted—the frontier shall be protected. We must first look to the General Government. If that fails, then [we will] take the burden upon ourselves." The North Texan continued, "I shall urge upon the Legislature the passage of such measures as will give me the power to defend the border, in the event of failure on the part of the General Government to afford adequate and permanent protection." The governor-elect then asked the people on the frontier to send him as much information as possible on the condition of their area.[2] In his inaugural address, the governor reiterated these themes.[3]

The ink had barely dried on his inaugural address when the governor's office was inundated with letters from the frontier describing the intensity and horror of the Indian attacks on whites. Each correspondent asked for the same thing—protection for white settlers until the Native Americans could be removed or exterminated.[4]

On August 14, the governor received a report from the Cherokee Nation that "a party of thirty Osage Indians on their return from Texas with a large number of [stolen] horses passed" nearby Washita "about a week ago and thence came two miles in the direction of this place where they turned north towards the Osage Country."[5] Another report of stock theft detailed that four white men ran across two different groups of Indians near the "mouth of the Concho [River]" and that the Indians were in possession of a large number of stolen horses and cattle. According to this report, "cattle in that section of country were nearly all driven out," and "many settlers have left the country" because "a general feeling of uncertainty prevails."[6] Numerous letters such as these crossed the governor's desk, and financial loss due to theft was a commonly reported occurrence. However, these accounts were not as terrifying as the reports of violent acts committed against the pioneers.

On August 16, T. Smiley, a trader in the Cherokee Nation, sent Governor Throckmorton the grave news that a potential Indian war against Texas seemed evident. Relaying information he had obtained from Major R. Miller, a former U.S. Indian agent in the Indian territories, Smiley reported that "the Indians of the prairie (Kiowas & Comanches) have had their usual annual council and being represented by the Arapahos and others. They have determined to make war on the state of Texas with renewed vigor." Smiley continued, "I need not explain to you the small amount of interest that the agents and other officials on this side of Red River take in the welfare of the state of Texas, and it would appear from the slow movement of the Government troops that the protection of the frontier is almost lost sight of." The Indian trader then warned Throckmorton that "unless there is some active measures taken, the people of the border counties [of Texas] are bound to suffer."[7] Undoubtedly, this report, as well as other accounts of Indian depredations that continued to trickle into his office, strengthened the governor's resolve to protect settlers living on the Texas frontier.

Believing that one of the primary responsibilities of government was to protect and to aid the people it served, Throckmorton turned to the federal military for a solution to the frontier problems. Apparently, he was not bothered by the crimes being committed against the freedmen and their white allies in the interior of the state.[8] However, most of the correspondence reaching the governor's desk during his early months in office was from frontier settlers who were pleading for the state government to provide relief from Indian depredations. As a result, the governor called on the U.S. Army to move its troops to the frontier counties, leaving the freedmen to fend for themselves.

Throckmorton's appeal to the federal government for frontier protection faced two major obstacles. First, U.S. Army commanders believed that reports of hostile activities on the Texas frontier were exaggerated. Second, the occupation forces distrusted the loyalty of the Texas government, inferring that the state officials were only trying to move the U.S. forces from the interior where soldiers were protecting freedmen and white radical Unionists from ex-Confederates and former secessionists. Throckmorton quickly realized that he would need to gain the trust of the occupying forces if the frontier was to be rid of Native Americans.[9]

In August, Throckmorton sent a request for frontier troops to Maj. Gen. Horatio G. Wright, who had replaced General Granger as commander of the District of Texas a year earlier. General Wright replied to Throckmorton that he had no authority to send troops to the western region of the state but that he would send the governor's request to his superior, Gen. Philip Sheridan, commander of the Department of the Gulf. Wright also informed Throckmorton that there were few available troops for the frontier service and that current hostilities in Texas against the freedmen and Unionists warranted keeping all available forces in the interior of the state.[10]

The governor was disappointed in Wright's reply, believing that federal troops were no longer needed in the interior. Throckmorton undoubtedly weighed the evidence that crossed his desk. The majority of the reports reaching his office were concerned with Indian depredations on the frontier, while reports of the injustices perpetrated against freedmen and Unionists were primarily limited to a few military reports.[11] Thus, while waiting for General Sheridan to respond to Wright's message, the governor wrote to President Johnson on August 25, informing him of the conditions on the frontier.

Throckmorton's decision to write the president was a logical move considering that the governor had earlier pledged support for his plan of reconstruction and considering that the president's views of the freedmen were closely aligned with his own. Neither man was willing to afford the ex-slaves more than freedom from slavery. Thus, the governor may have entertained the idea that Johnson would order the military from the interior where its primary function was to protect the freedmen. In his letter to the president, Throckmorton strongly suggested that the settlers' safety hinged on troop deployment to the frontier, especially in the northern part of the state. He voiced his opinion that only a show of force could prevent future Indian raids on white settlements.[12]

Meanwhile, Wright forwarded Throckmorton's request to General Sheridan with an endorsement of the governor's petition for frontier troops.[13] Sheridan was not convinced by his subordinate's assessment of the frontier conditions in Texas, believing that Throckmorton was purposely exaggerating the severity of the Indian depredations in an effort to obstruct the military's effort to protect blacks and Unionists from their ex-Confederate neighbors. Nevertheless, the general promptly informed the governor that he had "directed the District [of Texas] commander to send a cavalry force to Fredericksburg or vicinity, from thence to operate against such Indians and white men as are committing depredations on this portion of the frontier." Sheridan also noted that "as soon as additional troops are sent me to establish forts on the frontier, it will be done."[14]

While Throckmorton was trying to secure a federal presence in West Texas, the state legislature attempted to provide relief to the settlers by creating three mounted regiments for service on the frontier. In an effort to win federal approval for their act, the legislators placed the newly formed regiments under the direction of the federal military with the stipulation that the volunteers could not be removed from the state for detached service. The Texas Legislature justified the creation of the frontier troops by arguing that a majority of the federal soldiers were posted along the Rio Grande due to political unrest in Mexico. At the instigation of Napoleon III of France, Maximilian was attempting to establish himself as emperor of Mexico, and federal authorities were concerned that Maximilian might contemplate an invasion of Texas if he were successful in seizing the reins of power. Therefore, the legislature deemed it necessary to authorize the enlistment of the Texas frontier troops for use in the northern and western regions of the state.[15]

The legislature's debates regarding the formation of frontier regiments were published in various newspapers throughout the state, and even before the legislature officially passed the act, the governor received numerous letters from individuals who recommended various men to command ranging companies that might be raised in their region of the state. Typical of these letters was the one received from John Baylor on September 1, 1866, recommending Capt. John Pulliam for command of one of the proposed Frontier Regiments: "Capt Pulliam was with me during the late war and was a most efficient and excellent officer. Should you think proper to authorize him to raise a Company, I have no hesitation in saying that he will prove in every way worthy of your confidence."[16]

Throckmorton continued to receive reports throughout September from settlers on the frontier outlining new Indian depredations and letters from frontiersmen requesting that he provide immediate and adequate protection of their homes. In one such letter, Jack J. Cureton, a noted Indian fighter, wrote that people "in all parts of the country" were continually asking him what he thought the governor would do to protect them. "I answer them as I did when talking about the election," Cureton explained. "Throckmorton will do all in his power to protect us. I assured the frontier people if we elect Throckmorton we will have a friend on whom we can depend." Cureton then moved on to the central point of his letter: "I have been solicited time and again to [write] to you on this subject. We want some organization of a military character to compel men to there duty . . . all eyes are directed towards Austin for relief. They hope to hear of our own countrymen being called out in addition to the troops sent by the Federal Government." These are, the frontiersman concluded, "the sentiments of frontier people who are willing to shoulder their arms to protect their property, wives, children, fathers & mothers if they are permitted to take part in the work. . . . [T]hey think that there are no men in the world so capable of doing justice to the service as those who have lived and battled with the enemy for the last eight years."[17]

Throckmorton replied to Cureton on September 8 and reaffirmed his determination to help the people of the frontier, but he also revealed the obstacles that confronted him in providing relief. "I can assure you that I will give every exertion in my power to the protection of the frontier," Throckmorton declared, adding that "the legislature is now considering a bill for this purpose, and I hope they will do something. But unless they provide the means to pay for it, it is useless to give me the power to raise men." The governor prophetically concluded that "after the legislature does all it can, it may be that the General Government will not permit us to call out men for this purpose. I have already called upon the President and Military authorities for protection, and shall continue to press it in every conceivable way until it is accomplished."[18]

A more alarming report of depredations in Montague and Cooke counties reached Governor Throckmorton's desk at about the same time Cureton's letter arrived. According to J. T. Mosby, "a man by the name of Box was killed and his family consisting of a wife & four daughters were carried off." Mosby stated that "immediate action in reference to frontier protection" was necessary. "Something must be done," proclaimed the frontiersman, because "the settlements on the frontier will be abandoned."[19] After receiving numerous letters like these and reading the many newspaper accounts of the same stripe, Throckmorton strengthened his resolve to provide relief to the people living in the western counties.

At the end of September, Throckmorton informed both secretary of war Edwin M. Stanton and General Sheridan of the legislature's act that authorized him to raise state troops for the frontier. The governor urged Sheridan to accept the frontier regiments as part of his command and stressed the need for troops on the frontier. In his letter to Stanton, Throckmorton was more forward. He stated that if the federal government failed to adequately protect the frontier settlers, then the "state will be compelled to undertake it." The governor expressed his opinion that "the troops stationed in the interior of the state are of no service whatever. The laws can be enforced, and every class of our population can be protected in all their rights, without the aid of the military, and I most respectfully ask that the troops be withdrawn."[20] He requested again that federal troops, especially black soldiers, be removed from the interior of the state, blaming them for inciting unnecessary violence. The governor's appraisal of the troops in the interior seemed to reflect his own racist views. He unfairly blamed black troops for the atrocities occurring in the interior of the state, rather than properly faulting unreconstructed white Texans.[21]

At the end of September, Maj. Gen. George W. Getty replaced Wright as the commander of the District of Texas. Still waiting to hear from federal authorities in Washington, Throckmorton immediately wrote to Getty apprising him of the situation on the frontier and requested that he use his influence to ensure the protection of the settlers. Additionally, the governor wrote to Gen. U. S. Grant requesting that Texas be allowed to raise state troops to protect the frontier. By early October, Throckmorton's campaign to procure troops was being closely scrutinized by federal officials and military commanders.[22]

The governor soon received disappointing news. On October 11, Secretary Stanton wrote to him that the president had considered the circumstances in Texas in a recent cabinet meeting and was disposed to provide the Texas settlers all possible aid. Stanton continued by informing the governor that the president believed that the U.S. military would be able to provide adequate protection to the settlers without the help of the Texas volunteers. Stanton's letter reaffirmed an earlier telegram that General Sheridan sent the governor on October 9, 1866. Sheridan informed Throckmorton that he would not accept the Texas volunteers as part of his command. However, despite his suspicion that the Texas Legislature was conspiring to remove the federal troops from the interior, General Sheridan stated that "I have the pleasure of informing you that additional troops have been ordered to your state; that an inspector will be at once sent to the northern frontier of Texas and that as much protection as we possibly can give to the frontier will be cheerfully given, and also, that in the early spring the frontier posts will be established."[23]

The federal authorities' refusal to allow the state to raise frontier troops created an embarrassing situation for the governor because he had already issued an order to begin organizing companies for frontier service on October 6.[24] In many of the frontier counties, the inhabitants enthusiastically responded to the governor's call for troops and immediately began to volunteer for service. In early November, with federal troops on their way to the frontier, Throckmorton was forced to rescind his earlier order. In writing to the frontiersmen, Throckmorton put the best possible interpretation on his predicament. For example, the governor wrote to Thomas F. Mosby that "I do not contemplate at this time, being forced to the necessity of using them [state troops]. Yet, I desired very much that the company should be organized so that should the absolute necessity occur I could order them out." Throckmorton then updated Mosby on the federal army's efforts to protect the frontier citizens: "eleven companies [of] regular cavalry, under

Lt. Col. Oats, an old experienced frontier officer, are ordered to concentrate immediately at Jacksboro. I have asked and believe I will succeed in the request, to have four companies stationed in Montague, one or two in Cook [County]." Finally, the governor stated that he had "such hints from Sheridan that I am satisfied it would not do for me to order out the frontier reg's at this juncture. This will explain the reason of my not rushing them in the field."[25] Despite his awkward situation, Throckmorton had reasons to be optimistic about the federal government's protection of the frontier.

In mid-October, Sheridan initiated a plan to provide protection to the western and northern counties of the state. The commanding officer wrote to Bvt. Maj. Gen. Samuel P. Heintzelman authorizing him to post troops under his command on the frontier if he deemed it necessary. Sheridan also informed Heintzelman that additional infantry troops were en route to Texas. On October 16, General Sheridan informed Throckmorton that he had transferred command of the District of Texas to General Heintzelman and that he had authorized the new commander to concentrate the entire cavalry force under his command, approximately two thousand men, on the frontier.[26]

Furthermore, Sheridan ordered Maj. G. A. Forsythe to the northwestern part of the state to ascertain the true nature of the Indian threat.[27] Throckmorton sent a dispatch to Major Forsythe after learning of his mission. The governor urged the army scout to closely examine the circumstances in Montague, Jack, Palo Pinto, Erath, Comanche, Brown, San Saba, Llano, and Mason counties, which seemed to be the areas most devastated by Indian raids. The governor wrote to J. P. Dumas of Sherman informing him that Major Forsythe was en route to the area to examine possible locations for additional fortifications. In essence, Throckmorton asked Dumas to function as a guide for Forsythe and to inform him of the Indians' devastating effect on the northern frontier. Naturally, it took time for Forsythe to complete his task. As a result, the deployment of troops was delayed several weeks.[28]

Desiring that troops be deployed to the frontier as quickly as possible, Throckmorton wrote to the commander of the Sixth U.S. Cavalry on November 5, 1866, and inquired as to why federal forces had not started their march to the frontier. The governor warned the commander that additional delays and continued raids would force him to muster the Texas volunteers into service.[29]

Throckmorton's impatience was unfounded. Even as he wrote to the commander of the Sixth Cavalry, General Sheridan ordered troops deployed to the frontier. On November 6, he instructed General Heintzelman to post the second battalion of the Seventeenth U.S. Infantry at Austin and to send the Fourth and Sixth U.S. Cavalry units to the northern and western counties of the state. Sheridan ordered Heintzelman to move troops without orders from the headquarters in cases of emergency.[30] After receiving these instructions, the Texas commander ordered eleven companies of the Sixth Cavalry to take winter quarters in Jacksboro while he sent five companies of the Fourth Cavalry to Fort Mason. Of the companies sent to Fort Mason, one was to remain there while three were to proceed to Camp Verde and one to Fort Clark. While Heintzelman relocated troops, he left some soldiers in the southern part of the state: one company remained at Fort Inge, while two others relocated to the subdistrict of the Rio Grande border. Additionally, the general sent troops to reinforce interior posts. Ten companies in the first battalion of the Seventeenth Infantry were sent to major points in southeast Texas: two companies were sent to Hempstead; two to Brenham; two to Houston; and four to Galveston.[31]

The deployment of troops proceeded slowly, but it appears that the U.S. Army reacted in good faith to protect the citizen on the Texas frontier. By the end of December 1866, the northern and western counties had been adequately supplied with U.S. soldiers, and the troops seemed to have been effective in curbing Indian raids. The number of reports of new depredations declined in 1867. As a result, the frontier ceased to be a major issue of concern for the Throckmorton administration. The governor could boast that he had been the driving force behind protecting the settlers. However, the governor's threat to use Texas volunteers obviously produced distrust between his administration and the military authorities. Throckmorton's persistence in demanding that the troops be removed from the interior of the state to frontier fortifications and the tactics of appealing to General Sheridan's superiors in Washington were two contributing factors that eventually led to the governor's removal from office in August 1867.[32]

Throckmorton's problems with military authority went well beyond conflicts over the deployment of troops to the frontier. A wider rift between the Throckmorton administration and the military authorities developed over the governor's insistence that civil rule was superior to the military's authority. After President Johnson's proclamation on August 20, 1866, the governor immediately set out to solidify the civil government's control over the state. Throckmorton's task was nearly impossible, especially considering that the Radical and Moderate Republicans in Congress had forged an alliance to challenge President Johnson's plan of Reconstruction. The infighting in the nation's capital caused delays in transferring sovereignty of the state from military to civilian rule. In addition to the problems in Washington, D.C., events in Texas suggested that state officials were unwilling to accept the dictates of Reconstruction policies, especially recognition of the newly won status of freedmen and the protection of white Unionists.[33] It was clear that Throckmorton and other like-minded Texans wanted an end to Reconstruction.

In his effort to reinstate civil control of Texas, Throckmorton repeatedly informed local officials of the necessity of maintaining law and order. The governor requested county sheriffs and judges to practice impartiality at the local level. He reinforced his directive by stating that Union men, ex-Confederates, and freedmen should receive equal justice before the law. However, it is doubtful that Throckmorton acted out of a sense of humanitarianism; rather, it seems more probable that he simply desired to bring Reconstruction to an end.[34]

One of Throckmorton's earliest battles with the military authorities occurred less than a month after the governor's inauguration. This clash was with the Bureau of Refugees, Freedmen, and Abandoned Lands, commonly known as the Freedmen's Bureau. The federal government created the bureau on March 3, 1865, and charged it with helping the freedmen make their transition from slavery to freedom. The bureau officially began its task in Texas in December of 1865. The first assistant commissioner of the bureau in Texas was Gen. E. M. Gregory, but Gen. J. B. Kiddoo replaced him in May 1866 prior to Throckmorton's gubernatorial election. On July 16, 1866, Congress passed an act that allowed the bureau to continue operating in the southern states and gave its officers complete authority over all matters relating to the former slaves. After Throckmorton was officially elected, General Kiddoo wrote to him explaining the bureau's purpose and seeking the governor's cooperation in helping the freedmen of Texas.[35] The governor responded favorably to Kiddoo's correspondence, assuring the bureau commander of his "readiness to cooperate . . . in lending all aid in my power, that the duties required of you may be discharged in such a manner as will ensure justice to that class of people who are placed under your charge."[36]

While Throckmorton and Kiddoo exchanged pleasantries, a crisis erupted at Brenham that would test the good intentions of both sides. Local bureau agent Capt. Samuel Craig arrested the editor of the *Brenham Banner,* Dan L. McGary. The editor had published several unflattering editorials about James Whann and his wife, two bureau teachers working near

The Freedmen's Bureau. A Freedmen's Bureau agent is depicted standing between a group of angry white southerners and a group of freedmen. The Freedmen's Bureau played a major part in protecting Texas Freedmen against former Confederates, including Governor Throckmorton, who attempted to preserve white supremacy in Texas society during the late nineteenth century. *Originally published in* Harper's Weekly, *July 25, 1886. Library of Congress.*

Brenham, and had criticized Craig's efforts to protect the interest of local freedmen. Fearing that the editor's comments would arouse the ire of local whites against the freedmen and the bureau, Craig warned the editor that the military would arrest him if he continued to print slanderous rhetoric about the bureau and its teachers. McGary ignored the agent's warning and proceeded to publish his defamatory rag. As a result, Craig arrested the editor and assessed a fine of two hundred dollars against him. Instead of paying the fine, McGary chose to remain in jail, perhaps viewing himself as a loyal defender of the South's "lost cause."[37]

After receiving word of the incident, Throckmorton wrote to General Kiddoo protesting the arrest of the editor as an infringement of the Constitution's guaranteed right of freedom of the press. Kiddoo responded by informing Throckmorton that the editor had constantly used his newspaper to unnecessarily abuse the character of the freedmen, the bureau, and the soldiers stationed at Brenham. However, in an effort to secure peace, General Kiddoo reluctantly ordered Craig to release McGary. Subsequently,

Kiddoo transferred Captain Craig to the bureau office in Seguin, Guadalupe County.[38]

While the problems with McGary were seemingly resolved, Captain Craig found himself once again at the center of a controversy in Guadalupe County. The bureau agent actually had inherited the problems of his two predecessors, Judge William Longworth and Lt. James B. Moore of the U.S. Colored Infantry. Longworth was an ardent protector of the freedmen in Guadalupe County, and as a result, General Gregory appointed him as the bureau agent for the county in December of 1865. The judge, however, was unfamiliar with bureau policies and began to use questionable tactics in achieving his noble goal of protecting the freedmen. Apparently, Longworth had even stepped outside the law: a bureau investigator looking into complaints levied against Longworth stated that the judge had reopened cases that had already been settled to the satisfaction of both sides; compelled citizens to testify even when there were no formal complaints; kept freedmen from work for days until their cases had been heard; charged illegal fees; and made unnecessary, vitriolic speeches to the freedmen, which served to disrupt the agricultural pursuits in the county. Judge Longworth's actions understandably caused the white citizens of the county to side against not only him, but also against the bureau and the freedmen under its protection. Longworth became such a liability that General Kiddoo replaced him with Lieutenant Moore. After being removed from office, Longworth returned to his home in Sutherland Springs, Wilson County. Lieutenant Moore soon proved to be just as much a liability to the bureau as had Longworth. The bureau inspector who investigated the complaints against Moore described him as a man of little principle and a drunk. It was reported that Moore solicited prostitution from freedwomen on the street and that he was under indictment for gambling within the city limits of Seguin.[39]

After arriving at Seguin, Captain Craig, under orders from General Kiddoo, informed the judge that he should return to Seguin and face the possibility of arrest for his illegal activities. Longworth informed Craig that he feared for his own safety, given his past actions as subassistant commissioner. The captain assured the former bureau agent that he would be protected under General Order No. 3 of the Adjutant General's Office in Washington and General Order No. 5 of the District of Texas. Both these documents protected military personnel from prosecution in state courts while performing their duties. Craig also ensured Longworth that he would take personal responsibility for his safety. After the commander of the District of Texas intervened on Longworth's behalf, the judge was exempted from any arrest and was shielded from future prosecution.

With Longworth safe for the time being, Craig turned his attention to Lieutenant Moore's indictment for illegal gambling. After Craig posted bond for Moore, the lieutenant made a clandestine escape from the town. While disappointed that Moore had escaped prosecution, the citizens of Seguin took some comfort in the fact that the lieutenant's last paycheck of $143 was intercepted and distributed to people in the town to whom Moore owed money. All seemed well, but when Captain Craig visited Judge Longworth at his new home in Electo, Karnes County, the former agent expressed despair that the ex-Confederates would eventually prosecute him for real and unsubstantiated crimes against the county.[40]

Captain Craig, who was sympathetic to Longworth's circumstances, attempted to save him from further prosecution by securing all the court records relevant to both the Longworth and Moore cases. When the local district clerk of Guadalupe County, James Wilcox, refused to turn the records over to Craig, the bureau agent had him arrested. Wilcox eventually surrendered the requested documents, and Craig promptly destroyed them. In early December, the grand jury in the county indicted the bureau agent for "stealing" state records and placed him in jail without bail. After three days, the military forced the local authorities to release the captain.[41]

Throckmorton protested the military's actions in Guadalupe County to General Kiddoo and General Sheridan, but both believed that the governor's protest was invalid given the circumstances of the cases. By this time, Craig had grown weary of the troubles in Texas. As a result, he retired from the military. Once Craig left the state, the controversy faded.[42]

At the same time that he was battling the Freedman's Bureau, Throckmorton was contesting the authority of the U.S. Army. His first opportunity to challenge the army's command came in early September when he protested the actions of federal troops stationed in the coastal community of Victoria. The chief justice of Victoria County, C. Carson, wrote to Throckmorton claiming that the federal commander stationed in Victoria refused to recognize local authority and was protecting black troops from criminal prosecution. According to Carson, federal troops were not upholding the law. They stood accused of aiding the escape of African Americans from the county jail; of hanging a white man accused of murdering a black man; and of arresting and imprisoning various citizens of the county on false charges. Carson stated that all of Victoria was experiencing a reign of terror. Furthermore, the chief justice reported that Captain Spaulding, commander of the forces at Victoria, refused to turn over two black soldiers accused of murdering William Walker, a white citizen of the county.[43]

Reacting to evidence presented in Carson's letter, Governor Throckmorton wrote to General Heintzelman stating that "these things are hard to be borne and I must earnestly beg of you, that not only those soldiers be arrested and held for trial by the civil authorities if there is any proceedings against them, but also ask that Captain Spaulding be arrested and tried by Court Martial for not discharging his duty in this case."[44] Heintzelman informed Throckmorton that he was "satisfied that many illegal & unlawful acts have been committed by Capt. Spaulding's command" in Victoria and that he would turn the matter over to General Sheridan.[45]

In November, Sheridan ordered that one of the soldiers be turned over to the civil authorities for trial. The governor was pleased with the military's response to the circumstance in Victoria and believed that he had effectively secured official recognition from the military that civil authority was once again superior in the state. However, Throckmorton's euphoria was short-lived, as another conflict soon erupted between the civil and military authorities in Brenham.[46]

On September 7, 1866, just two days before Captain Craig left Brenham, a group of federal soldiers of the Seventeenth Infantry under the command of Bvt. Maj. George W. Smith apparently went to an African American dance. When they were asked to purchase a ticket to the social function, the soldiers reportedly forced their way into the dance hall and caused the breakup of the party. Some of the African Americans left the dance and went to Duke's Dance Hall, where whites in the community were holding their own party. The soldiers followed the African Americans and proceeded to break up the white gathering. Sometime after the arrival of the troops at Duke's Dance Hall, a white citizen fired at the soldiers, wounding two of them. Major Smith appeared on the scene with his company shortly after twelve o'clock and arrested two citizens involved in the disturbance and demanded that others be surrendered to his command. Smith stipulated that the town would suffer if the citizens did not carry out his orders within the hour. While waiting for the surrender of additional men, Smith's troops were reported to have patrolled the streets of Brenham. Once the hour had passed and no one was brought forth, the soldiers gathered at Wyatt's saloon and then proceeded to ransack the town, breaking into Compton's general store and pillaging it. At some point, the store was set afire, and before the blaze could be brought under control, the inferno spread to several adjacent buildings, destroying a large section of the town.[47]

After receiving word of the crisis in Brenham, Governor Throckmorton directed the sheriff of Washington County to restore law and order in the town, and he dispatched a telegram to Maj. Solon H. Lathrop, who was stationed at Houston, asking the army officer to investigate the events that had transpired at Brenham. The governor sent a special message to the state legislature recommending that they appoint a joint committee to investigate the matter. They were instructed to take testimony regarding the origin of the fire and to estimate the property damage that resulted from the blaze. Throckmorton then wrote to Lt. Col. E. C. Mason, regimental commander stationed at Galveston, and asked that Smith and his company be removed from the area. Additionally, Throckmorton requested that Mason turn over the soldiers who were involved in setting the fires for civil prosecution. Much to the governor's surprise, Lieutenant Colonel Mason's official report of the incident exonerated the army of any wrongdoing. He further stipulated that citizens disguised in military uniforms were actually responsible for starting the fire. On September 20, General Sheridan telegraphed the governor that he had ordered Smith not to turn himself or any of the men in his command over to civil authorities until the matter had been properly sorted out. Sheridan asked Throckmorton to aid him in calming the excitement surrounding the crisis. Throckmorton responded to Sheridan stating that his office would cooperate with the military but stressed that Smith and his men should be removed from Brenham to avoid further turmoil. Throckmorton sent word to Rep. James Shephard, who was in charge of the legislative committee investigating the fire, not to arrest any of the federal troops stationed at Brenham.[48]

Fearing that the military would not turn over the soldiers, Throckmorton wrote two letters to U.S. attorney general Henry Stanbery. In the first, he sent evidence suggesting that soldiers were involved in burning the town and asking Stanbery to bring them to justice. He also mentioned the problems that had occurred in Victoria. Generally, Throckmorton wanted an order handed down from Washington that would force the military authorities to recognize the supremacy of civil officials in the state.[49]

The governor's second letter was more direct. He stated that "these cases in addition to others heretofore sent to your office will show the necessity for the authorities of the General Government to make known to the State authorities how far State laws and the laws and Constitution of the United States are to look to for protection." The governor asked whether the military was subject to the president's proclamation of August 19, or was it going to be allowed to "continue to disregard and override the rights of the loyal citizens of the U.S., leaving them powerless, and at the mercy of every petty military upstart, who may chance to have bayonets to enforce the edicts of a heart and mind too callus to be touched with a single aspiration for the peace and prosperity of a suffering country, and so benighted as never to have had flashed upon it a single ray of intelligence."[50] Attorney General Stanbery replied rather promptly to Throckmorton, stating that "orders have been issued to the military authorities as will prevent the recurrence of collision between the military & civil jurisdictions in the State of Texas."[51] While Throckmorton was pleased with the response from Washington, the governor's vitriolic attack on the military did little to improve relations between his administration and the army commanders in Texas.

The legislative committee proceeded to Brenham but found the military to be less than cooperative; Major Smith refused to allow the legislators to question his soldiers. The committee's official report claimed that Smith was responsible for the incident and recommended that civil authorities should detain him. Subsequently, a Washington County grand jury indicted the commander for arson and burglary. At that point, Throckmorton asked Gen. Charles Griffin to turn Smith over to the civil authorities. However, the military took no immediate action to solve the matter.[52] As the relations between the civil authorities and the military deteriorated, Sheridan wrote to General Grant that the soldiers involved in the incident at Brenham were reported to be unarmed and inoffensive and that the townspeople's insolent and threatening attitude toward the army was the root cause of the confrontation. He added that the damage to the town was minimal and that the buildings as well as the contents inside them were not particularly valuable anyway.[53]

Sheridan ordered Lieutenant Colonel Mason to come to New Orleans and give him a detailed report of the Brenham incident. After interviewing Mason, Sheridan decided to travel to Texas to investigate the matter personally. Upon arriving in Brenham and examining the facts more closely, the general wrote to Grant again. Sheridan conceded that Union soldiers had indeed set the fire. Nevertheless, despite continued protest from Throckmorton, the general did little to prosecute the matter.[54] Though Major Smith appeared to be at fault, the military authorities reassigned him to duties outside Brenham, rather than turning him over to the civil courts.

In July 1867, the Department of Texas put an end to the matter by issuing a special order that formally cleared Smith of all charges against him.[55]

One more incident occurred in September of 1866 that afforded Throckmorton another opportunity to confront the military authorities. However, this case proved detrimental to the governor's call for federal troops to leave the interior. In a Bell County court case, Johnathon Lindsey was accused of conspiring to murder two men named Duncan and Davis. Apparently, the case originated during the Civil War. Lindsey, a rabid secessionist, was found to be connected with a gang of horse thieves in Collin County and was forced to leave North Texas during the war.[56]

At the close of the war, Lindsey returned to his former trade in Lampasas County. Fearing that two Bell County men might have incriminating evidence against him, Lindsey hatched a plan to save his neck from the hangman's noose. He approached the federal authorities and claimed that Duncan and Davis had led a mob in North Texas during the war which hanged his son for pro-Union views. Given the widespread knowledge of the Gainesville hangings, the federal authorities believed his story probable, and as a result, the military arrested the two suspects, planning to bring the men before a military court. Unfortunately for Duncan and Davis, Lindsey was with the military unit that arrested them. At some point, he shot and killed the two suspects for attempting to escape. The grand jury in Bell County issued warrants for the arrest of both Lindsey and the officer in charge of the military escort, but the military authorities insisted that a military commission try the case. Furthermore, they refused Throckmorton's request to allow his attorney general to attend the military trial. All parties in the Lindsey affair were acquitted of wrongdoing. However, Lindsey was later arrested in Bell County, and despite Governor Throckmorton's assuring the military authorities that Lindsey was safe in the hands of the local authorities, a mob broke into the jail, seized the accused murderer, and lynched him. The inability of the Bell County authorities to secure the safety of Lindsey was prejudicial to Throckmorton's claim that the state and local governments could administer fair justice in civil affairs. It seems certain that General Sheridan would have used this case to illustrate the necessity of maintaining troops in the interior of Texas, but the events that had transpired in Brenham seriously weakened his own position.[57]

During the early days of Throckmorton's governorship, Texas became a virtual killing field. The frontier was out of control, with Indian raids threatening the lives of settlers in the west. Ex-Confederates nefariously terrorized the freedmen and their white allies in the interior of the state.

While these atrocities developed, state authorities and military commanders vehemently disagreed over which citizens were in greater need of protection. Though underfunded and undermanned, soldiers and the agents of the Freedmen's Bureau did their best to preserve the peace. With some exceptions, the federal troops served admirably and remained true to their mission to protect the rights of all loyal men in the state regardless of ethnicity. Throckmorton, on the other hand, fought to ensure that white Texans dominated the social, political, and economic institutions of the state. For him, as well as many ex-Confederates, the lives and rights of the freedmen or the Plains Indians mattered little. There is little doubt that the governor's attitude toward the nonwhite population made him an impediment to Reconstruction.

## CHAPTER SEVEN

# *An Impediment to Reconstruction, 1867*

As the confrontation between the civil and military authorities unfolded, the legislature was in session and was debating laws designed to restrict the rights of Texas freedmen. Concerned about the controversies between the military and civil authorities and worried that Congress might establish complete military rule over the state, former Confederate cabinet member John H. Reagan wrote to Throckmorton on October 12, 1866. Reagan candidly told the governor that Texas had yet to fulfill the North's wishes, and he reminded his colleague that the state had not yet made provisions for black testimony in all court cases, nor had the legislature granted suffrage rights to the freedmen. The East Texas politician questioned whether whites understood that such actions would lead to the possible loss of their own political rights, the perpetuation of territorial status, and the continued rejection of their elected officials in Washington. Reagan reminded Throckmorton of his earlier letter sent from prison at Fort Warren on August 11, 1865, and observed that the predictions he had made from his prison cell were materializing. He suggested that the continued existence of the Freedmen's Bureau and military rule were the direct result of the South's failure to act judiciously. Reagan then warned that the state government might be terminated at any time and suggested that further hardships might be avoided if the state legislature would grant blacks full civil rights, equal access to the courts, limited suffrage rights, and equal but separate educational facilities for African American children.[1]

After receiving Reagan's letter, Throckmorton questioned the appropriate course that the state should follow concerning the adoption of the Fourteenth Amendment. As a result, the governor sent a telegram to President Johnson on October 29, asking the nation's chief executive for advice.

The next day, Johnson replied, informing Throckmorton that he had "nothing to suggest further than urging the legislature to make all laws involving civil rights as complete as possible, so as to extend equal and exact justice to all persons without regard to color, if it has not been done." The president then attempted to reassure Throckmorton that the Union would soon be united again: "we should not despair of the Republic. My faith is strong, my confidence unlimited in the wisdom, performance, virtue, intelligence . . . of the great mass of the people." The president continued, "their ultimate decision will be uninfluenced by passion and prejudice engendered by the recent civil war, for the complete restoration of the Union, by the admission of loyal Senators and Representatives from all States to the respective Houses of the Congress of the United States."[2]

Throckmorton saw some validity in Reagan and Johnson's arguments. On October 31, he delivered an address to the state legislature in which he denied that ex-Confederates were preying on Unionists and freedmen and claimed that federal troops were no longer needed in the interior of the state. The governor suggested that the legislature pass a resolution pledging law and order without racial distinctions, and he urged the lawmakers to extend the witness provision to include blacks in all court cases. To strengthen his position, he submitted the letter that President Johnson sent to him the day before so that the legislators could read it for themselves. However, he stopped short of calling on the legislature to give suffrage rights to African Americans. Despite the governor's recommendations, the legislators were unwilling to give black Texans anything more than nominal freedom. As a result, they refused to ratify the Fourteenth Amendment and instead decided to pass the infamous Black Codes, which, as mentioned earlier, severely limited the civil rights of black Texans.[3]

Soon after the legislature passed the Black Codes, state officials learned that Republicans had swept the midterm congressional election in November. The Republicans were now in a position to force the southern states to provide civil rights to the freedmen. The Radical Republicans' success demoralized Throckmorton. In a lengthy letter to H. G. Hendricks, the governor prophetically stated that "our political prospects are to my mind, quite gloomy. The Radicals have the majority [in Congress] and from what we know of them, we cannot doubt they will use it. But there are some very powerful causes that will perhaps make them somewhat cautious." Throckmorton continued with the observation that "the safety and stability of the public debt in which their interests are much greater than ours, will perhaps keep them within bounds."

Throckmorton, however, understood that the South would experience changes. He stated, "I incline to the opinion that Hamilton and his especial friends, [Benjamin] Butler, [Nathaniel] Banks, and [Thaddeus] Stevens, will make a serious effort to destroy our State government," but the governor did hold out hope that "the more conservative among the leaders, [Horace] Greeley, [James] Bennett, [Henry] Raymond, and [Henry] Beecher and those who agree with them, will not consent to this, and their influence will be thrown to sustain the President in his veto of any bill that the extremists might pass for this purpose."[4]

Throckmorton commented to Hendricks on the probability that universal suffrage for the freedmen would soon become a reality: "Greeley, [William] Smith, Beecher, and some others are and have been all the strive, in favor of universal suffrage and a general and full amnesty. I incline to the opinion that Chase and a number of the other prominent radical leaders are for this plan." The governor added, "I believe that many leading democrats in the North will side in the same way. They go upon the hypothesis that there will be no restoration, no peace, no stability of trade, no safety for the public debt, until a compromise is made." Throckmorton was convinced that "the Northern democracy will yield on the suffrage question for the purpose of getting the electoral vote of the South in the next presidential canvas. How far the President may be disposed to harmonize on this point, I am not able to judge. But I believe he will agree to advise the South to accept such terms, but standing firm upon his doctrine that the States have the right to fix such qualifications as they may deem proper." Throckmorton also believed that "the proposed amendments will not be adopted by three-fourths of the States. And I do not believe the radicals will go so far as to contend that three-fourths of the States represented in Congress are competent, though this is their theory. But the truth is they prefer negro suffrage to those amendments. I am of the opinion that such will be the solution of our difficulties." For the governor the final question to be answered was whether "we will agree to accept this, or be afflicted with the Freedmen's bureau, and a semi-military government—and run the risk of losing our State organizations and the disfranchisement of the largest portion of our leading men to the extent of voting [or] holding office State or federal."[5]

In a letter to Charles R. Breedlove, Throckmorton contemplated the way southern states should vote regarding the issue of the suffrage amendment. He asked the rhetorical question, "Will enough of the Southern States vote for the suffrage amendment to the Constitution to carry it?"

He then answered, "I believe they will. For instance: Kentucky, Maryland, and Delaware would, having nothing to lose except the principle, as there are not sufficient blacks in these States, for any risk to be run. The same may be said of Missouri and Tennessee, and I think Arkansas and North Carolina, would also adopt it." Throckmorton concluded that "the other southern states would run too much risk in being onslaughted by negro voters, unless such qualifications should be adopted as would exclude them and at the same time exclude many white citizens."[6] Without knowing it, Throckmorton had visualized a plan of disfranchisement that would become all too common in the New South of the 1890s and early 1900s. Furthermore, he revealed his innermost fear that black suffrage might lead to his loss of political power.

Throughout December, Throckmorton continued to be consumed with the prospect that freedmen would be able to vote in Texas. He slowly began to frame his arguments against universal suffrage in a format that had served him well in the past: he claimed that Congress was going to coerce the South to accept black voting rights. Throckmorton wrote to Epperson that "if coercive measures are resorted to, if the best citizens are to be degraded by the laws of their country, if they are to be prescribed with a mark upon them, denied the same proud and high privileges . . . there can be no prosperity, no harmony, no restoration." He then warned that "the poor negro will be the greatest sufferers."[7]

The congressional victories of the Radical Republicans brought about rumors that Throckmorton might soon be removed from the governor's office. He addressed these rumors in a letter to one of his longtime friends in Collin County. He wrote that "if it was not for the great injury that would result to the country, so far as I am concerned, I would be glad to be relieved from my position. . . . [I]t makes me sad to realize that I am not my own man, and cannot control my own actions but must continue [to be] the slave of the public."[8] Throckmorton even stated that he would resign his position, but he was afraid that a radical would replace him. Therefore, he believed that he had to remain in office for as long as possible to thwart the radical agenda.

Throckmorton knew that his standing with military authorities was tenuous at best and that General Sheridan would welcome the governor's resignation. Writing to Charles R. Breedlove, the governor stated that "Sheridan . . . has some reason for making a lick at me. I have denounced his course in my correspondence to Washington. In one of my letters, I said that the great misfortune the south labored under was being cursed by

Gen. Charles Griffin. General Griffin and Governor Throckmorton were at odds over the issue of military and civil rule. Throckmorton's obstructive actions during 1867caused Griffin to call on Sheridan for the removal of the governor. *Civil War Glass Negative Collection, Library of Congress.*

military satraps, who had not the sense to appreciate the condition of the Country and whose hearts never had a patriotic emotion."[9] Assuming that Radicals in Congress would soon strengthen military rule in the South, Throckmorton attempted to repair his reputation with General Sheridan and his subordinate officers by recognizing their authority. Nevertheless, while Throckmorton believed it necessary to appease the military authorities, he still attempted to ensure the removal of federal troops from the interior of the state and to restore civil rule as soon as possible.

The governor's first opportunity to work more closely with the military came in December of 1866 when troubles erupted in Prairie Lea, Caldwell County. A group of Unionists sent a memorial to the Freedmen's Bureau stating that whites were persecuting the freedmen in the community and requesting that the military come to their aid. At about the same time, W. C. Phillips wrote to the governor that whites frequently were intimidating, cheating, and murdering black citizens.[10] Throckmorton immediately wrote to Gen. Charles Griffin, who had replaced Heintzelman as commander of the District of Texas, and asked him to investigate the reported atrocities taking place in Caldwell County.[11] The governor also sent a dispatch to the county judge in Caldwell County, stating that "information from various persons has convinced me of the necessity of asking from the military authorities assistance in maintaining laws in the neighborhood of Prairie Lea in your county." Throckmorton continued, "I deem it just and proper that you should know of my request, not to take the administration of the law into their hands, but when called upon by the civil authorities to render assistance as may be necessary to insure the arrest and trial of offenders." The governor concluded, "I need not remind you of how much the good people of Texas suffer on account of the occasional acts of lawlessness of bad & vicious men. I sincerely trust you will impress upon the civil authorities, and upon your fellow citizens, the necessity of the laws—It must be done."[12]

Additionally, Throckmorton attempted to repair his relationship with the Freedmen's Bureau. During the temporary absence of bureau commissioner General Kiddoo, William Sinclair contacted the governor about the ill treatment of a freedman accused of murder in Wharton County. After receiving Sinclair's correspondence, Throckmorton dispatched a communication to the county judge, requesting him to check into the matter. He informed the judge that Sinclair believed that "a freedman confined in jail for the killing of 'Jake' a freedman" was not "properly treated as a prisoner &c." Throckmorton instructed the judge to make sure "that the prisoner receives such treatment as is contemplated by the law, and the same given to white men under similar circumstances."[13] The extent of the governor's sincerity cannot be measured, but it seems likely that Throckmorton sent this letter with the knowledge that he could later use this incident to strengthen his argument that his administration was making an honest effort to protect the freedmen.

Despite Throckmorton's maneuvers to salvage his administration, events in early 1867 prevented the two sides from cooperating with one another. The Freedmen's Bureau continued to intervene in cases where civil officials failed to protect the rights of African Americans. As a result, Throckmorton appealed to General Griffin in several cases where local authorities accused bureau agents of making illegal arrests and of their refusal to obey the writs of habeas corpus issued by county judges. One such case involved the arrest of J. C. McCrary of McLennan County, Dr. John Bell of Bosque County, and a Dr. Irving of Milam County. According to the citizens in McLennan County, Lt. Alfred Manning, the subassistant agent for the county, arrested the men without informing the accused of the charges against them. Even though he was not familiar with the particulars of the case, Throckmorton immediately protested Lieutenant Manning's actions. Perhaps if he had investigated the case more closely, Throckmorton would not have sided so quickly with the supporters of the accused men because the governor was politically astute enough to avoid confrontations that he could not win. Dr. Bell's crime was inexcusable. He had helped the other men castrate a young black male living in McLennan County, alleging that the youth had attempted to rape a white woman.[14] This case undoubtedly jeopardized what little credibility Throckmorton had left with the military authorities, especially General Griffin.

The commander of the District of Texas was outraged by the McLennan County case. As soon as his subordinates informed him of the castration of the young man, Griffin sent a letter to the governor. He stated that "I have directed with view to bringing these parties to trial and it appear[s] that the civil authorities are unable to hold them." The general informed Throckmorton that the accused would be detained "by the sub agent of the Freedmen's Bureau, at Waco, Texas, until otherwise ordered from these Headquarters." Griffin concluded his letter with a stern warning: "If the civil courts are prepared to try this case and can be relied upon to give impartial justice, I will direct these citizens to be turned over to the proper civil officer of the state. If this negro boy cannot receive full justice, so far as the law is qualified to give reparation for the great crime done him, and the parties guilty of the same punishment for their barbarity, I shall be obliged to take action as laid down in Sec. III of the Civil Rights Bill."[15] The incident apparently ended when Lieutenant Manning was ordered to consult with the prosecuting attorney of his district and to take the "proper measures and turn over Dr. Bell and [others] to the civil courts for trial."[16] Since the accused men were tried by a group of their peers, the results of the trial were predictable. The defendants were set free. The outcome infuriated and disgusted Manning to the point that General Griffin reassigned him in February 1867.[17]

By January 1867, General Sheridan had become increasingly concerned with the political conditions in Texas. As a result, he sent a scathing report to the War Department. The general questioned the legitimacy of Throckmorton's repeated request to have the military removed from the interior to the frontier counties. Sheridan reported that during the last six months of 1866, Indian depredations had indeed taken place on the frontier, but the extent of those raids was yet to be determined. The general theorized that the attacks were not very alarming and that the Texas governor was purposely exaggerating the reports to convince federal authorities of the necessity of stationing troops in the northern and western counties and thereby improving the economic circumstances of the frontier population by providing them with army contracts for their crops and livestock. Additionally, Sheridan alleged that Throckmorton desired to remove troops from the interior as part of a plot to leave freedmen and Unionists defenseless against lawless ex-Confederates.[18]

As reports of violence continued to reach General Sheridan's office, he became more convinced that the freedmen and Unionists in Texas were in grave danger. Sheridan wrote to Throckmorton stating that "there are more casualties occurring from [ex-Confederate] outrages perpetrated upon Union men and freedmen in the interior of the state than occurs from Indian depredations on the frontier." Fearing that troops would remain in the interior of the state, Throckmorton assured Sheridan that many of the men who professed to be Unionists were actually criminals and sought the protection of the military from civil authorities by claiming to be persecuted for their political beliefs. In an effort to prove Sheridan's accusations false, Governor Throckmorton called on county judges to inform his office of the conditions of freedmen and Union men within their jurisdiction. The judges universally replied that all citizens received justice before their courts, including secessionists, freedmen, and Unionists. The judges stated that the crimes committed against freedmen often were perpetrated by individuals who had drifted into their jurisdiction during and after the war. For example, the judge of Grayson County revealed that many foul murders had been committed in his county but insisted that they were the work of a band of outlaws that resided across the Red River in the Indian Territory.[19] Throckmorton seemed assured that the crime rate in Texas was no worse than other states in the Union and claimed that the military's charges were basically groundless.

As late as February 12, Throckmorton felt that he had appeased the federal authorities sufficiently to save his administration. In a letter to Richard B. Hubbard, the governor analyzed the circumstances confronting the state. "We cannot refer to the past for a parallel by which to form a judgement as to our future," he suggested. "To your inquires I answer, 1st, I do not believe our present State government will be abolished, and territorial ones in place thereof be established." Throckmorton continued, "2nd, I believe negro suffrage will be forced upon us by Congressional action. 3rd, I do not believe the Amnesty Proclamation of the President and the pardons granted thereunder will be declared null and void." The governor concluded, "4th, I do not believe any confiscation measure will pass. In regards to the 2nd proposition of negro suffrage I believe it is coming upon us in some shape. It is the very least of all the ills which we are threatened by the Radical majority in Congress."[20]

Throckmorton's statements to Hubbard suggested that he underestimated the Radical congressmen's desire to reconstruct the southern states. On March 2, 1867, Congress claimed that President Johnson's plan for the South was essentially a failure and therefore passed the first of a series of Reconstruction Acts over the president's veto. This act declared that no legal government existed in the southern states; that Congress planned to divide the South into five military districts, with Texas and Louisiana comprising the Fifth Military District; and that President Johnson should appoint an army officer to command each district. The acts further stated that the southern states would have to hold another constitutional convention and to adopt a new state constitution that was in accordance with the U.S. Constitution. In addition, each state had to adopt the Fourteenth Amendment, requiring the states to ensure due process and equal protection under the law for African Americans. When these requirements were met, the state could officially apply for readmission to the Union. General Sheridan, who commanded the Department of the Gulf, was appointed commander of the Fifth Military District, and General Griffin was made commander of the District of Texas.[21]

The Reconstruction Acts placed Throckmorton in an awkward situation. The laws provided that only loyal Union men could hold office or vote in elections. Thus, the governor and many of those in his administration did not qualify to hold office. The laws also gave the military commanders more authority to carry out Congressional Reconstruction policies. This naturally proved problematic for the governor, considering he had obstructed the military's efforts in the months prior to passage of the acts. Thus, Throckmorton realized that the military would now exercise greater control over the civil affairs of the state.[22]

Because the military's authority was strengthened in the southern states, Throckmorton redoubled his efforts to give the appearance of aiding the military's efforts to reconstruct the state. He seized the opportunity to aid the Freedmen's Bureau in investigating alleged crimes committed against freedmen in Marshall, Texas. The governor wrote to the county judge in Harrison County, requesting an official report of any "violations of the rights of property or person of freedmen by the white race and any violation of law by freedmen upon freedmen." Throckmorton requested that the judge send him "an official statement as to the correctness of the charge made by the agent that the civil authorities will not, and does not, act in cases of shooting & robbing, as in fact in any case of any imprudence unless the freedmen is the defendant, for fear of disfavor." Throckmorton concluded that "I trust civil authorities of your section will [make every effort] to punish crime of any shade and character, and if these charges are slanderous furnish me the evidence." This call for a report on the crimes against freedmen might have served the governor well had he not expressed his own biases in his letter to the Harrison County judge. Throckmorton stated that he did not "believe one word" of the bureau agent's reports concerning criminal activity in the county.[23]

The next day, Throckmorton reported to General Griffin about cases involving crimes against white Unionists and freedmen in Travis County. He stated that "I enclose you the response of the county [attorney] of Travis County to inquiries made by me in reference to the freedmen, Edward Parsons & Mat Hewling, one of whom was wounded & the other killed, and reported to you by Capt. Porter from this place on the 18th December last." The governor then defended the civil officials in the county: "you will observe, General, that the civil authorities here [have] done their duty in these cases." Throckmorton informed Griffin what he believed to be the true nature of the criminal activities in Travis County. He wrote, "I am familiar with all the facts in regards to the murder of Hewling. [The perpetrators] are noted robbers & murders and through my exertions, aided by the sheriff, Mr. Zimplerman of this county, in addition to the offence already named, are also confined for justification in the murder & robbery of Judge Doyle of Hill County." Furthermore, the governor revealed that "it was given out that Judge Doyle & his son were murdered & robbed because they were Union men when nothing could be further from the truth. The band who murdered them . . . are notorious scoundrels who have been fugitives from justice for a year past."[24]

Despite his attempts to reestablish the credibility of his administration, Throckmorton could not resist the opportunity to make an impolitic jab at the federal authorities. The governor stated in his letter to Griffin that "I am not aware that Capt Porter's fear of robbery of freedmen during Christmas week were realized, but I am aware of the facts that the robberies committed upon them the previous Christmas were made by U.S. Soldiers, and that the same class have repeated the offence frequently since, not only upon the freedmen, but upon the white persons also." Throckmorton then attempted to smooth over his comments by stating that "I do not mean this as any reflection upon the U.S. army, but I mention to show that Capt. Porter would have more fairly discharged his duty if he had stated that the soldiers were the parties who robbed freedmen."[25] It seems certain that these comments did little to improve relations between the civil and military authorities.

When Throckmorton first learned of the Reconstruction Acts, he began to ponder the new circumstances confronting his state. In a letter to Ashbel Smith, the governor wrote that "it is certain to my mind that Texas cannot long delay action. If we do[,] 25–50 or 100 or more radical[s] and negroes will call a convention, adopt a constitution, elect officers &c." He continued, "We must make up our minds to this State of things, or we must act at once, and take the initiative, and produce [a] concert of action, and energy as well, among our friends. Action under this military bill is forced upon us, we do not adopt it as our action—we do not accept it as the best thing we can get, or approve it." Nevertheless, Throckmorton stated that "it is forced upon us by a maddened and infuriated Congress, and put through by the bayonet. Therefore, as the house is burning, and the soldiery are around with bayonets and will not let us stop the fire, had we not better save what little they will allow us, instead of . . . standing by doing nothing, and permitting the flames to devour the women and children." The governor concluded that "we must act, or the radicals and negroes will act, and when they make a constitution without hindrance, Tennessee and Missouri will be the example."[26]

Apparently, the governor believed it would serve the state well if he continued his campaign to heal his relationship with the military. As a result, Throckmorton redoubled his efforts to establish more cordial relations with General Sheridan. The governor sent a telegraph to the general on March 27, asking for a conference with him to discuss how the civil authorities might cooperate more fully with the military in executing the newly passed Reconstruction Acts. Sheridan sent a straightforward reply that the civil authorities could assist in the reorganization of the state only by rigorously supporting General Griffin and by advising the people of Texas to participate fully in the work of reorganizing their state.[27]

Throckmorton believed that it might also prove beneficial to court black political leaders, convincing them to align black voters with the Democratic Party and thereby disrupt Radical Republicans' efforts to do the same. In April 1867, he called on Jacob Raney and Anderson Scroggins, two black leaders in Texas, to meet with him and discuss the political situation of freedmen. At the conference, Throckmorton attempted to persuade the black leaders to move the freedmen into the conservative camp. The governor claimed that conservative Democrats were the true friends of the freedmen and that they were deeply concerned about the welfare of the state's black citizens. Throckmorton proposed that the freedmen should hold a rally and allow prominent conservative politicians, such as Judge John Hancock and Col. George W. Carter, to speak to them. He also suggested that organizers of the rally should give copies of his inaugural address and the acts of the Eleventh Legislature to the attendees as evidence that conservative Democrats were sincerely concerned about the well-being of the freedmen. Both Raney and Scroggins saw through the governor's ruse. Instead of calling for a rally, they condemned the governor for his opposition to the franchise bill introduced in the Constitutional Convention of 1866; his approval of a school bill that excluded freed children from its provisions; his failure to prosecute outrages against Union men and blacks; and his opposition to Congressional Reconstruction.[28]

While attempting to gain the favor of the military and black leaders, other problems continued to plague Throckmorton. On April 26, General Griffin notified him that sixty Unionists in Jack and Parker counties had informed his office that the local courts were prosecuting Unionists' cases where they had already been acquitted by the courts during Governor Hamilton's administration. In addition, the general charged that the courts failed to prosecute those individuals who murdered and robbed honest Union men in both counties. Griffin concluded by saying, "such grave charges of maladministration if false should be disproved without delay; if true the remedy must be swift and effectual."[29] Throckmorton agreed with Griffin and replied:

> In this sentiment I beg to concur most heartily. If the officers of the law are guilty, they should not only suffer the penalty of such guilt, but they should be removed from office as soon as their guilt can be established. It is but simple and unadorned justice that they should have an opportunity to acquit themselves of the guilt charged—they now have that opportunity—should they fail to do so or should an investigation show the truth of the statement, the law has clothed the military with power and authority to make the remedy swift and effectual. I shall by no act of mine seek to smother investigation, screen guilt, or avert the blow where justice demands it should fall.[30]

On April 29, 1867, Throckmorton wrote John J. Good, judge of the Fifth Judicial District, to call his attention to the charges levied against the courts in Parker and Jack counties. The governor urged Judge Good to fully investigate the matter and, if necessary, to prosecute the offenders. Then Throckmorton revealed his desire to restore law and order in the counties:

> It is hardly necessary for me to impress upon you the absolute necessity that exists that all good law-abiding citizens of the country should unite in allaying excitement and prejudice and that no ill feeling should be indulged in towards those of our fellow citizens who adhere to the general government during the war. I am aware of the fact from unquestioned information that there were persons adhering to the Confederate cause in Parker County who during the war committed many serious violations of the law—doubtless the same has been true since the war—and while this is true I know it from equally good authority that persons in the same region who adhered to the general government have committed the same character of offences and it matters not who have been thus guilty[,] they should be punished by the law.[31]

On the same day, the governor made it a point to write the county judge in Parker County. Not only did he enclose a copy of Griffin's communication in his correspondence, but he also included a copy of the petition that the Unionists had sent to the District of Texas headquarters. The governor's intentions seemed clear: he wanted the judge to know exactly who the Unionists were in Parker County. Throckmorton stated that "the charges therein made against yourself and the county commissioners and other officers of the county—as well as citizens[—]renders it but an act of justice that you should be made fully acquainted with them—the laws must be enforced and every person be prosecuted in person and property. If this cannot be done in your county, I shall deem it a duty to call upon the military and see that it is so."[32] Throckmorton's actions endangered the lives of the Parker County Unionists by sending their petition to the county judge. At best, his actions represented poor judgment. At worst, the governor sent the information knowing that the local officials would silence their accusers.

Throckmorton continued to monitor the situation in Parker and Jack counties, and he eventually requested that Griffin send a small force of twenty-five soldiers under the command of an officer of discretion and good judgment to Parker County. The governor continued to correspond with officials in the county reaffirming the sentiments that he had expressed in his letter to Judge Good.[33] As the events unfolded in Parker and Jack counties, Throckmorton began to realize his efforts to work with the military authorities were not producing any tangible result. Thus, the governor became less cooperative with federal authorities.

At the same time he was working to solve problems in Parker and Jack counties, Throckmorton turned his attention once again to Prairie Lea, Caldwell County. Following the initial troubles in Caldwell County and Throckmorton's request that federal troops be stationed there to protect the freedmen, General Griffin sent 1st Lt. S. C. Plummer to the scene with a small contingent of men. While stationed there, Plummer reported to Griffin that the whites were orderly and that his only opposition came from a disgruntled freedman, whom he gunned down.[34]

However, evidence suggests that conditions in Caldwell County were not as calm as Plummer had reported to Griffin, and the military had indeed run into conflict with whites. Throckmorton realized that events in Prairie Lea presented him with an opportunity to embarrass the military. In a letter to John Ireland, a district judge whose region included Caldwell County, he stated, "yesterday I wrote to Genrl. H. E. McCulloch and requested him to see you and confer with you in regard to getting up all the facts in relation to Lt. Plummer's proceedings at Prairie Lea in ordering off the citizens of that vicinity and as to the death and killing of Burns [a freedman]." Throckmorton continued to inform Judge Ireland that he wanted "sworn statements as to Hoppler's [who had been ordered off his land] character—also any facts that will go to prove the bad character or good conduct of Plummer. The sworn statement of any facts that will show the true state of the case relating to the death of Burns." Throckmorton concluded by stating that "it strikes me that Plummer and his men who killed Burns should be indicted for murder—if the facts warrant such a conclusion, but as a matter of course this depends upon the facts." Throckmorton made clear that he "would try and expose all the villainy they [radicals and federal troops] commit, though it may cause my removal—therefore any information in regard to affairs at Prairie Lea, I desire."[35]

As events unfolded at Prairie Lea, the governor became engaged in more disagreements with the military authorities. Nowhere was this more evident than in the Huntsville prison controversy. In early 1867, Gen. William H. Sinclair visited the state prison and reported to General Griffin that nearly three-fourths of the black convicts were unjustly imprisoned.

Sinclair revealed that one black prisoner had received a two-year sentence for the theft of a single dollar. In all, the general reported 209 such cases. General Griffin requested that Governor Throckmorton investigate the unjust imprisonment of African Americans, and when appropriate, issue pardons. The governor flatly refused. Although most of the prisoners in question eventually received pardons or at least reduced sentences, the prison controversy illustrated the conflict that existed between the military and civil authorities. The military clearly was attempting to enact equitable social reforms, which the civil government and the majority of white Texans were not willing to accept.[36]

In late March, the military authorities began to carry out the dictates of Congressional Reconstruction. On March 28, General Griffin began the process of reorganizing the state government and registering voters. He requested that the governor supply his office with a list of the counties and county seats. Throckmorton complied with Griffin's request and offered to help aid the general in his task of reorganizing the state.[37]

On April 3, the governor wrote to Griffin to inquire if the new reconstruction law allowed him to appoint individuals to vacancies in the state and county offices, or whether he should call for elections to fill the positions. Unsure of how these vacancies should be filled, Griffin forwarded Throckmorton's inquiry to General Sheridan, who in turn informed the governor that he could neither make appointments nor call for elections. Furthermore, Sheridan revealed that Congress had taken the power of calling elections and taking appointments away from the civil authorities and placing those duties in the hands of the military commanders.[38]

On April 4, Griffin continued his efforts to register loyal voters, requesting that the governor furnish his office with a list of all men, irrespective of color, who could qualify to act as voter registrars. These men had to take the oath of office as prescribed by Congress on July 2, 1862.[39] Four days later, Throckmorton issued a circular address to the county judges asking them to furnish him with a list that would fulfill Griffin's request.[40] The judges apparently completed their task in a timely fashion, and Throckmorton promptly forwarded their reports to General Griffin. The governor took pride in the fact that the local judges had quickly complied with his request, and he commented to the general, "I respectfully invite your attention to the promptitude of this action of the county judges, and especially to the spirit manifested to observe the law and aid in its executions."[41]

Despite the prompt actions of the governor and the judges, Griffin distrusted the true motives of Texas officials. On March 28, the Texas commander wrote to Sheridan that none of the civil officers in the state were trustworthy. He pointed out that Throckmorton was unwilling to punish individuals who committed crimes against Union men and freedmen. As a result of the governor's inability to carry out the laws of the state, General Griffin recommended that Throckmorton and all members of his administration be removed from office and replaced with good Union men. On April 2, General Sheridan wrote to his superior, Gen. U. S. Grant, that he believed Griffin was correct in his assessment of the Texas officials and that he agreed that many of the state officials should be removed from public office. Grant promptly replied to Sheridan that no elected officials should be removed from office because there were still legal questions about whether or not the military had the authority to take such actions.[42]

On April 22 and 24, Throckmorton transmitted to Griffin the applications of people who qualified to serve as the assessor and collector of taxes for Bastrop and Comanche counties and a list of citizens who had taken the loyalty oath. Griffin immediately returned the applications to the governor with a message that stated "daily applications are made to me by many, and you have recommended so many persons as qualified to take the oath as registrants that I am disinclined and have decided not to appoint any to vacancies, who cannot take the oath of July, 1862." Throckmorton replied to the commanding general that he had made no recommendations and that his intention was merely to aid the general in his task of reorganizing the state. This incident clearly illustrated the growing divide between the Throckmorton's administration and the military authorities.[43]

On April 27, the next controversy between the civil and military officials centered upon General Griffin's Circular Order No. 13, also known as the Jury Order. It stated that only those individuals who had taken the iron-clad oath, which claimed that an individual had never voluntarily borne arms against the United States or voluntarily supported the Confederacy in any way, were allowed to serve as jurors in the civil courts of Texas. Additionally, the order reaffirmed that loyal citizens should not be excluded from the jury box on account of race. Griffin instructed Governor Throckmorton to distribute copies of the order to the county judges and to see that they were enforced. The general hoped that juries would soon be filled with loyal Union men and that they would be able to protect radicals and freedmen in the local courts. It seems certain that Throckmorton did not share Griffin's enthusiasm for giving Radical Republicans and freedmen the unrestricted right to serve on juries. More likely, the governor shared the same view as the editor of the *Galveston Daily News,* who stated that it "would be [better] to leave the active duties of the government, political and judicial, in the hands of the white race . . . [and] it would be much the better plan to give the negroes, for the present, no more rights than they now enjoy."[44]

The governor complied with Griffin's order but sent a communication to President Johnson expressing concern over the matter.[45] The state's chief executive promised the president that the Jury Order would be properly executed if it were found to be constitutional. Furthermore, he made the case that "federal judges holding courts of the United States for this state have ruled the petit jurors of their court are not required to take the oath contained in the order referred to." In addition, Throckmorton expressed the belief that the execution of the order would result in the confusion and demoralization of the state's court system.[46] Perhaps hoping to intimidate Griffin into rescinding his order, Throckmorton sent the general a copy of his letter to the president.[47] However, it is likely that the governor's letter only served to widen the rift between his administration and the military commander.

Just as Throckmorton predicted, the courts found it difficult to function under Circular Order No. 13. Judge Good could not hold court in Parker County. He succeeded in getting one petit juror in Tarrant County and a few in Dallas County. Judge Harrison failed to organize a jury for Coryell County. In McLennan County, he was more successful, compiling a jury of both black and white citizens. Reacting to citizen complaints, General Griffin requested that Throckmorton send him a list of the judges who could not organize their courts under the Jury Order. Throckmorton smugly replied that he had no accurate and complete information concerning the matter, which undoubtedly served to raise the ire and suspicions of the general.[48]

Throckmorton was not oblivious to Sheridan and Griffin's disdain for him and his government. Since he had written many unflattering letters to Sheridan and Griffin's superiors often referring to them as "military satraps," the governor clearly understood that his position with the commanders was tenuous at best.[49] His comments as well as his obstructive acts no doubt led the military commanders to renew their efforts to remove him.

Benjamin Epperson, who remained in Washington after Congress refused to let him take his seat in the House of Representatives, wrote to Throckmorton warning him that he was in political danger. He informed his friend that Sheridan had demonstrated his power to strike at top public officials by removing Gov. James M. Wells of Louisiana from office. Epperson felt that a lack of public outcry concerning Sheridan's removal of the Louisiana governor ensured that Throckmorton would experience a similar fate.[50]

Epperson's fears proved well founded because on July 25, Sheridan wrote to Grant again, stating that the crime rate in Texas was up and that Throckmorton was partly responsible for the atrocities committed against the freedmen and their white allies. Furthermore, the general stated that the governor had obstructed the ability of the military to maintain peace and had remained an obstacle to black suffrage. As a result, Sheridan stated that Throckmorton's removal from office was absolutely necessary if the freedmen's political rights were to be protected.[51]

Sheridan's contention that the crime rate had risen in Texas was accurate. Between 1865 and 1867, the number of homicides had increased from 77 to 331. The highways were infested with bandits who were willing to kill for plunder. Many of these desperadoes were ex-Confederate officers and soldiers who were unwilling to accept Congressional Reconstruction policies. Thus, the primary targets of the outlaws tended to be freedpeople, white Unionists, and federal soldiers stationed in the state. Furthermore, Sheridan was correct that Throckmorton did little to bring the lawbreakers to justice. However, the governor did not have at his disposal an effective law enforcement agency: federal authorities had prevented the state from organizing a state militia or ranging companies. Even if Throckmorton would have had such an agency, he likely would have sent the state troopers to the frontier, leaving the freedpeople in the interior of the state to fend for themselves.[52]

With the passing of the summer of 1867, it became evident that Throckmorton would be removed from office. On July 19, a second supplementary reconstruction act became law. The new law gave military commanders of the military districts full power to remove uncooperative state and local officials. The way was now legally clear for the governor's removal. On July 30, General Sheridan issued Special Order No. 105 ending Governor Throckmorton's term as governor after less than a year in office.[53] Sheridan sent the governor the following message:

> A careful consideration of the reports of Brevet Major General Charles Griffin, United States army, shows that J. W. Throckmorton, Governor of Texas, is an impediment to the reconstruction of that state under the law;

> he is thereby removed from that office. E. M. Pease is hereby appointed in place of J. W. Throckmorton, removed. He will be obeyed and respected accordingly.[54]

Thus, Throckmorton's term as governor of the Lone Star State came to an abrupt end. The governor's inability to accept the freedmen as the equal of white men and his repeated attempts to obstruct the military's efforts to carry out the Reconstruction Acts led to his political downfall. His views toward Reconstruction policy had caused him to side against white Unionists who supported the Radical Republicans' agenda of extending civil rights to African Americans. The North Texan could not bring himself to support even the moderate position of E. M. Pease, who called for limited suffrage rights for the freedmen. Throckmorton believed that the radical Unionists' position would eventually lead to equal rights for blacks and would provide them the necessary mobility to move en masse to North Texas.

The deposed governor, however, did not go quietly into the night. As stated in a letter to Epperson, he announced his intention "to fire a few shots that will place the military in their true light, and show the condition of affairs in Texas."[55] Throckmorton immediately prepared an "Address to the People of Texas," which reviewed his relations with the military authorities and refuted the charges that he was an impediment to Reconstruction. The outgoing governor wrote that he had exhibited every effort to follow federal laws, had aided General Sheridan and his subordinates in Texas, and had maintained peace in the state. Furthermore, he declared that the military had interfered with the civil courts and juries. Throckmorton claimed that the actions of the military had thrown civil administration of the state into disorder and had aroused bitterness and apprehension in the hearts of the people. Despite the vitriolic commentary he aimed at the military, Throckmorton concluded his address by advising the people to abide by the laws, to be kind to the freedmen, to refute by their conduct the Radical charges of disloyalty, to register if allowed to do so, and to elect good conservative men to office.[56]

At his Collin County home, the ex-governor could take some comfort that his administration was unofficially exonerated by President Johnson. During an interview, a reporter asked the president if he believed Throckmorton "had attempted to thwart the General in a proper execution of the law." Johnson answered, "No sir, the records prove the reverse. The Governor of Texas also placed the whole machinery of his State at the disposal of the military power, and aided in every way possible, except in the manufacturing of a Radical majority of voters, and in securing negro supremacy."[57] If Johnson's comments were not enough to please Throckmorton, it is certain the ex-governor took satisfaction that the president relieved General Sheridan as commander of the Fifth Military District in mid-August.[58]

While the president's comments reveal more about his own bitterness toward the Radical Republicans in Congress than the realities of the deposed governor's political actions in Texas, they do reveal an important aspect of the ex-governor's removal from office. Like President Johnson, Throckmorton's racial biases against the freedmen and his unwillingness to accept Congressional Reconstruction ultimately led to his removal from office.[59]

## CHAPTER EIGHT

# *Fueling the Fires of Redemption*

## THE STRUGGLE TO BRING DOWN RADICAL RULE IN TEXAS, 1867–73

Once removed from office, Throckmorton returned home and resumed his law practice. However, the ex-governor soon found himself drawn back into the political arena. Believing that Sheridan with the aid of Radical Republicans in Congress unjustly removed him from office, the North Texas politician began to seek ways to oust the Radicals from state and local offices. Because he was barred from holding political office, Throckmorton now had to work behind the scenes to achieve his political objectives. By the end of 1867, Throckmorton was committed to aiding the Democratic Party's efforts to reclaim control of the state. In part, his motivation was fueled by racism. In a letter to Epperson concerning economic and railroad development in Texas, Throckmorton stated that "our political condition must be vastly mended before capital will venture here, and if the State should be turned over to the ignorance & insolence of the negro race and radical hatred and vengeance it never will come."[1] The ex-governor's hurt pride and his disdain for African Americans led him to oppose Radical Republicans in the state. His opposition led him to take an active role in both local and state politics between 1867 and 1876.

Throckmorton's first opportunity to challenge Radical rule came in September 1867. According to the Reconstruction Act of March 23, 1867, the commanding officers of the Fifth Military District had to carry out two tasks: First, they had to register all qualified voters in their districts. General Griffin had successfully completed this chore in Texas during the summer and early fall of 1867. Second, once the qualification and registration of voters was completed, the military authorities and provisional state government had to call for a statewide election to decide whether the state should convene a constitutional convention to write a new state constitution that conformed to the dictates of Congressional Reconstruction. This element of the Reconstruction Act was not yet fulfilled in Texas. The delay in calling for the county elections resulted from the changes in command that occurred in the Fifth Military District during August and September 1867. President Johnson replaced Gen. Philip Sheridan with Gen. W. S. Hancock on August 27, and General Griffin, who died of yellow fever on September 15, was replaced with Gen. Joseph J. Reynolds. The reorganization of military command took several weeks to complete and presented conservative Democrats, including Throckmorton, with the opportunity to defeat the call for a new constitutional convention. If the conservatives were successful, the Constitution of 1866 would remain in place.[2]

Throckmorton headed the conservative charge. Frustrated by his personal political misfortune, Throckmorton called on conservative Democrats to thwart the Radicals' plans to reorganize the state government. The ex-governor claimed that Radical Republicans had perpetrated a great injustice to Texas by removing elected officials from statewide offices and by replacing them with loyal Union men. Also, Throckmorton was disturbed by the methods that federal authorities used in registering voters. The *New York Times* reported that "Throckmorton . . . opposes the holding of a Convention under the terms of the military reconstruction bills. He expresses regret at the apathy and indifference of the people, saying that they have scarcely heeded the last act of Congress, and the arbitrary manner of the Administration of the recent acts by the military authorities." The *Times* quoted Throckmorton as saying, "the impertinence and outrages of the county Boards of Registration pass by unheeded; with scarcely a remark made concerning them, they are sunk into insignificance in consequence of the highhanded outrages of Sheridan and Griffin." Throckmorton continued, "the recent instructions of the latter, which ought to have filled the whole State with a howl of indignation, have scarcely received a comment or passing notice."[3]

Because the Reconstruction Act of March 23 stipulated that individuals who had held executive or judicial offices in the state during the war were no longer qualified to vote, the North Texan claimed that many of the state's most able politicians were unfairly barred from holding office or voting in elections. Throckmorton was also irritated because Radicals supported unrestricted suffrage rights for African Americans. Thus, the former governor believed that a constitutional convention would result in a state constitution that would elevate the freedmen to an equal status with white men. In addition, Throckmorton believed that disenfranchised ex-Confederates might never regain the right to vote or hold state office. As a result, he began a relentless assault against the Radicals' efforts to call a constitutional convention.[4]

Despite the advice of friends to remain aloof from public life, Throckmorton could not refrain from entering the fray. The allure of power was too great. Thus, he engaged in a letter-writing campaign to editors of leading state newspapers expressing his opposition to a constitutional convention. Generally, his letters expressed the same sentiments that he had conveyed before: he called on conservative voters to defeat the convention by staying away from the polls. If voters refused to abstain from voting, the ex-governor believed that they should at least vote against any constitution that provided suffrage rights to the freedmen. On December 18, General Hancock, now in command of the Fifth Military District, issued the order for county elections to be held in February 1868 to vote on the proposed constitutional convention. Hancock instructed the election officials in the counties to elect delegates to the constitutional convention in case it was approved by a majority of the voters statewide. In addition, the general stipulated that the registry lists of voters should be reopened and revised during the first five days of January. The order to register new voters made conservative politicians panic, as they feared most of the added voters would favor the Radical agenda.[5]

Many conservatives believed Throckmorton's plan of defeating the convention by simply staying away from the polls was too risky. The plan assumed that conservative voters represented a majority of registered voters in Texas. Thus, if the county elections did not have a plurality of registered voters casting ballots, the convention could not be legally convened. As long as the conservatives represented a majority of the registered voters in Texas, Throckmorton's plan could effectively block a call for a constitutional convention. However, conservative leaders became increasingly alarmed that the absence of Democrats from the election would ensure a Radical victory. As a result, the leading conservatives called for a conference to meet at Houston on January 20, 1868, to discuss new strategies for thwarting the Radicals' plan to write a new state constitution. Throckmorton did not attend the conference and disagreed with the actions of his political colleagues. He deemed that there was not enough time to enact any new plan to defeat the constitutional convention. When conservatives convened in Houston, only twenty counties were represented. The conference adjourned after a relatively brief session, but its members issued a lengthy resolution that called on white conservatives to cast ballots in the upcoming elections. Because the county voters were required to vote for delegates to the constitutional convention during the same election, the Houston conferees suggested electing a slate of delegates who supported creating a new constitution but who also opposed giving the freedmen suffrage rights. The Houston plan proved ultimately to be a failure. In fact, the strategy influenced enough conservatives to go to the polls that a plurality of voters participated in the election, thus ensuring that a constitutional convention would be held in the state.[6]

The election was held in February, and Radicals were overwhelmingly victorious. The results indicated that 44,689 voters approved the constitutional convention and 11,440 opposed it. Ironically, if the conservatives had followed Throckmorton's advice, it is likely that the call of a convention would not have passed. The total number of registered voters casting ballots in the election numbered 56,129. The number of registered voters who did not cast ballots in the election was 52,964. Thus, 51.5 percent of the registered electorate participated in the election. If 1,583 of the voters against the convention had remained at home, the election would not have had a plurality and the call for a constitutional convention would have failed.[7]

The constitutional convention convened on June 1, 1868, and quickly organized. Delegates elected Edmund J. Davis, a noted Texas Radical who fought in the Union army during the war, as president of the convention. While most of the delegates were members of the Republican Party, they were divided along ideological and sectional lines. Provisional governor Pease and Andrew Jackson Hamilton led one group, which was closely identified with the interests of conservative Republicans. Another contingent of delegates was led by A. J. Hamilton's brother, Morgan Hamilton, and E. J. Davis and represented the interests of the central and southern counties of the state. Another faction of Republicans was headed by J. W. Flanagan and represented the interests of East Texas. Finally, George T. Ruby, a noted black politician, led a group of delegates who supported the rights of African Americans. Throughout the convention, these various factions formed alliances that shifted as the convention debated specific issues. However, the Republican contingents tended to remain loyal to their sectional interests.[8]

The first issues addressed by the convention did not concern the creation of a new constitution; rather, the delegates debated the ab initio question, civil rights for freedmen, the viability of dividing the state into three separate states, and the permanent disfranchisement of ex-Confederates. The ab initio issue was the first major issue before the convention and was supported by Morgan Hamilton and George Ruby's factions but was opposed by Pease and Flanagan's supporters. The primary concern about the question for Hamilton and Ruby was the fact that the Texas Legislature during the last year of the war had allowed the railroad companies to use worthless Confederate notes to pay part of the $1 million in interest that they owed on the $2 million they had borrowed from the state's school fund between 1858 and 1861. Hamilton argued that the debt should be paid back in full with U.S. currency. Though he based his argument on the need to replenish the school fund, Hamilton also hoped to use the money for future railroad development in West Texas. Ruby's support seemed nobler. He was more concerned with strengthening the school fund, which could be used to educate African American children.[9]

Likewise, the Pease and Flanagan factions differed on the ab initio question. Pease supporters claimed that the motives of ab initio adherents were selfish and did not represent the interests of the state. Flanagan's bloc sought to protect the major railroads built in East Texas, including those that had made interest payments during the war. In the end, the divisions in the Republican convention prevented the passage of ab initio, and the issue was finally tabled so the members could address other matters. However, the delegates soon found it just as difficult to work together on other questions. In regard to providing social equality to the freedmen, the members of the convention only agreed to recognize the equality of all persons under the law, which offered the freedmen no more protection than they had prior to the convention. Likewise, the delegates were divided over the disenfranchisement of white voters who could not pass the loyalty oath.[10]

For three months, the members of the convention diligently worked on these critical issues but made little progress. By mid-August, they had yet to draft a new constitution, and with the passing of each month, conditions in the state continued to deteriorate. As a result, several of the delegates called on their colleagues to adjourn the convention until after the 1868 federal election and after the newly elected Congress convened. Republicans primarily wanted to adjourn the convention because ex-Confederates were engaged in widespread violence against white Republicans and freedmen, a development that illustrated the need for congressional intervention to sustain their efforts in reorganizing the state government. Therefore, the delegates adjourned, agreeing to reconvene on December 7.[11]

When the convention met in December, it soon became evident that the divisions of the previous session were even more entrenched, and the delegates once again found themselves bogged down over the issue of permanently disenfranchising the ex-Confederates. Also, the attendees reached a stalemate over a proposed plan to divide Texas into three additional states, after which the delegates deferred the matter to Congress. On the issue of white disenfranchisement, conservative Republicans banded together and passed a resolution that granted all men in the state the right to vote except those specifically disqualified by the U.S. Constitution. While both of these issues created a wider rift among Republican leaders, delegates were able to draft a new state constitution and call for a referendum to be held on the first Monday in July 1869. Texas voters would decide the fate of the Republican constitution and would elect a new slate of state officers.[12]

Following the adjournment of the convention, the Republican Party divided into two well-defined camps. Provisional governor Pease and his close ally A. J. Hamilton were the leaders of the conservative element of their party. This faction lost the support of black members during the course of the convention because African Americans believed that white conservatives had taken positions that failed to guarantee black equality. Thus, the conservative Republicans were forced to explore alternative sources of political support in order to maintain their influence in state politics. As a result, conservative Republicans became more open to the idea of working with conservative Democrats. In contrast to the conservative element, Radical Republicans consisted of a coalition of blacks and West Texans. To achieve their objectives, West Texas Radicals were willing to support social equality for the freedmen. However, black support proved to be a double-edged sword, because racial biases throughout the state made it difficult for Radicals to attract white voters to their causes. Finally, Republicans from East Texas, including J. W. Flanagan, remained uncommitted to either the conservative or radical factions of their party. They were concerned that the conservatives' plan for internal improvements and commitment to racial politics would limit support for their agenda. As a result, the coalition of East Texas Republicans decided to remain in the shadows, waiting to see how events developed after the upcoming election before aligning themselves with either faction in their party.[13]

Immediately following the convention, a controversy ensued over the date of the forthcoming state election. Radicals were enraged because the elections were scheduled to be held in July, rather than in November when

Texas elections had normally occurred. Apparently, Radicals were not satisfied with the results of the constitutional convention and were afraid it would be adopted. One of their primary concerns was that Radicals would be deprived of state offices in future elections, especially since the proposed constitution prevented the widespread disenfranchisement of ex-Confederates. The Radicals were relieved when President Grant, who had won the presidential election of 1868, ordered the postponement of the election until November 30, 1869.[14]

While the Republicans were working through their differences, Texas Democrats prepared for the federal elections of 1868 and the state elections that they assumed would follow the adjournment of the constitutional convention. On May 18, 1868, the Democratic state executive committee met in Austin. The following day, its members announced the names of the delegates who were appointed to represent the Texas Democratic Party at the National Democratic Convention in New York on July 4, 1868. The delegates included Benjamin Epperson, Ashbel Smith, S. Powers, and Gustave Schleicher. The committee members also named Throckmorton as one of four alternate delegates. Furthermore, the committee called on conservatives from both political parties to meet in Bryan, Brazos County, on July 7.[15]

Conservative Democrats and Republicans attended the called meeting in Bryan, and they chose Throckmorton to preside over the gathering. After attending to issues related to the upcoming national election, the attendees turned their attention to state affairs. Since many of the ex-Confederate Democrats remained disenfranchised, the delegates conceded that it would be impossible for a Democratic candidate to win a major state office. Thus, they agreed not to field any candidates in the upcoming state elections. Instead, the delegates decided to support a representative of the conservative faction of the Republican Party. However, the Bryan convention did produce a conservative platform, which was created by a committee of both moderate Republicans and Democrats. The platform called for more effective cooperation between the state and national Democratic parties in order to escape disfranchisement, black supremacy, and the degradation and ruin threatened by Radical Republicans. It declared slavery and secession dead issues and pledged the allegiance of Texas to the federal government and the U.S. Constitution. At the close of the convention, Throckmorton addressed the delegates, denounced the Radicals, and urged the conservatives to mount a united front against them.[16] One of the primary concerns for Throckmorton seemed to be the Radicals' willingness to allow African Americans the right to vote and to participate in state politics.

After the Bryan convention, Throckmorton and Epperson returned to their homes in North Texas. The duo arrived in Dallas on the evening of July 18 and addressed a crowd that had gathered to hear the latest news regarding the outcome of the conservative meeting. The ex-governor once again denounced the military authorities and urged conservatives to band together against the Radical leadership of the Republican Party.[17] In the days that followed, Throckmorton made numerous stump speeches against Radicals. His speeches consistently criticized the new constitution, but he also argued that conservatives should vote to approve it. The North Texan clarified his position by stating that conservatives should support the constitution because the Radicals were opposed to it. Furthermore, he believed the adoption of the constitution would ultimately lead to a victory against Radicals in Washington, who supported the postponement of the upcoming election. During an interview with a reporter from the *New York Herald,* Throckmorton said that "the extreme Radicals do not want an election at all. The constitution is not to their liking, although there were only eight democrats in the convention which framed it. What might suit the Radicals would be a constitution framed in Washington and conferred by Congress on the state."[18]

The elections of 1869 proved to be a bitter contest between the radical and conservative factions of the Republican Party. The Radicals had earlier nominated Edmund J. Davis as their candidate, and conservatives had put forth Andrew J. Hamilton. Conservative Democrats, including Throckmorton, called on their followers to support Hamilton. The editor of the *Dallas News* claimed that the Collin County politician "expressed a decided conviction that the best interests of the State would be promoted by the election of Hon. A. J. Hamilton." Furthermore, he stated that Hamilton "had a very just and proper appreciation of the condition of the country, and would labor to restore good feelings among all classes of our people."[19] While they did not completely dismiss conservative support of Hamilton, Radicals believed that African American voters would assure their candidate's victory. After the four-day election ended, voters approved the new state constitution by a count of 72,466 to 4,928, and E. J. Davis defeated Hamilton by a vote of 39,901 to 39,092.[20]

Following the election, Hamilton and his supporters claimed that the federal government had helped Davis win the governorship. According to the accusers, General Reynolds during the election campaign had convinced President Grant that Hamilton and his supporters had aligned themselves with ex-Confederate Democrats. As a result, the president looked the other way while Reynolds directly aided the Davis campaign. The general made sure that Davis supporters controlled the polling places and that military personnel supervised the election. Moderate Republicans stated that under such conditions voter fraud was widespread. Supposedly, the commanding officer's actions were so blatant that provisional governor Pease felt compelled to resign his office, believing that Reynolds had thwarted the democratic process. General Reynolds did not appoint a replacement for Pease but instead chose to assume the duties of the office himself until after the 1869 elections. On January 8, 1870, Reynolds appointed Davis to the office of provisional governor pending his formal inauguration. Additionally, Reynolds called for a provisional session of the Twelfth Legislature to ratify the Thirteenth, Fourteenth, and Fifteenth amendments to the Constitution and to elect U.S. senators. The legislators met briefly in February and followed the general's orders, ratifying the amendments and electing James Flanagan and Morgan Hamilton to the Senate. Congress passed a bill that President Grant signed on March 30, bringing an end to Military Reconstruction in the state. Despite protests that A. J. Hamilton and his supporters made to Washington officials over the gubernatorial election of 1869, Davis was officially inaugurated on April 28, 1870.[21]

According to historian Dale Baum, Hamilton's supporters and subsequent generations of Texas history scholars have exaggerated the role that General Reynolds played in helping Davis win the election of 1869. Reynolds refused to delay the election until 1870, as Radicals in the state had requested, and he refused to remove pro-Hamilton officeholders who had been targeted for replacement by radicals. Additionally, the general's appointment of new voter registrars in the state had a minimal impact on the voter roles. If anything, it appears that General Reynolds may have been guilty of trying to move the election forward as quickly as possible. Regardless, the controversy sparked by the outcome of the gubernatorial election became a roaring fire during the course of the next three years as conservatives unfairly blamed all the state's problems on the Davis administration. Throckmorton proved to be one of Davis's most vociferous critics. The North Texan did not approve of the governor's willingness to give freedmen full civil rights, and he disagreed with the governor's economic and taxation policies.[22]

The Twelfth Legislature soon proved as unpopular as the newly elected governor. Radicals who dominated it passed several laws that raised the ire of conservative Democrats and Republicans. The most hated of these new laws were the Militia Act, the State Police Act, the Enabling Act, and the Public Printing Act. Of these measures, conservatives and moderates found the Militia Act and State Police Act the most vexing. The former provided that all able-bodied men were liable for military service if called to duty by the governor, the commander-in-chief of the state militia. The law also allowed the governor to declare martial law at his own discretion. In addition, racist Texans did not accept the fact that the state police was a biracial force, with approximately 40 percent of the officers being African Americans.[23] Conservatives unfairly claimed that the state police committed more crimes than they solved. However, this charge seemed to be politically motivated because the historical record suggests that the state police was an effective law enforcement agency. In a period of fourteenth months, the state police arrested almost 3,500 persons and jailed 638 persons on charges of murder or attempted murder. Furthermore, the force recovered approximately $200,000 in stolen property. While carrying out their duties, eight policemen were killed and four wounded in the line of duty.

Though conservatives were unsuccessful in defeating Davis in the gubernatorial election, they continued to fight the Radicals on other political fronts. On July 9, 1870, a conservative Democratic meeting was held at Austin in the office of Maj. John A. Green. The attendees chose Benjamin Epperson to chair the meeting. After he called the conclave to order, several men made presentations that called for greater organization of the Democratic Party in the state. Following their brief presentations, Throckmorton introduced a resolution that eventually led to the creation of a list of grievances that would serve as the Democrats' mantra against Governor Davis until he was voted out of office in 1873. Throckmorton stated that the attendees should call for a state Democratic convention. In addition, the members selected a committee, following Throckmorton's suggestion, to draft an official list of grievances against the Davis administration, and then they voted to adjourn the meeting until the committee had time to complete its task.[24]

On July 21 the political leaders reconvened to hear the committee's report. The grievances outlined against the Davis administration were numerous and undoubtedly reflected the views of Throckmorton as well as most conservative Democrats in the state. They claimed that Davis and his supporters expelled duly elected members from the legislature and seated in their places men who were not elected by majorities; delayed economic recovery in the state by deterring immigration; created a multitude of new offices and appointed Radicals to them; delayed legislation favorable to the people of Texas and ensured the passage of laws deemed favorable to Radicals; authorized the creation of the state police, which preyed on honest citizens; aided in organization of secret political parties representing primarily African Americans; centralized the control of government by giving the governor tyrannical power; established newspapers to expedite the Radicals' political heresies; planned to extend Davis's term in office beyond constitutional limits; arbitrarily arrested members of the legislature, thus depriving them of a voice in pending legislation; and amassed an enormous state debt. Accompanying the list of charges, the committee presented a draft of an address to the people of Texas that called on them to hold public meetings to protest against Radical rule in Texas.[25]

Following the meetings in Austin, Throckmorton made an out-of-state business trip on the behalf of the Memphis, El Paso, and Pacific Railroad.[26] Unfortunately, scholars are left to speculate about Throckmorton's trip, because no record of it exists in the historical record. Nevertheless, it was likely that his efforts centered on bringing the Memphis, El Paso, and Pacific Railroad through Texas. The historical record does indicate that Throckmorton did not return until the latter part of 1870. In his absence, conservative Democrats accomplished little, and the call for a Democratic convention did not materialize. On August 5, 1871, conservatives held another political meeting in Austin. The members of this conclave called on leading Democrats to hold local meetings to protest the allegedly exorbitant expenditures of the state and to elect delegates to represent the state's counties in a convention at Austin on September 22, 1871. The purpose of the popularly called state convention was to protest the Davis administration's fiscal and tax policies.[27]

Ninety-five counties sent delegates to the convention, commonly referred to as the Taxpayers' Convention. Collin County voters elected Throckmorton as their representative. The delegates began to arrive in the state's capital in mid-September and immediately aroused the criticism of the Davis administration. The *State Journal,* a Radical newspaper, noted that "the tax-howlers are gathering much to the delectation of whiskey sellers. These fellows can't pay their taxes, but have enough [money] to travel hundreds of miles and pay heavy bar room bills in order to add a little fuel to the Ku-Klux disaffection and hostility that disfigures and disgraces the state."[28] The next day, the editor claimed that no good would come from "any movement supported by Throckmorton, Pease, Hamilton, and others of the unreconstructed rebel type."[29]

State officials allowed the members of the convention to use the House of Representative chambers for their sessions but stipulated that the delegates had to hold their meetings during the afternoon and night. The first meeting of the Taxpayers' Convention convened at two o'clock in the afternoon on September 22, 1871. After being called to order, the delegates elected E. M. Pease as the permanent chairman. While Pease's election suggested the convention was bipartisan, most of the 217 delegates were members of the Democratic Party. Besides preliminary organization, little else was accomplished on the first night of the convention. Judge John Ireland made a motion to create a committee of twenty-one to consider and to report the business of the convention. The motion was seconded and approved by a majority vote, but no one was immediately appointed to serve on the committee. Realizing that the convention would have to work with the Davis administration as well as the state legislature to produce any real reforms, Throckmorton introduced a resolution calling for a "committee of seven to be appointed to confer with his excellency E. J. Davis upon the subject of the reduction of expenditures of the state government . . . and that the same committee also confer with . . . the legislature."[30] The resolution was adopted, and shortly afterward the convention adjourned until that evening. During the next few hours, officers of the meeting selected leading conservatives to serve on the newly created committees.

The convention reconvened at seven o'clock, and Pease announced the names of those men selected to serve on the committees. Among the individuals chosen to serve on the Committee of Twenty-one were A. J. Hamilton, the chairman of the committee, Morgan C. Hamilton, William M. Walton, John Ireland, Thomas J. Chambers, and Throckmorton. Members of the Committee of Seven included Throckmorton as chairman, W. M. Walton, John Ireland, J. T. Harcourt, M. C. Hamilton, A. J. Hamilton, and C. S. West. In addition to announcing the members of the two committees, Pease appointed a third committee on statistics with Judge William Upton as its chairman. At this point, the convention was adjourned until two o'clock the next day. When the convention reconvened, the committees reported that they had not completed their task and asked the convention for a two-day delay. Pease and the other delegates agreed and rescheduled their next session for seven o'clock in the evening on September 25.[31]

Following the adjournment of the convention, an incident took place that further tainted future relations between the Davis administration and conservatives in the state. A crowd collected at Buass Hall on Congress Avenue and proceeded to the capitol grounds. It was reported that among their ranks were about one hundred African Americans. When the crowd reached the state capitol, Governor Davis addressed them, making reference to the purification of the capitol after the adjournment of the convention. The *Democratic Statesman,* a conservative newspaper, quoted Davis as saying, "fellow citizens . . . in ancient times it was the custom of the people to purify their temples when defiled, by burning and sprinkling incense round about the same. This temple, our Capital, has been polluted by the presence of the tax payers of the state." Davis allegedly added, "therefore it devolves upon you, my colored brethren, to purify the place. As we have no incense, I would suggest that you form in double ranks and march around the capitol singing those glorious hymns of freedom with which you are so familiar." According to the editor, the freedmen followed Davis's suggestions and marched around the state capitol singing, "John Brown's Soul Is Marching On" and "Rally Round the Flag, Boys."[32]

When the convention reconvened on Monday, C. W. West resigned his position on the Committee of Seven, stating that he considered Davis's actions on Saturday night an "insult to the memory of the able men who [held] that office before him." West further stated that "I feel that personal respect and the duty I owe my constituents demand that I resign from [this] committee, and I trust the first act of this convention will be to rescind the appointment of the committee of conference with the Governor."[33] Throckmorton agreed with West and offered a resolution calling for the release of the Committee on Conference with the Governor "in view of the flagrant indignity offered the convention by Governor Davis on Saturday evening last, in remarks made by him as to the purification of the capitol after the sitting of the convention, and his conduct in connection therewith." The resolution was tabled by a vote of 71 to 56.[34]

The remainder of the session was dedicated to hearing the committees' reports. The grievances listed by the Committee of Twenty-one were identical to those enumerated by the private committee organized in Major Green's office the previous year. In connection with the charges, Throckmorton read a series of recommendations and asked the convention to adopt them. He proposed that the taxpayers should refuse to pay the new taxes imposed by the Davis administration and the legislature. Additionally, the committees suggested that the convention should prepare an address to the people advising them how to resist paying certain state taxes that the convention defined as illegal and stated that if the governor or legislature disregarded the convention's recommendations, the committee should prepare a memorial to the Congress of the United States asking for federal intervention on behalf of the state's citizens.[35]

The resolution calling for congressional intervention caused great debate among the delegates. There was considerable disagreement concerning what mode of redress should be taken if the governor and the legislature refused to comply with the demands of the taxpayers. Judge Upton opposed the resolution calling for federal assistance because he could not bring himself to recognize the right of Congress to interfere in the affairs of the state. He favored the election of delegates by the sovereign people of the state to a convention to form yet another state constitution. Upton firmly believed that a direct appeal to Congress forfeited the rights of sovereign people to act in such a crisis; however, he conceded that conservatives might have to call for federal assistance if Radicals refused to allow the people of the state to publicly call a new constitutional convention. Throckmorton disagreed, and considered Upton's stance as impractical. He stated that a constitutional convention would not be allowed to meet and that Congress would consider such an act open rebellion and would help the Radicals remain in power. Throckmorton clarified his position by stating that he did not question the people's right to handle the affairs of their state but that he did not feel it was the right policy to pursue at that time. The resolution to appeal to Congress was adopted.[36]

The convention then directed the Committee of Seven to write an address to the people of Texas and a memorial to the state legislature. Before adjourning, E. M. Pease was added to the Committee of Seven upon the request of Throckmorton. The members also instructed the committee to meet with Governor Davis. Following these last-minute changes, the convention adjourned on September 25. The Committee of Seven quickly finished their task and issued an address to the people and a memorial to the legislature on September 30. The address to the people stated that the 1 percent school tax was illegal and could not be collected because the tax law failed to name the property on which the tax was levied.[37]

On October 2, 1871, the Committee of Seven completed its memorial to the legislature. The petition called on the legislators to reduce the state and county tax rates and to repeal the school tax. In addition, the memorial requested the repeal of the police bill, the registration law, and the enabling act. With this, the Taxpayers' Convention officially ended.[38]

While confronting Radicals at the state level between 1869 and 1871, Throckmorton was also actively involved in local politics. Collin County's favorite son became a central figure in the 1869 Second Congressional District race, where J. C. Conner was running on the Democratic ticket. Despite Conner's affiliation with the Democratic Party, many North Texans considered him a carpetbagger. He was born in Noblesville, Indiana, and was a Union military officer during the Civil War. Following the war, Conner had returned to Indiana and unsuccessfully made a bid for the state legislature on the National Union ticket in 1866. When the Union army was reorganized as an occupation force in the fall of 1866, he applied for and received a captain's commission of the Forty-first Colored Infantry. Conner served with the unit until General Reynolds transferred him to civil service, appointing the captain as the new county clerk of Grayson County.[39]

Because Conner was a northerner and an appointee of the military authorities, Throckmorton considered him unfit to represent the people of the Second District. As a result, he supported Joshua Johnson for the congressional nomination. However, once the Democratic Party officially endorsed Conner, Throckmorton ceased all open opposition to him but he did not actively campaign for the candidate. When Reynolds reported the election returns on January 11, 1870, Conner was declared the winner. On March 20, 1870, Congress passed an act readmitting Texas to the Union, and consequently, the state's senators and representatives took their seats in Washington. However, this did not produce political calm in the state. During the fall of 1870, the Davis administration extended the term of office for Radicals elected in 1869 by postponing the 1870 congressional elections until 1871. This move caused a stir among the Texas Democrats and led to continued controversy in the Second District.[40]

Given the political divisions within the Republican Party and the Democrats' attempt to regain control of the state, the congressional race in North Texas gained statewide attention. As A. J. Hamilton and E. M. Pease sought political alliances between conservative Republicans and Democrats, Throckmorton began to calculate his own return to political office. It was natural that he set his eyes on winning the congressional seat in his home district. On October 14, 1870, the editor of the *Houston Union,* a Radical Republican newspaper, surveyed the political environment of North Texas:

> North Texas opposes Conner. Dissatisfaction is being spread. Collin County, the *Enquirer,* and the *McKinney Messenger* are all against him. This means Throckmorton wants to go to Congress himself. But there is something deeper than all this. Conner is straight out Democratic and down on *Fusion* and so is all North Texas. Hamilton, Walton, Pease, Webb, and the coalitionists generally are seeking to get Conner out of the way to give North Texas to the *Fusion.* The *Fusion* is much the weakest party in that region, but it has all the old strong politicians with them, and then, too, the straight Democracy are at a disadvantage in having committed themselves to a little adventurer like Conner.[41]

On November 9, 1870, the editor of the *Union* again commented on the political environment of North Texas and suggested that Throckmorton might run against Conner in the upcoming congressional race. The editor commented:

> We sometime ago intimated that the little political monstrosity, Captain Conner, Yankee adventurer, Federal soldier, nigger Captain, state rights, secession, rebel, anti-reconstruction, southern chivalry candidate for Congress was going to have opposition. We understand that ex-Governor Throckmorton has determined to be a candidate to represent the Second Congressional District.[42]

The editor suggested that Throckmorton might be eligible to hold political office once again and that he would be easily elected to office, especially considering that the Democratic Party had chosen Conner as their candidate in 1869 only because he opposed the reconstruction policies of the military. The political circumstances in North Texas would have suggested an easy victory for Throckmorton, except for one major obstacle: the Democrats and Fusionists in the district pledged their loyalty to Conner's reelection. Conner had worked hard to gain the favor of his constituents. Throughout September and October, he had canvassed his district, denouncing the Davis administration, Congressional Reconstruction, and the Republican Party. Ironically, he had even wrapped himself in the Confederate flag by praising the South's lost cause and the veterans of the Confederate Army. Despite their attachment to the Union prior to the war, many North Texas voters gravitated toward their congressman and gathered in large crowds to hear him speak.[43]

Given Conner's popularity with the people of the Second District, Throckmorton moved cautiously in putting his name before the voters. The ex-governor might have acted more definitively, but he still had not received a federal pardon that would allow him to hold political office again. As a result, Throckmorton did not initiate plans to enter the race until February 1871. On February 1, Throckmorton wrote to Epperson:

> I have been studying some way to get the [Galveston] *News* and [Houston] *Telegraph* to occasionally urge the necessity of sending me from this district, but I have not clearly seen the way. They are friendly. How would it do for you to write Ashbel Smith and make known Conner's calibre and suggest my disinclination and the propriety of the *News* and *Telegraph* speaking out.[44]

Five days later, Throckmorton wrote to his friend again and presented a more explicit plan for challenging Conner:

> Our friends—yours and mine—should be active in making me the candidate—this will tend to break Conner down—already the talk of my candidacy has greatly weakened him—should my disabilities be removed and he vote against it, it will settle his hash. The moment my disabilities are removed I should be nominated by county meetings where it can be done. This would give a start at least. A convention would help. If you can manage to have the friends in Jefferson and the lower counties to take such steps it would help.[45]

Unfortunately for his political ambition, Throckmorton's bid for Congress ended abruptly when Congress did not approve his pending pardon. Members of the Republican Party attempted to use the ex-governor's political misfortune to their own gain. In an effort to gain Throckmorton's political support, Republicans blamed Conner for obstructing the pardon. According to the *Houston Union,* the bill for Throckmorton's pardon, which came before Congress on March 12, 1871, "was never read but passed the House very late in the session without reading through the efforts of General Clark." The editor of the paper continued, "Conner clamored for the reading of the bill which would consume time. Foiled in this Conner took the bill from the clerk to delay engrossment. Defeated in this, he resorted to the Senate saying that the Amnesty bill with Jim Throckmorton's name on it should not pass and prevented its being called up in the Senate."[46] Conner denied the charges in a letter to the *Bonham News,* a Fannin County newspaper. He stated, "I see the *Houston Union, Austin Journal, McKinney Enquirer,* etc., charge that I voted against the removal of the disabilities of certain gentlemen. The charge is untrue. Please correct the error."[47] Conner's denial spurred the Republicans to redouble their efforts to bring Throckmorton into their camp. The *Houston Union* wrote that "Governor Throckmorton has long been considered the leading public man in North Texas. Now the Democracy has suddenly thrown him overboard for a carpet bag adventurer and Union Renegade." The newspaper further stated, "North Texas has disgraced herself, and Throckmorton is not the man we thought him if he submits to this open insult in favor of his pigmy enemy, Conner."[48]

While Conner and the Republican newspapers were embroiled in a political battle, Throckmorton conceded that he would not become a candidate in the 1871 congressional race. As a result, he became actively involved in searching for a suitable challenger to Conner. While seeking a worthy opponent, the ex-governor made numerous stump speeches against the incumbent and called for a congressional convention to meet in Dallas to nominate a new candidate. Apparently, the call for a convention was successful because a meeting was held in Denton County for the purpose of electing precinct delegates to the proposed Dallas convention. The people of Precinct No. 2 elected Hugh J. Throckmorton, the ex-governor's eldest son, as their representative.[49] Countering his opposition's actions, Conner took to the stump and began circulating the story that the former governor was hatching a plan to secure the nomination of his son when the convention met in Dallas. This prompted the Collin County politician to respond that "these dirty scamps, with Conner at their head, are the most damnable set of liars out of Hell."[50] The stage was set for a bitter campaign battle.

Early in July 1871, the Democrats held the Dallas convention and nominated Conner without serious opposition. With the added prestige of a convention nomination, the incumbent was virtually assured reelection. Throckmorton continued on the stump, making pro-Democratic speeches, but as he had done in 1869, the former governor refused to endorse Conner. When the election took place in early October, the Democratic nominee easily defeated his Republican challenger by a vote of 18,285 to 5,948.[51]

When the election concluded, Throckmorton supporters began to make preparations to nominate him as the congressman-at-large in 1872.

Because the Texas population had increased, the state was granted two additional congressional seats designated as congressman-at-large. The state now had six congressional seats but it still had only four congressional districts. In addition to reapportionment, Congress indirectly aided the North Texan's bid for the nomination by passing the Amnesty Act of 1872, which removed Throckmorton's political disabilities. In January 1872 the *Dallas Herald* was already calling for the ex-governor's nomination, but the editors of the *Sherman Patriot* and the *Denton Monitor* questioned the political viability of the Collin County politician. Undoubtedly, the editors were aligned against Throckmorton because he had opposed Conner in 1869 and 1871. The editor of the *Dallas Times* quickly pointed out that following Conner's nomination at the Dallas convention, Throckmorton had supported the Democratic candidate, even if his support was less than enthusiastic.[52]

While the editors penned their differences, plans for the state elections proceeded. In early 1872, Texas Democrats called for a state convention to convene at Corsicana on June 17, and held preliminary district meetings to select delegates to the meeting. At these local gatherings, the citizens also decided whom they would support in the upcoming congressional race. At the Dallas meeting on May 6, locals passed a resolution that recommended Throckmorton as one of the congressional candidates-at-large. Later the same month, a similar meeting was held in McKinney. After a few hours of deliberation, Throckmorton read a draft of a resolution compiled by members of the meeting. The resolution called for the redemption of the state from the misrule, oppression, and bankruptcy of the Davis administration; invited the citizens of the state, regardless of political affiliation, to join in their cause; and endorsed the state convention at Corsicana. Another member of the committee then presented a resolution calling for Throckmorton's nomination as congressman-at-large. The attendees at the assembly overwhelmingly endorsed the resolutions.[53]

The Corsicana convention met as scheduled on June 17, and early balloting seemed to suggest that Throckmorton was a favorite for the congressional nomination. On the first ballot he garnered more votes than Asa Willie and Roger Q. Mills, his two leading opponents. After six ballots, the North Texas politician was still in the lead. However, on the seventh ballot his opponents' supporters struck a deal that allowed Willie and Mills to secure both of the congressional nominations. Many delegates were dissatisfied with the chosen candidates because both came from the Third District, a voting district containing a small Democratic majority.

Nevertheless, when the balloting was concluded, Throckmorton graciously congratulated the nominees and made a motion to make the nominations unanimous. The *Dallas Herald* commented on Throckmorton's defeat: "we are free to express our surprise of the defeat of Gov. Throckmorton, the stronger man in the State as the voting at first plainly showed. The adoption of the two thirds rule, the number of candidates, and the various combinations formed, explain the matter." The *Herald* continued, "It was the natural consequence of the union of the weaker to defeat the stronger. We have not a word to say against the gentleman selected—they are both worthy men." However, the editor did express his concern that "the two candidates for the State at large should have been taken from the 3d District, which cast the smallest democratic majority of all. It would look as if a combination of delegates was made to defeat the favorite candidate [Throckmorton] of the 2d District, which can give a majority more than all the others together."[54]

Even though the Corsicana convention proved to be a disappointment, Throckmorton's supporters wasted no time in placing him before the people for the governorship in the next election. The *Sherman Courier* expressed the belief that many votes had been withheld from him at the Corsicana convention because leading politicians hoped to make him governor when the opportunity arrived.[55] They would not have to wait long. The Thirteenth Legislature convened in January 1873 and called for the next gubernatorial election to be held on the first Tuesday in December. As a result, the editor of the *Dallas Herald,* J. W. Swindells, wrote to Throckmorton and urged him to run for office. Throckmorton, however, declined to become a candidate. He replied to the editor: "you, as well as other friends, know that the support of my family depends upon my daily labor. For twenty years and more I have in one capacity or another, been in public harness." Throckmorton continued, "Whilst I have been devoted to the public interests, and particularly to those of my immediate section of the state, my public affairs have well nigh gone to ruin."[56] Despite his desire to take care of his personal financial situation, it also seems likely that Throckmorton planned to campaign for a seat in the U.S. Senate, rather than attempt to recapture the governor's office.

Regardless of his motivations, the ex-governor's refusal to seek the governorship did not deter his supporters, nor did it stop his opponents from attacking him in the newspapers. During the first week of September, the Democratic nominating convention met in Austin. The people of Collin County elected Throckmorton as their delegate to the convention. At the convention, many politicians throughout the state believed that he would receive the party's nomination for governor even if he did not seek the office. However, he brought an end to such rumors. In a letter to the *Democratic Statesman,* the North Texan stated "that there may be no misunderstanding in regard to my position I desire to say, through your paper, that I am not a candidate for governor—that under no combination of circumstances will I be before either the Democratic State Convention or the people." Throckmorton continued, "I came to Austin as a delegate to the convention from my county, with no other view than to work in the ranks and to promote democratic success."[57]

With Throckmorton refusing to run in the upcoming race, the convention nominated Richard Coke as their candidate for governor. In the December election, Coke overwhelmingly defeated the unpopular Republican incumbent, E. J. Davis. Coke's victory virtually brought an end to the Republican Party's influence in the state. Texas voters not only ushered in a new executive to Austin in 1873, but they brought forth a new era of Democratic dominance in the state. According to the Democrats, the state was officially redeemed.

Once the Democrats had successfully removed Republicans from office, they solidified their rule of the state by replacing the Constitution of 1869 with one more favorable to their political agenda. Voters approved a constitutional convention in early August 1875 and elected ninety delegates to frame a new governing document for the state. The conservative Constitution of 1876 effectively swept away the last vestiges of congressional directives, military rule, and Republican leadership from the state government. Even though the new government did not completely disenfranchise the freedmen, it allowed Democrats to dominate statewide politics and to relegate African Americans to second-class citizenship. Also, between 1874 and 1875, the U.S. Army successfully brought an end to the last major Indian resistance in Texas, defeating the Comanches, Kiowas, and Southern Cheyennes in a series of battles collectively known as the Red River War. The Plains Indians would never threaten the Texas frontier again. Thus, two of Throckmorton's goals were achieved. The freedmen and Native Americans were no longer a threat to white supremacy in the state. As a result, the ex-governor's future political endeavors concentrated less on racial issues and more on the economic development of North Texas.[58] In the end, conservative Democrats won the war of Reconstruction.

## CHAPTER NINE

# *The End of the Line*

## FAILED RESTORATIONS AND CONGRESSIONAL MEDIOCRITY IN THE POST-RECONSTRUCTION ERA, 1873–94

At first glance, James Webb Throckmorton appears to be something of an enigma in nineteenth-century Texas political history. Between 1861 and 1867, his political positions seemed contradictory, self-serving, and irrational. In part, this assessment holds some validity. Like most politicians of his times, Throckmorton pursued policies that benefited him personally, especially the development of railroads in North Texas. However, a detailed examination of Throckmorton's public life reveals that his political views exhibited a high degree of consistency. Four factors influenced Throckmorton's political development: his experiences on the frontier, his belief in white supremacy, his adherence to political conservatism, and his commitment to the economic development of North Texas. These factors shaped Throckmorton's actions throughout five decades of political change in the Lone Star State.

Throckmorton's frontier experiences undoubtedly played a critical role in defining his political ideology and his racial views. Having lived on the southern frontier most of his life, he witnessed firsthand many of the hardships confronting pioneer families, especially the devastating impact that Indian raids had on their settlements in the northern counties of the state between 1845 and 1870. Like many white settlers living in north-central Texas, Throckmorton concluded that the Native Americans were standing in the way of progress. As a result, he consistently supported the removal of the Native Americans to reservations and sought ways to protect the settlers of North Texas. Throckmorton's concern for the white settlers along the Texas frontier eventually led him to develop a racial hatred for Native American peoples. Thus, Throckmorton believed that the frontier was a refuge for whites, and he went to extremes to protect white domination over the region.

Throckmorton's hatred of Native Americans was consistent with his racial views of other minority groups, especially African Americans. In line with the views of most nineteenth-century white southerners, Throckmorton believed that African Americans were inferior to Anglos, and he attempted to prevent black migration to the north-central counties of Texas following the Civil War. Thus, he consistently supported policies designed to prevent blacks from receiving full civil rights and supported laws, such as the Black Codes, that were designed to keep African Americans tied to East Texas lands where they had lived in bondage.

In part, Throckmorton's racial animosity toward African Americans initially rested with his disdain for the antebellum southern planter class. Throughout the 1850s, Throckmorton sought to protect the social, political, and economic institutions of the settlers of North Texas. After proving his loyalty to the early settlers by helping them retain title to their lands during the Peters Colony fiasco, Throckmorton worked throughout the 1850s to prevent slaveholding planters from encroaching on the northern frontier. His plan to fend off the planters included measures designed to advance the economic development of Red River counties. He was especially concerned with the building of railroads in the region. Railroads were critical to the continued prosperity of North Texas wheat farmers. Without the railroads, these farmers lacked adequate access to distant markets and suffered continued economic hardships. The consequences of frontier poverty were self-evident. Small farmers would eventually be forced to sell their landholdings to migrating planters from the east. Such circumstances would ultimately give large slaveholders complete control over the social, political, and economic institutions of North Texas. In this environment, Throckmorton's racial hatred of the black slaves partly resulted from his disdain of the planter class itself.

Throughout the antebellum era, the slaves were the most visible representation of the planters' wealth and social dominance. In Throckmorton's mind, the slaves were the mechanism that allowed large planters to take advantage of small farmers. Aside from his own racist views, Throckmorton believed that the economic advantage that blacks provided to the planters was a compelling enough reason to hate the slaves. After the slaves were emancipated, Throckmorton's disdain for African Americans grew as black voters threatened conservative Democrats' hold on the state government.

While serving as governor of the state, he nearly ended his political career by supporting policies that tried to prevent the freedmen from gaining full equality with whites under the law. If it had not been for the failures of Reconstruction, it is likely that his public career would have ended in 1867 when military authorities removed him from the governorship.

Even though the views of frontier settlers toward minority groups needs further scholarly examination, the concept of frontier racism remains important to the evolution of Texas as a southern state. We cannot begin to understand Throckmorton, or others like him, unless we first come to realize the differences that existed between the various regions of the South. In many ways, the frontier served as an escape valve for settlers who wanted to avoid a society dominated by large slaveholders. These settlers moved to North Texas from the Upper South and attempted to forge a new white society. As a result, they developed an intolerance for nonwhites and sought to protect their region from what they deemed an infiltration of inferior humans. In the Red River counties, Throckmorton became one of the most prominent advocates of this form of racism.

In addition to his frontier experiences and the desire to uphold the ideals of white supremacy, Throckmorton adhered to a conservative brand of politics. Evidence suggests that his political conservatism stemmed from his early political affiliation with the Whig Party. During the 1840s and early 1850s, Whigs in the Upper South adhered to three basic party principles: they favored economic development through internal improvements and tariffs; they expressed a certain disdain for political extremists, such as the northern abolitionists and southern secessionists; and they remained faithful to the Union. After being introduced to the party's ideology at an early age, Throckmorton never abandoned the party's principles even after he left the Whig Party to become a member of the Democratic Party in the mid-1850s.

Scholars have labeled Throckmorton's reaction to change in Texas politics as contradictory and ironic. Academicians are puzzled by the fact that the North Texan voted against secession in 1861 only later to join the Confederacy and oppose Radical Reconstruction. However, his positions were more consistent than contradictory. Throckmorton's support of the Union during the secession crisis stemmed from his opposition to extremists in both northern and southern states. Like Sam Houston, he realized that secession would bring economic ruin to Texas. It also would prevent northern capitalists from investing in southern railroads, which were vital to the North Texas economy. Furthermore, he understood that the slaveholding planters would likely hold key positions in the Confederate government and thereby would continue to dominate the political, economic, and social institutions of the South. As previously mentioned, this was a proposition that he and other Texas Unionists were unwilling to accept.

However, once the majority of Texas voters approved secession, Throckmorton realized that the people on the frontier were exposed to two potential dangers. With the U.S. Army abandoning their western forts, the people of his home region were once again left unprotected from Indian raids. Additionally, Unionists in the North Texas were vulnerable to the charge of being traitors to the Confederacy, a circumstance that could have led to the eruption of a civil war within the state. While he was attempting to reconcile these differences, the Confederate military attacked Fort Sumter, prompting President Lincoln to issue a call for seventy-five thousand volunteers to put down the rebellion in the southern states. The president's actions led Throckmorton to join the Confederacy, believing that the federal government did not have the *right* to coerce the southern states back into the Union. For Throckmorton, coercion was a form of political extremism. Thus, the North Texan reluctantly joined the Confederate cause. However, his experience in the Confederate military was mostly limited to fighting Native Americans in the Indian Territory and on the Texas frontier, thereby allowing him to fulfill his self-proclaimed role as defender of the northern frontier.

Throckmorton was the first democratically elected governor during the Reconstruction era in Texas. Throughout his tenure in office, he continued to act as a guardian of the frontier. In fact, his confrontations with the military authorities were the result of his pursuit of policies that were designed to shield the frontier settlers from continued Indian raids and to prevent the migration of freedmen to North Texas. These policies, coupled with Throckmorton's lack of concern for the freedmen's general welfare, eventually led Gen. Philip Sheridan to remove the governor from office, charging that he was an impediment to Reconstruction.

Throckmorton's racism proved detrimental to black Texans' struggle for equal rights during the Reconstruction era. As governor, he did not actively prosecute whites who committed crimes against blacks in the state. While he was willing to accept emancipation of the slaves, Governor Throckmorton could not consent to granting freedmen suffrage. As a conservative Democrat, Throckmorton understood that the disenfranchisement of ex-Confederate voters and the enfranchisement of African Americans would swing the balance of political power in the state in favor of Radical Republican candidates and their Reconstruction policies. Given that the governor believed Radical Republicans were extremists who subverted the constitutional powers guaranteed to the states, he refused to accept Republican control of the state and did his best to sabotage Gov. E. J. Davis's administration.

Throckmorton seemingly condoned the crimes committed against the freedmen for two reasons: First, white oppression of blacks forced the freedmen to accept second-class citizenship, thereby allowing East Texas landowners to effectively force the freedmen to sign unfair labor contracts, which prevented them from escaping the cotton fields that they had worked as slaves. In effect this fulfilled Throckmorton's plan to prevent blacks from migrating to other regions in the state, especially North Texas. Second, the violence eventually stifled the freedmen's participation in the political process. Without the support of black voters, Republicans were weakened. When the federal government lifted its voting restrictions on the majority of ex-Confederates with the passage of the Amnesty Act in 1872, Radical Republicans lost their grip on the state, and Democratic redeemers regained political prominence once again.

Following his failed attempt to win the Democratic nomination in the election of 1873, Throckmorton focused his efforts on the 1874 Senate race. He became an early favorite in the election as did his old political friend John H. Reagan. According to local newspaper reports, the race hinged on competing factions of railroad men. The editor of the *Daily Journal* commented: "The great senatorial railroad war is now intense. The Texas and Pacific has its favorite in ex-Governor J. W. Throckmorton. . . . The International and Great Northern has John H. Reagan."[1] Though it was true that both men were invested in their respective railroad companies, the newspaper editors tended to exaggerate the railroad companies' influence in the election and downplayed the idea that the contest hinged on a growing rivalry between northern and southern counties in the state. Beginning with Texas' entry into the Union in 1845, state senators had primarily been residents of counties in the eastern and southwestern parts of the state. Now with more than half of the state's population residing in the northern counties, the people of North Texas wanted what they deemed fair representation in the state.[2]

As political wrangling took place in the state legislature, the candidates prepared themselves for the final outcome. Throckmorton appeared to be the strongest candidate when balloting began on January 27. After the first ballot, Throckmorton received thirteen votes in the senate and

John H. Reagan. Shown here in his later years, Reagan gave lukewarm support to Throckmorton's bid to become the U.S. senator from Texas. Still, Reagan and Throckmorton remained allies during their latter political careers. *Texas State Library and Archives Commission.*

thirty-four in the house, a total of forty-seven votes, which was well below the fifty-eight votes needed to fulfill the two-thirds majority rule. The other candidates faired worse: Reagan received only thirty-nine total votes; Samuel Bell Maxey received seventeen; and Webster Flanagan was only able to garner ten votes. With no clear victor, several of the Democrats decided to hold an informal caucus to determine a course of action that would lead to the election of a single candidate. They decided to abandon John H. Reagan and planned to oppose Throckmorton with their support of Samuel Bell Maxey. Apparently, conservative Democrats had not forgiven Reagan for writing the Fort Warren letter warning the South nor Throckmorton for his vote against secession. The next day, when the second ballot was taken, Maxey won the election, defeating Throckmorton by a vote of fifty-nine to forty-four votes. Within the course of a year, the North Texas favorite had lost his second bid for a major political office.[3] Nevertheless, Throckmorton had not completely given up on the idea of reviving his political career.

Based on the 1870 Census, the legislature had created the Third Congressional District composed of the counties of Grayson, Collin, Rockwall, Kaufman, Dallas, Ellis, Johnson, Hill, Hood, Erath, Eastland, Palo Pinto, Parker, Tarrant, Denton, Wise, Jack, Cook, Montague, Clay, and eleven more counties that were yet to be created in the northern frontier of Texas. This newly created congressional district provided Throckmorton with a unique opportunity. Even during the Senate election, he made plans to run for a seat in the House of Representatives for the newly created district if he lost his bid for the Senate. Because the counties were located in the northern region of the state, Throckmorton immediately became the favored candidate. Nevertheless, he still had to defeat several candidates for his party's nomination, including Judge Silas Hare of Grayson County and John J. Good of Dallas.[4]

During the campaign, the editor of the *Sherman Courier*, who was a loyal supporter of Judge Hare, repeatedly published scathing attacks against Throckmorton's character and affiliation with the Texas and Pacific Railroad Company. On June 17, the editor called a meeting of Hare supporters to convene at Sherman. At the meeting, a resolution was drafted stating that the people "wanted to send a man to Congress who has no personal tastes, ambitions, or interests to gratify except those of his people; a man who thinks as we do, and who will act in accordance with our expressed desires." The resolution concluded by stating that "we desire a man who is disconnected from all monopolies and money schemes and therefore free at all times to act for the whole people."[5]

Shortly following the Sherman meeting, Judge Hare officially announced that he would accept the Democratic nomination if elected. He then attempted to divide the people of the district along class lines. He made a direct appeal for the labor vote by declaring that labor was the foundation upon which the economy was erected. In a show of support for labor, Hare condemned government subsidies to railroad companies. He stated, "These companies subsidized by the Federal government, pocketing their ill-gotten gain, soon build up vast monopolies, become rich, insolent, and overbearing—enter the halls of Congress and by a judicious distribution of their favors control the passage of laws." Hare called on the laborers "to resist these encroachments, to throttle these insolent vampires that are sucking their life blood."[6] Hare's statements undoubtedly were early reflections of the growing agrarian discontent with the railroad companies and were directed against Throckmorton as a known railroad man.

Rep. James Webb Throckmorton. This photograph was taken during Throckmorton's tenure as the U.S. representative from Texas. While serving in the House of Representatives, Throckmorton primarily worked to secure legislation that would aid the Texas and Pacific Railroad. His influence was minimal, however, and he failed to aid the company in any tangible way. *Brady-Handy Photograph Collection, Library of Congress.*

Adding to Hare's class rhetoric, the *Sherman Courier* continued its attacks on Throckmorton, stating that he had only been a Democrat since 1869 and up until that time had remained a devoted Whig; that he was currently a paid attorney of the Texas and Pacific Railroad; that his principal object in going to Congress was to promote the endorsement by the government of the bonds that the company held; that the interest of the people in Texas would remain secondary to the interest of the company that employed him. Finally, the newspaper stated that Throckmorton was a director and stockholder of the Texas and Pacific, making him a friend of monopolies and therefore hostile to the common people of North Texas.

While some of the charges against Throckmorton were true, the editor of the *Sherman Courier* had twisted the facts. Throckmorton had been a member of the Whig Party, but he had served the conservative element of Democratic Party faithfully beginning as early as 1857. Throckmorton was an attorney for the Texas and Pacific Railroad and received an annual salary of ten thousand dollars for his services. Likewise, he served as a director for the railroad in Texas and was a stockholder with approximately two thousand dollars invested in the company. All this Throckmorton openly admitted. In a lengthy speech printed in the *Dallas Weekly Herald,* he thoroughly answered questions concerning his involvement with the Texas and Pacific. He stated that some of the greatest politicians in Texas, including Sam Houston and Thomas Rusk, had been strong supporters of railroad companies. As further evidence, Throckmorton outlined several occasions when he took legislative actions aligned against the interests of the Texas and Pacific Railroad for the benefit of his constituents, for example, his defense of North Texans' land titles in the Memphis and El Paso Railroad Reserve in 1858. In closing, Throckmorton argued that the railroad had been a positive force for economic growth in North Texas and that it would be completed up to Fort Worth within a year.[7] Apparently, Throckmorton's explanations carried weight because he received the nomination and won the subsequent general election by a landslide.[8]

In Congress, Throckmorton primarily worked to secure federal funding for the Texas and Pacific Railroad Company. Congress had originally incorporated the company to build a railway from Marshall, Texas, to San Diego, California, in March 1871. After suffering financial woes, the railroad was on the verge of bankruptcy. Thus, Thomas A. Scott, the president of the company, prepared a plan for submission to the Forty-fourth Congress when it convened in December 1875. Scott's plan called on the federal government to guarantee the interest on bonds of the company to the amount of $70 million in exchange for a mortgage on the company and all of its rolling stock and lands. The company would issue bonds at a rate of thirty-five thousand dollars for every mile of new track laid, except in mountainous regions where the amount would be forty thousand dollars.[9]

When Congress assembled, it seemed that Scott's plan would pass easily through the House, especially since Throckmorton earned an appointment to the Committee on the Pacific Railroad. The Texas representative immediately began touting Scott's plan but grew disappointed when his fellow congressmen showed little interest in the proposal or in amending the Texas and Pacific's original charter. Thus, Throckmorton established his own plan to fund the railway. He proposed a bill that called on Congress to extend the time allowed for the completion of the transcontinental line between Marshall and San Diego. In addition, he proposed that the company be required to complete the main, or trunk, line from Marshall to Fort Worth within a year, and that it build at least twenty miles a year from San Diego, the western terminus.

While the new bill dropped Scott's request that the government guarantee the company's bonds, it did include the land-grant system present in the company's earlier charter. Unfortunately for the Texas and Pacific, Throckmorton's new bill did not generate any more enthusiasm than Scott's plan. As a result, Scott began to focus his attention and efforts on completing the line from Marshall to Fort Worth with the hope that Congress would once again become interested in the project if the company extended its existing line. As the session came to a close, congressmen began to focus on the upcoming elections and little else was accomplished concerning the funding of the railroad.[10]

While Throckmorton was in Washington, opposition to his reelection to Congress began to emerge in his home district. The anti-Throckmorton faction initially evolved out of a controversy between the Texas and Pacific Railroad Company and the people of Fort Worth. In an effort to obtain prime farm land north of Dallas, the company had built a branch line from Sherman to Fort Worth. Naturally, the people of Fort Worth blamed Throckmorton for influencing the company to construct this northern route, as it would bring prosperity to his home region. The editor of the *Weatherford Times* asked, "Is Throckmorton partial to a particular place or people and does he ignore with impunity the great interest and importance of our country, or is his actions to be attributed to a positive want of brains?" The editor continued to stress the economic necessity of the railroad in Fort Worth, observing that while the citizens of Fort Worth and its surrounding communities waited for the rail line to reach them, their "lands remain unsettled, capital discouraged, improvements delayed, and activity slumbers."[11] The editor had clearly underlined the economic importance of the railroad to his community and vividly expressed his displeasure with Throckmorton's affiliation with the Texas and Pacific.

The railroad was only one of the obstacles standing in the way of Throckmorton's reelection bid. Many of his constituents found it disturbing that he had openly opposed his party's nomination of Samuel Tilden, the Democratic candidate in the 1876 presidential election. According to the editor of the *Fort Worth Democrat,* a Democratic rag that was unfriendly to Throckmorton at the time because of his perceived involvement in the delay in the railway coming to Fort Worth, Throckmorton had used his skills as orator against the nomination of Tilden because corrupt politicians had successfully bought his support of Hayes. These charges seemed more politically motivated than grounded in truth. More probably, Throckmorton's opposition centered on his support for the repeal of the specie resumption act, a law passed in Congress in 1875 that demanded the government buy back all greenbacks (paper money issued after the Civil War without specie backing) with silver or gold coins within the next four years. Additionally, Throckmorton probably questioned whether an easterner could win a party victory in the general election.[12]

On August 30, the Third District held its nomination convention. Throckmorton had returned the night before from Washington and had delivered a spellbinding speech that addressed many of the charges levied at him, restoring confidence in his candidacy among those present. Despite the efforts of delegates from Dallas, Ellis, and Johnson counties, Throckmorton was the nomination by a landslide. In the ensuing general election, Throckmorton defeated the Republican challenger, J. C. Bigger, by a vote of 14,814 to 1,962.[13]

Once Congress had reassembled in Washington, the Committee on the Pacific Railroad met in executive session to consider a new bill that proposed the completion of a line from Fort Worth to San Diego. The Texas and Pacific Railroad Company was to lay tracks from Fort Worth to the Rio Grande near El Paso and then from El Paso to one hundred miles inside the border of New Mexico, to a yet-to-be-determined junction with the Southern Pacific. The Southern Pacific was to build a line eastward from San Diego toward Fort Yuma on the Colorado River, and from there the company was to build along the thirty-second parallel until it connected with the Texas and Pacific line. Additionally, the Atlantic and Pacific Company was to extend its line from its terminus in Vinita, Indian Territory, to a location between 99° and 100° west longitude where it would connect with the main trunk line of the Texas and Pacific. However, the Atlantic and Pacific would have to forfeit claim to 33 million acres of congressional land grants promised to the company in the Indian Territory, relieving Congress from the difficult task of extinguishing Indian titles to the land.[14]

Furthermore, the new bill provided that the companies should build the line in ten-mile sections. With congressional oversight, the U.S. Treasury would deliver the company its own bonds not to exceed $35,000 per mile on the main trunk line; $30,000 per mile on the San Diego line; and $25,000 on the feeder lines. The federal government would guarantee the interest on these bonds up to 5 percent. In return, the government's investment would be secured by a first mortgage on the road and all of its assets.[15]

The committee approved the bill and sent it to the floor of the House for a vote. Rep. John A. Kasson of Iowa wrote the committee's minority report for those who disapproved the bill, arguing that government funds should not be given to aid the construction of the Pacific Railroad because the company had not complied with its original charter, which required that two hundred miles of track be laid by May 1875. Kasson noted that in 1877, the Texas and Pacific had built only 179 miles of track and the Southern Pacific had laid no track from its western terminus. Also, Kasson pointed out that the security the company offered to the government was insufficient, and he doubted that any federal funds directed to the project could be recovered. Finally, Kasson pointed out that the proposed Vinita line was a waste of resources because the railway would traverse a large, unsettled area that was not in need of such a road. In other words, only a limited amount of goods and people would travel the line, virtually ensuring its failure.[16]

Predictably, Throckmorton refuted Kasson's charges. In a speech delivered from the floor of the House on March 1, 1877, he painstakingly covered the potential benefits that would result from the passage of the bill. First, he argued that the Vinita line would reduce the expense of delivering supplies to Native Americans living on reservations in the Indian Territory. Next, the new railway would provide the U.S. military with more efficient access to the frontier regions of Texas, New Mexico, and Arizona. Also, the line would open the possibility of foreign trade with Mexico and would further promote trade between the Atlantic and Pacific coasts. Finally, Throckmorton argued that the new line would break up the monopoly of the Central and Southern Pacific line, the only existing transcontinental railway at that time.[17]

The bill languished in the Forty-fourth Congress for the remainder of the session without coming to the floor for a vote. Even after Pres. Rutherford B. Hayes called a special session of Congress, little progress was made toward its passage. However, the bill was amended and brought up for consideration once again in December 1879 during the Forty-fifth Congress. Throckmorton made a passionate speech from the floor of the

House in favor of the bill, arguing that the Texas and Pacific Railroad was a sound investment and that federal funds appropriated to the project would be secure. In essence, Throckmorton was making the same basic argument before Congress that he had made every year since 1874. Despite his oratory, the bill failed to get congressional approval. As a result, the Texas and Pacific was reorganized into the Pacific Railway Improvement Company, and Grenville Dodge was made its new president.[18]

While Throckmorton battled to gain funding for the Texas and Pacific, faithful supporters in Texas were circulating his name as a potential candidate in the 1878 gubernatorial election. By March of 1878, Throckmorton was convinced that he had enough support to make a serious bid for the governorship. He left Congress and returned home, believing that he had a decent chance at winning the Democratic nomination. In part, Throckmorton probably felt that his removal from the governorship might give him a decided edge in the upcoming election. Many Texans had expressed their belief that the military had unjustly removed Throckmorton from office during Reconstruction. Because of the public sentiment for the former governor, a small group of Democratic leaders supported his nomination for a second term as the state's chief executive. However, their support was not enough to sustain him in the Democratic Party's state convention, and he lost the nomination to Judge Oran M. Roberts, who subsequently went on to win the gubernatorial race. One factor that led to Throckmorton's failed attempt to capture his party's nomination was his association with railroad magnates. As the agrarian protest movement against railroad companies began to gain ground in Texas, the North Texan's affiliation with the Texas and Pacific Railroad Company had a negative affect on his candidacy.[19]

After his defeat, Throckmorton continued practicing law and participated in various public-speaking engagements. In 1880, Throckmorton once again became politically active. By the end of that year, he let it be known to close associates that he intended to run for the U.S. Senate. However, earlier in the year, his focus was on national politics. At the state Democratic convention, Throckmorton was elected to serve as a delegate to the national convention that was slated to meet in Cincinnati later in the year. At the national convention, Throckmorton led the delegates who were in support of Winfield Scott Hancock's nomination for president. The *Galveston Daily News* reported his reasons for supporting Hancock. First, Hancock had not been involved in recent congressional debates concerning the issuance of hard or soft currency. Next, he believed in the supremacy

Sen. Samuel Bell Maxey. Senator Maxey foiled Throckmorton's chances to fulfill his aspirations to represent Texas in the U.S. Senate in the 1881 state elections. *Brady-Handy Photograph Collection, Library of Congress.*

of civil over military authority. Finally, he could carry Pennsylvania for the Democrats as well as garner the votes of thousands of Union Civil War veterans.[20] Although Throckmorton led a successful campaign to nominate Hancock, the candidate lost the general election to James A. Garfield.

Throckmorton was also interested in the Texas gubernatorial race in 1880. Perhaps hoping to gain favor with the incumbent and gain the governor's support for his senatorial bid, Throckmorton campaigned vigorously for O. M. Roberts. With the support of men like Throckmorton, Governor Roberts was easily reelected to office. Throckmorton must have been slightly disappointed that his efforts did not pay great dividends. In the senatorial race in January 1881, Throckmorton lost to the incumbent, Sen. Samuel Bell Maxey.[21]

In 1882 Throckmorton was once again elected to the House of Representatives, and he was reelected in 1884 and in 1886. However, ill health prevented him from vigorously fulfilling his duties in office. In fact, he spent much of his last months in Congress on granted leaves of absence.

At the end of his fifth term in Congress, poor health eventually forced him into retirement. Apparently, he continued to suffer from the same kidney problems that had plagued him throughout his life.[22]

In 1890 Throckmorton's supporters persuaded him to seek the Democratic nomination for governor, but he was not physically strong enough to effectively campaign for office. Additionally, his longtime ties with the railroad continued to prove a political liability in an era when many Texas voters had grown to distrust the railroad companies and big business. Following a few brief weeks of campaigning, the aging North Texan quietly retired from the race. With Throckmorton out of the race, the younger and more energetic Jim Hogg received the nomination and later won the general election.[23]

Throckmorton returned to his home in McKinney, where he became a receiver for the Choctaw Coal and Railroad Company. Apparently, he was enthusiastic about his new position because the main office of the Choctaw Company was located in McAllister, Oklahoma, which was fairly close to his home. For the first time in his life, the old politician envisioned spending his latter days near his family. Throckmorton assumed his duties at McAllister in the summer of 1893, and all seemed well. He ran his office smoothly and efficiently, and there were even rumors that he might soon be made president of the company. However, tragedy struck before these plans materialized.

In April 1894, Throckmorton was playing cards with friends when he excused himself momentarily, explaining that he needed to go to his office to send a telegram. He completed his task and left his office to rejoin the card game. As he made his way down the street, the elderly statesman lost his footing and fell to the ground. The fall left Throckmorton unconscious and broke two of his ribs. After a reasonable time passed, his friends became worried and headed toward the Choctaw office. Near there, they found the ex-governor lying on the ground. After he regained consciousness, Throckmorton returned to his home in McKinney, where he remained a few days before going back to McAllister to reassume his duties. But he soon became sick and once again had to return to McKinney. This time, he was confined to his deathbed.[24] Throckmorton's last hours were recorded in the following newspaper account:

> Early last night Gov. Throckmorton was asked how he felt. He had been in a stupor for two days with only temporary periods of consciousness and it was during one of these the question was put. He replied: "Very well," and

> nodded his head. Immediately after that he went to sleep as quietly and peacefully as a child. The men of medicine who had been in attendance day and night for many days dozed off, leaving a few watchers to await developments with sleepless eyes. The clock ticked off the minutes with depressing monotony and the hours crept on leaden heels. The sick man slept on. So did the doctors. The clock struck 12. The dying man turned over, opened his eyes once or twice, gasped a little and then went back to rest. The minutes crept along and the watchers by the bedside conversed in low whispers. Just as the clock struck 1 the sleeper awoke with a gasp. His face was drawn and wrinkled with pain and his body was writhing in agony. The physicians were at once aroused and went to work. A crisis was at hand. The slender thread of life vibrated, the convulsion passed, the patient rallied. But there was no more sleep. It was evident that the strength which had withstood death nigh a hundred times was exhausted and the beginning of the end was at hand. From 1 o'clock till daylight stole over the hills the departing spirit tarried awhile in peace. But about 6 o'clock another convulsion as violent as the first shook the weakened frame. He never rallied. At 8:30 he died without having spoken for hours and hours, perfectly unconscious alike [of] the pangs of suffering and the farewells of those whom he had loved so well and who had so well loved him.[25]

Throckmorton's life provides scholars with a glimpse into five decades of Texas history: his life experiences reveal much about southern society as it existed during the latter half of the nineteenth century. Most importantly, Throckmorton's biography reveals that the South was never a homogeneous society. For example, during the antebellum and Civil War years, southern whites were not united in a defense of slavery. The frontier settlers clearly represented a challenge to the South's slave-owning aristocracy." On numerous occasions, Throckmorton challenged the authority of the planters in Texas. However, this is not to say that the Texas frontier was not a viable part of the South. On the contrary, North Texas represented a clear extension of the cultures and customs of the Upper South, while East Texas represented an extension of the Lower South. In fact, while this study only alludes to the fact, Texas represents an excellent case study on the social, political, and economic differences between the states of the Upper and Lower South.

The North Texas politician's disdain for African Americans during the Reconstruction era illustrates that southern racism was multifaceted. During this period of racial strife, Throckmorton, unlike the former planter

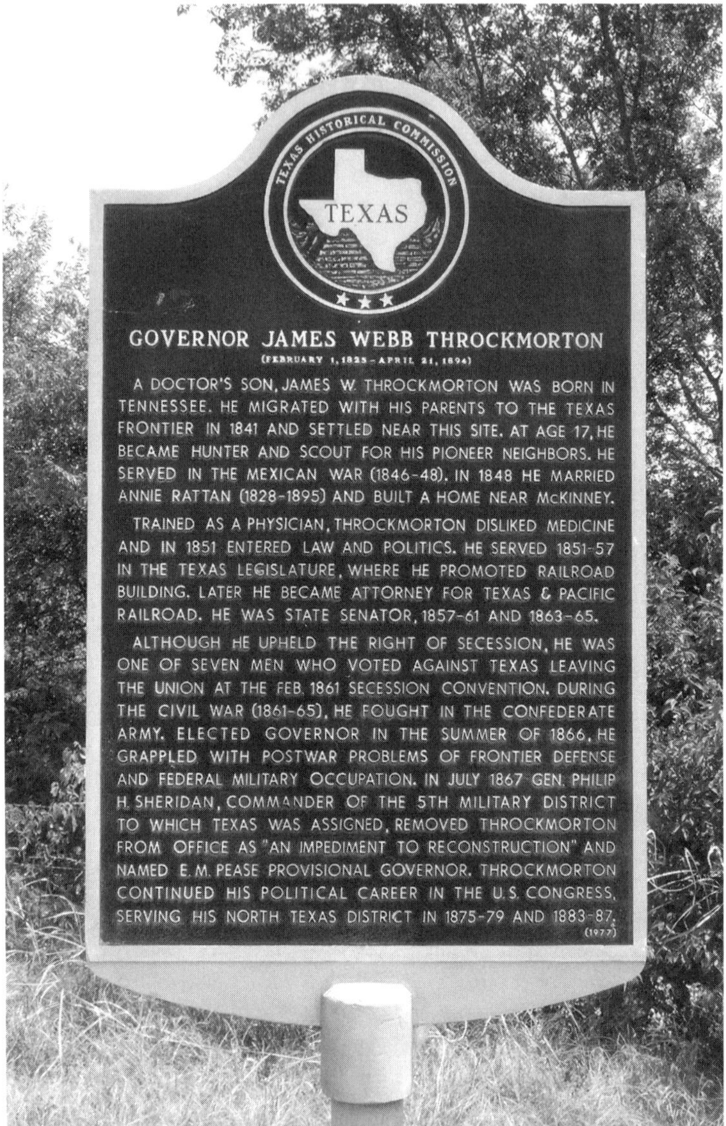


J. W. Throckmorton Historical Marker. The marker is placed near the homestead of James W. Throckmorton and provides a brief account of the governor's life. *Courtesy of Kenneth W. Howell.*

J. W. Throckmorton Monument. Standing prominently in one corner of the downtown square in McKinney, Texas, this monument is a reminder to all who pass and take time to read the inscription that Throckmorton was once a favorite son of Collin County. *Courtesy of Kenneth W. Howell.*

class, did not attempt to oppress black Texans out of a desire to revive the institution of slavery. Throckmorton's oppressive views of freedmen were directly related to his quest to ensure that conservative Democrats retained political, economic, and social control of the state. While Throckmorton's racist views and his desire to protect white rule in Texas eventually led him to work hand in hand with former antebellum political foes such as Oran Roberts, he was not an ardent proponent of the South's "lost cause." In fact, he almost certainly viewed the end of slavery following the Civil War as a positive *good* for small farmers in North Texas. Settlers no longer had to worry about falling under the complete control of elite slaveholders in the eastern part of the state.

Finally, Throckmorton's career exposes the complexity of southern society. Scholars cannot fully appreciate the historical significance of this nineteenth-century politician by examining his racial views alone. Although his racism influenced his political decisions, we cannot overlook the influence of his personal political ambitions, his commitment to the economic development of Texas, and his conservative political ideology. This examination of the life experiences of southern frontier politician James Webb Throckmorton, and the attempt to explain how these experiences influenced his public life, make him less of an enigma in nineteenth-century Texas politics.

# NOTES

INTRODUCTION

1. Winkler, *Journal of the Secession Convention,* 46. The resolution preventing debate was made by Allison Nelson.

2. This group of Unionists shared some common characteristics: they represented North Texas and East Texas counties, except for Hughes, who was from Williamson County; they or their fathers had ties with Upper South states, migrating to Texas from either Tennessee or Kentucky; and they were all members of the Texas bar.

3. Elliott, *Leathercoat,* 53.

4. *The True Issue* (La Grange, Texas), February 7, 1861.

5. Ibid.; Holbert, "Public Career of James Webb Throckmorton," 36–37; Wooster, *Texas and Texans in the Civil War,* 13; Schlameus, "Secessionist Thought in Texas," 64; Sandbo, "First Session of the Secession Convention," 191. There is some discrepancy about the actual wording of Throckmorton's response to the hiss in the gallery. Wooster states that Throckmorton said, "Mr. President, when the rabble hiss, well May patriots tremble." However, according to the report found in *The True Issue* (La Grange), February 7, 1861, Throckmorton stated, "Mr. President, the rabble May hiss when patriots tremble."

6. Winkler, *Journal of the Secession Convention,* 48–49; Wooster, *Secession Conventions of the South,* 130; Elliott, *Leathercoat,* 54–55; Chapin, "Presidential Reconstruction in Texas," 12–13; Holbert, "Public Career," 36; Wooster, *Texas and Texans in the Civil War,* 13–14. For more information on the individuals who voted against secession in the convention, see Evelyn Calhoun Miller, "Seven Shouted 'No' When Secession Vote Taken Here," *Austin American-Statesman,* July 19, 1936, Throckmorton Papers, Texas State Library (TSL).

7. For other works that focus on Throckmorton's political career, see Holbert, "Public Career of James Webb Throckmorton"; Harrison, "J. W. Throckmorton's Administration"; and Buenger, *Secession and the Union in Texas.* For a more thorough discussion of the historiography relating to Throckmorton, see Howell, "James Webb Throckmorton," 1–34.

8. Elliott, *Leathercoat,* xi.

9. Ibid.

10. U.S. Bureau of the Census, *Eighth Census.*

11. Berlin, *Many Thousands Gone,* 8.

12. For a more thorough discussion of racism and for new studies of how whites form the concept of race, see Kolchin, "Whiteness Studies"; Doane and Bonilla-Silva, *White Out*; Schutte, *What Racists Believe*; and Babb, *Whiteness Visible.*

## CHAPTER ONE

1. Elliott, *Leathercoat,* 5–7; *McKinney Examiner,* October 3, 1940; Massey, "History of Collin County," 1–2.

2. Elliot, *Leathercoat,* 4–5; Lynch, "J. W. Throckmorton," unpublished manuscript, Throckmorton Papers, TSL; *McKinney Examiner,* October 3, 1940; Stambaugh and Stambaugh, *History of Collin County,* 206; Fulmore, *History and Geography of Texas,* 97–98; Holbert, "Public Career of James Webb Throckmorton," 2–3; Gary Throckmorton, unpublished genealogical register for William Edmund Throckmorton, 1–3; C. Wickliffe Throckmorton, *Genealogical and Historical Account,* 353. All accounts, except for those by Ruby Holbert, C. Wickliffe Throckmorton, and Gary Throckmorton, show that William E. Throckmorton was married first to Elizabeth Webb and that she was the mother of James Webb Throckmorton and three of his brothers and four sisters. I believe that Holbert, C. Wickliffe, and Gary are more accurate than the previous works, which seem to replicate the same mistakes first printed in Fulmore. Holbert and both Throckmorton genealogists agree that William married Susan Jane Rotan. In addition, Gary Throckmorton finds that William E. Throckmorton was born on November 1, 1796, while other authors are less exact about his date of birth, ranging from 1795 to 1800. Here again, I believe that Gary Throckmorton is more accurate.

3. For more information concerning western migration, see McDonald and McWhiney, "Antebellum Southern Herdsman," 147–66; Otto, "Migration of the Southern Plain Folk," 183–200; and Schaefer, "Locational Choice in the Antebellum South."

4. Bergeron, Ash, and Keith, *Tennesseans and Their History,* 92–130.

5. Elliott, *Leathercoat,* 4–5; Lynch, "J. W. Throckmorton"; *McKinney Examiner,* October 3, 1940; Holbert, "Public Career of James Webb Throckmorton," 2; Stambaugh and Stambaugh, *History of Collin County,* 206; Fulmore, *History and Geography of Texas,* 97–98; Massey, "History of Collin County," 72; Gary Throckmorton, unpublished genealogical record of William Edmund Throckmorton, 1–3.

6. Elliott, *Leathercoat,* 4–5; Lynch, "J. W. Throckmorton"; Stambaugh and Stambaugh, *History of Collin County,* 206; Fulmore, *History and Geography of Texas,* 97–98; Holbert, "Public Career of James Webb Throckmorton," 3; Gary Throckmorton, unpublished genealogical record of William Edmund Throckmorton, 1–3. The Stambaughs, Fulmore, and Holbert state that Susan Throckmorton died in 1837, but Gary Throckmorton records her death as December 28, 1838. Once again, it appears that the scholars have simply repeated an incorrect date in their different works, and Gary Throckmorton's work is more accurate.

7. Elliott, *Leathercoat,* 4–5; Lynch, "J. W. Throckmorton"; *McKinney Examiner,* October 3, 1940; Holbert, "Public Career of James Webb Throckmorton," 3; Stambaugh and Stambaugh, *History of Collin County,* 206. There is no mention of where William's older children stayed. Apparently, they were old enough to take care of themselves, or they lived with friends in Arkansas. William's oldest son, William Albion Little Throckmorton, was nineteen years old and John Augustus Throckmorton, second eldest son, was fifteen years old. In fact, James would have been old enough to stay with his father, but he probably was sent to Tennessee to look after his younger brother and sister.

8. Phillips, *Governors of Tennessee,* 62–65. The service prior to 1843 was only the beginning of Campbell's political fortunes: following valiant service in the Mexican War, he was unanimously elected to the judgeship of Tennessee's fourth circuit court. In 1851, Tennessee's native son was elected governor of his state. During the secession crisis, Campbell ardently supported the Unionists against the rebellious Confederates, and after shots were fired at Fort Sumter, he joined the U.S. Army, briefly becoming a brigadier general in command of the Tennessee Volunteers. Following the war, he was elected to represent his state as a conservative Unionist in the Thirty-ninth U.S. Congress. During Reconstruction, Campbell was a strong supporter of President Johnson and opposed Radical Republicans. Campbell's career is important to note when examining J. W. Throckmorton's own political career because the two men follow very similar paths to political prominence. For example, Throckmorton fights in the Mexican War, becomes an ardent Unionist opposed to the secession of Texas in 1861, and evolves into a conservative Unionist during Reconstruction who faithfully adhered to Johnson's Reconstruction policies and adamantly opposed Radical Republican rule in Texas.

9. Holt, *Rise and Fall of the American Whig Party,* xii–xiii.

10. Ibid., xiii.

11. Ibid.

12. Crofts, *Reluctant Confederates,* 47; Buenger, *Secession and the Union in Texas,* 23–25; Holt, *Rise and Fall of the American Whig Party,* 64–70. For other views on the Whig Party, see Cole, *Whig Party in the South*; Carroll, *Origins of the Whig Party*; Sellers, "Who Were the Southern Whigs?"; Howe, *Political Culture of the American Whigs*; and Brown, *Politics and Statesmanship.*

13. Gary Throckmorton, unpublished genealogical record of William Edmund Throckmorton, 4; Fulmore, *History and Geography of Texas,* 97–98; Elliot, *Leathercoat,* 4–5; Lynch, "J. W. Throckmorton"; *McKinney Examiner,* October 3, 1940.

14. Elliott, *Leathercoat,* 5–7; *McKinney Examiner,* October 3, 1940; Holbert, "Public Career of James Webb Throckmorton," 3–4; Stambaugh and Stambaugh, *History of Collin County,* 206; Massey, "History of Collin County," 1–2; Fulmore, *History and Geography of Texas,* 97–98.

15. For more information on slash-and-burn cultivation, which was the most common form of farming throughout the South, see Otto and Anderson, "Slash-and-Burn Cultivation in the Highlands South."

16. Stambaugh and Stambaugh, *History of Collin County,* 21–22.

17. Wilbarger, *Indian Depredations in Texas,* 436–37; Carter, *History of Fannin County,*

30–31; Pitts and Champ, *Collin County,* 2:55; Massey, "History of Collin County," 24. Massey reveals that few Indian attacks occurred in Collin County and that most of them were the result of Anglo encroachment upon their lands and the natives' need for horses. For other examples of Indian raids occurring in Fannin County in 1842, see Winfrey and Day, *Indian Papers of Texas and the Southwest,* 1:125, 127, 129, 131, 134.

18. Elliott, *Leathercoat,* 7–8.

19. It cannot be overstated that J. W. Throckmorton was raised in the conservative culture of the Upper South. As a result of his time in Tennessee and Kentucky, Throckmorton did not develop an affinity for slavery, although he did recognize the "right" of slave owners to protect their property. He also believed in the art of political compromise between radical fringe groups. In this light, his fundamental political ideology was similar to Henry Clay's core beliefs. Throckmorton, like Clay and other Upper South politicians, was devoted to the Founding Fathers' concept of the Union. Throckmorton also understood the necessity in supporting economic growth and therefore was a strong advocate of federally funded internal improvements.

20. *McKinney Examiner,* October 3, 1940; Stambaugh and Stambaugh, *History of Collin County,* 207; Lynch, "J. W. Throckmorton"; Elliott, *Leathercoat,* 8–9; newspaper clipping, possibly from a McKinney newspaper, Throckmorton Papers, TSL; Holbert, "Public Career of James Webb Throckmorton," 5; Massey, "History of Collin County," 72.

21. Tutorow, *Texas Annexation and the Mexican War,* 18; Calvert, De Leon, and Cantrell, *History of Texas,* 108.

22. Wilson, *Papers of John C. Calhoun,* 13 (*1835–1837*): 197–99, and 14 (*1837–1839*): 32, 96–101; Tutorow, *Texas Annexation and the Mexican War,* 19; Wortham, *History of Texas,* 4:147–50.

23. Tutorow, *Texas Annexation and the Mexican War,* 19–21.

24. Seager, *Papers of Henry Clay,* 897–99. In a letter to John J. Crittenden, Clay expresses his concerns over the annexation of Texas.

25. Saxon, "Politics of Expansion," 213–47; Tutorow, *Texas Annexation,* 85, 100–103.

26. Wortham, *History of Texas,* 186–88; Wallace, Vigness, and Ward, *Documents of Texas History,* 146–60; Tutorow, *Texas Annexation,* 115–16. Wallace and his coauthors include in their collected documents "The Annexation Offer Accepted" (July 4, 1845), "The Texas Constitution of 1845" (August 28, 1845), and a speech given by Anson Jones entitled "The Republic of Texas Is No More" (February 19, 1846). Congressional resolutions for annexation were extremely favorable to the people of Texas. Congress offered to admit the republic as a single state in the Union but with the option of dividing its vast lands into as many as four additional states in the future. The state would be allowed to retain possession of its public lands, which could be sold to help pay off its existing public debt. Additionally, the U.S. government agreed to assume responsibility for resolving the outstanding boundary disputes between Texas and Mexico regarding the southern and western borders of the state. Anson Jones, the newly elected president of the Republic of Texas, called for a special session of the Texas congress in June 1845 to consider the United States' annexation offer. At the same time, a constitutional convention convened and produced a state constitution which, along with the issue

of annexation, was placed before the citizens of Texas in a referendum. Voters overwhelmingly supported the new constitution and annexation. After reviewing the Texas constitution, Congress accepted it, and President Polk signed the Texas Admission Act on December 29, 1845, officially making Texas the twenty-eighth state of the Union.

27. Richardson, *Compilation of the Messages and Papers of the Presidents,* 2287–93; Wallace, Vigness, and Ward, *Documents of Texas History,* 161; Tutorow, *Texas Annexation,* 124. In his "War Message" to Congress on May 11, 1846, Polk recounts his instructions to John Slidell and the Mexican government's reaction to his arrival in Mexico City.

28. Richardson, *Compilation of the Messages,* 2287–93. James K. Polk's "War Message" to Congress on May 11, 1846.

29. "An Act Declaring a State of War Between Mexico and the United States," *Congressional Globe,* 29th Cong., 1st sess., 794 (May 11, 1846).

30. Wilkins, *Highly Irregular Irregulars,* 141–43.

31. *Dallas Morning News,* April 22, 1894. Wilson recounted this incident after Throckmorton's death; Elliott, *Leathercoat,* 9.

32. Holbert, "Public Career of James Webb Throckmorton," 5; Stambaugh and Stambaugh, *History of Collin County,* 207; Elliott, *Leathercoat,* 11; Lynch, "J. W. Throckmorton"; Wilkins, *Highly Irregular Irregulars,* 136–51; Spurlin, *Texas Veterans in the Mexican War,* 157. The record of Throckmorton's military service in the Mexican War has often been exaggerated by most scholars. Most of Throckmorton's five months in the military was spent in transit from Collin County to Mexico. It seems unlikely that Throckmorton could have served in the Battle of Buena Vista because the battle took place on February 22–23, 1847, when Throckmorton was still in San Antonio. Also, according to Wilson's account, Throckmorton did not travel forward with Chevallie's Battalion to Monterey. According to accounts of Throckmorton's medical discharge, the farthest point in Mexico the young physician reached was Camargo, Mexico, where he was physically unable to rejoin his battalion. Thus, Throckmorton's war experience was for the most part uneventful. Throckmorton apparently suffered from some type of kidney illness perhaps brought on by his experience in the desert between San Antonio and Camargo, Mexico.

33. Massey, "History of Collin County," 109. Collin County was formed out of Fannin County on April 3, 1846, following the annexation of Texas.

34. Holbert, "Public Career of James Webb Throckmorton," 6; Elliott, *Leathercoat,* 11. Elliott reveals that the couple returned to Texas in wagons and were accompanied by Ann's older sister and family friends. All settled in an area near the place where William Throckmorton had originally settled. J. W. Throckmorton and his wife lived in this area the rest of their lives, and like many of the frontier families of the mid-nineteenth century, they had a large number of children, ten in all.

35. Newspaper article "Tender Woman, After Braving Pioneer Day Perils, Presides as Mistress of Governor's Mansion," from the *San Antonio Express,* n.d., circa 1912, Throckmorton Papers, TSL.

36. Ibid.

37. Ibid.

38. Elliott, *Leathercoat,* 12–15; Massey, "History of Collin County," 72; Holbert, "Public Career of James Webb Throckmorton," 7.

39. Connor, *Adventure in Glory,* 146–49. For a more detailed examination of the Peters Colony, see Connor, *Peters Colony of Texas,* and Connor, *Kentucky Colonization in Texas.*

40. Connor, *Adventure in Glory,* 149.

41. Ibid., 149–50; Seymour, *Kentucky Colonization in Texas,* 8; Spaw, *Texas Senate,* 1:94.

42. Calvert, De Leon, and Cantrell, *History of Texas,* 94; Holbert, "Public Career of James Webb Throckmorton," 22–23. Immigrants' states of origin are defined as Ohio Valley (Illinois, Indiana, Ohio); northeastern United States (Pennsylvania, New York, Massachusetts, Connecticut, New Hampshire, Rhode Island); and Upper South (Missouri, Arkansas, Tennessee, Kentucky, Virginia, North Carolina). A large number of the immigrants came from the Upper South.

43. Connor, *Adventure in Glory,* 214–17. The Mercer Colony was a separate colony to the immediate southeast of the Peters Colony.

44. Richardson, et al., *Texas,* 149–50. Charles F. Mercer was awarded a colonizing contract just before the Texas congress discontinued the *empresario* contracts in early 1844. The Mercer Colony contract called for the location of families in a large area to the south of the Peters Colony. Unfortunately, the borders of the Mercer and Peters colonies overlapped, which caused further confusion regarding land claims.

45. "Proceedings of a Convention, of Delegates from the Counties in Peters and Mercer's Colonies, held in the Town of Dallas 21st day of May A.D. 1849," *Clarksville Northern Standard,* June 16, 1849.

46. "Public Meeting in Collin County," *Clarksville Northern Standard,* June 23, 1849. Many citizens wanted to move the capital from Austin, arguing that its frontier location made it less accessible to the people of East Texas; other Texans were content with leaving it in Austin. Almost everyone who promoted the relocation of the capital understood that the state capital would be an economic gold mine for the lucky town that won the honors. It was eventually decided to leave the capital in Austin.

47. Ibid.

48. Ibid. The committee recommended that "the Seat of Government should be located with a view to the convenience of a majority of the people" and "that object could best be obtained by the location of the Capital at some eligible place East of the Brazos River." The committee further deemed it "desirable to bring some one place permanently before the public and whereas we believe the best means of obtaining that end would be through the instrumentality of a convention." The committee concluded that "Palestine [was] a suitable place for holding said convention." The representatives who were later sent to Palestine from Collin County supported placing the new capital along the banks of the Trinity River in the town that served as the host of the convention. Unfortunately for their cause, state leaders eventually decided to leave the capital at its Austin location.

49. Stambaugh and Stambaugh, *History of Collin County,* 40–61.

50. Massey, "History of Collin County," 108–9.

51. Fowler, "Origins of the Texas Railroad Commission," 7–8.

52. Ibid., 8–9; *Seventh Census of the United States, 1850,* 515, 517. Collin County in

1850 produced 2,433 bushels of wheat. In the same year, the county reported producing one bale of cotton (four hundred pounds). Clearly, the interest of the county was not the same as that of their East Texas brethren.

53. Kingston, Attlesey, and Crawford, *Texas Almanac's Political History,* 72; Buenger, "Stilling the Voice of Reason," 96–97. Kingston and his coauthors report the presidential election vote in Collin County as follows: In 1848, Lewis Cass (Democrat), 99, to Zachary Taylor (Whig), 43. In 1852, Franklin Pierce (Democrat), 133, to Winfield Scott (Whig), 58. In 1856, James Buchanan (Democrat), 564, to Millard Fillmore (Whig), 302.

## CHAPTER TWO

1. Brands, *Age of Gold,* 246, 292.

2. Potter, *Impending Crisis,* 94; Cooper and Terrill, *American South,* 290–94.

3. Cooper and Terrill, *American South,* 294; Campbell, *Gone to Texas,* 235; Richardson et al., *Texas,* 165; Calvert, De Leon, and Cantrell, *History of Texas,* 133–34; Wooten, *Comprehensive History of Texas,* 2:29–30; Stegmaier, *Texas, New Mexico, and the Compromise of 1850,* passim. Clay's original proposal was rejected by both northern and southern politicians: neither side could accept the portions of the proposal that benefited their rival section. Exhausted from his efforts, Clay passed leadership of his resolution to Sen. Stephen A. Douglas, an able parliamentarian who supported the Kentuckian's compromise proposal. Douglas broke the resolution apart from the omnibus format and began to cajole the separate parts of compromise through Congress by creating a series of shifting coalitions for each part of Clay's original bill. As a result, Douglas succeeded in effecting a viable compromise in September of 1850. It appeared that the sectional debate over slavery was solved forever.

4. Potter, *Impending Crisis,* 109–12.

5. Texas Legislature, *Members,* 11, 18, 23, 26, 31. Throckmorton was elected to the Texas House of Representatives in 1851, 1853, and 1855. He was elected to the Texas Senate in 1857 and 1859. For further information on Throckmorton's various state elections and for verification of Throckmorton's election victories, see the following newspaper accounts: *Clarksville Northern Standard,* September 13, 1851, August 13, 1853, and August 25, 1855; *Texas State Gazette,* June 11, 1853, and August 20, 1853. Also see Elliott, *Leathercoat,* 15–16, for more information on Throckmorton's 1851 campaign and election victory. Throckmorton's membership in the Whig Party is evident from two different newspaper articles appearing in the *Texas State Gazette* describing the Texas Whig Party's presidential conventions held at Houston and Tyler. The newspaper accounts say that at the Tyler convention, Throckmorton was elected as a district elector for the eastern districts of the state. Also, Texas Whig principles were mentioned very briefly in the article, stating that the Whigs "adopted resolutions approving the administration of Mr. Fillmore; in favor of internal improvements by the Federal Government; and the Tyler convention also passed resolutions in favor of amending the State Constitution so as to permit the chartering of banks. This shows that Texas whiggery is no counterfeit, but that it is indeed and in fact . . . alive and ready to fight vigorously

for its ancient creed." For more on the Whig Party conventions in Tyler and Houston, see the *Texas State Gazette,* May 8, 1852, and May 22, 1852.

6. Holbert, "Public Career of James Webb Throckmorton," 11; Lynch, "J. W. Throckmorton."

7. Texas House, "Special Joint House and Senate Report," *Journal, Fourth Legislature,* 477–86; Spaw, *Texas Senate,* 1:229; Connor, *Peters Colony,* 137.

8. Elliott, *Leathercoat,* 20–21.

9. Ibid., 19–20. The legislature passed a law on December 2, 1850, that authorized settlers in the Peters Colony to intervene in colony contract suits where they had an interest. Litigation grew out of this law because land titles could not be issued by the state, and as a consequence the company instituted a suit against the General Land Office, which suit was pending when the Fourth Legislature met in November 1851.

10. Ibid., 21–22; Texas House, *Journal, Fourth Legislature,* 484; Gammel, *Laws of Texas,* 3:950–57; Stambaugh and Stambaugh, *History of Collin County,* 26–27; Connor, *Kentucky Colonization in Texas,* 56. Connor states that John H. Reagan, the primary legal representative of the settlers, strongly opposed the compromise law of 1852. Reagan believed that the report on which the legislature based the compromise law was fraudulent.

11. Good, "John Henninger Reagan," 70; Connor, *Kentucky Colonization in Texas,* 59; Elliott, *Leathercoat,* 22.

12. Elliott, *Leathercoat,* 22–24; Timmons, "Texas on the Road to Secession," 110.

13. Elliott, *Leathercoat,* 24; *Texas State Gazette,* September 11, 1852; Timmons, "Texas on the Road to Secession," 110; Stambaugh and Stambaugh, *History of Collin County,* 27.

14. Stambaugh and Stambaugh, *History of Collin County,* 27; Elliott, *Leathercoat,* 24–26.

15. Elliott, *Leathercoat,* 26–27; Connor, *Kentucky Colonization in Texas,* 59; Connor, *Peters Colony,* 143–45; Texas House, *Journal, Fourth Legislature, Extra Session,* 33–34; *Clarksville Northern Standard,* August 7, 1852, and September 10, 1853.

16. *Clarksville Northern Standard,* September 10, 1853; Connor, *Kentucky Colonization in Texas,* 59; Timmons, "Texas on the Road to Secession," 111; Elliott, *Leathercoat,* 27–28; *Austin Southwestern,* January 29, 1853. In a letter to the editor of the *Austin Southwestern,* Throckmorton agreed with the colonists that Hedgcoxe had been the center of their problems with the Texas Emigration and Land Company, but the delegates still called for his resignation from the Texas House of Representatives.

17. *Clarksville Northern Standard,* August 7, 1852; Timmons, "Texas on the Road to Secession," 111–12; Elliott, *Leathercoat,* 29.

18. Elliott, *Leathercoat,* 29–30.

19. Throckmorton to Gov. Peter H. Bell, September 15, 1852, Bell Records, TSL. According to the notation made on the letter, Throckmorton's resignation was accepted on October 6, 1852.

20. Texas House, *Journal, Fourth Legislature, Extra Session,* 4; *Clarksville Northern Standard,* November 13, 1852; Connor, *Peters Colony of Texas,* 143–45; Connor, *Kentucky Colonization in Texas,* 59; Timmons, "Texas on the Road to Secession," 112; Elliott, *Leathercoat,* 30–31.

21. Elliott, *Leathercoat,* 31–32; Texas House, *Journal, Fourth Legislature, Extra Session,* 252–54.

22. Texas House, *Journal, Fourth Legislature,* 477–86; Elliott, *Leathercoat,* 32.

23. Cooper and Terrill, *American South,* 305–6.

24. Ibid.

25. Russel, "Revaluation of the Period Before the Civil War," 346.

26. Russel, "Revaluation of the Period Before the Civil War," 346, 352; Buenger, "Stilling the Voice of Reason," 22; Sinclair, "Crossroads of Conviction," 34.

27. Schaefer, "Locational Choice," 163–64; U.S. Bureau of the Census. *Seventh Census,* Schedule XI (Agriculture). The census reports wheat production at 2,433 bushels of wheat in Collin County; the *Clarksville Northern Standard,* November 29, 1856, discusses the agricultural potential of North Texas. Russel, "Revaluation of the Period Before the Civil War," 346–47, mentions why the railroads were important to local merchants. Also see *Texas State Gazette,* November 1, 1853, and *Clarksville Northern Standard,* August 30, 1856, for specific motives of Texas residents concerning the development of a transcontinental railroad route through Texas. Schaefer's quantitative analysis of migration in the antebellum South clearly reveals the divide between yeoman farmers and planters. He correctly contends that small farmers could not economically compete with the planters and therefore moved to frontier regions in order to become self-sufficient. Schaefer also states that yeoman farmers did not want to live in areas numerically dominated by slaves and plantations. The author reminds scholars that settlers migrating from the northern states (Ohio, Indiana, Illinois, Michigan, and Iowa) were characteristically racist. Given that many of the settlers in North Texas migrated from those northern states and from the Upper South, it seems likely that Schaefer's conclusions are valid for the Red River counties.

28. Fowler, "Origin of the Texas Railroad Commission," 9; Sinclair, "Crossroads of Conviction," 34.

29. Campbell, *Gone To Texas,* 212; Brockman, "Railroads, Radicals, and Democrats," 2–5.

30. Gammel, *Laws of Texas,* 3:72–79, 4:12; Texas House, *Journal, Sixth Legislature,* November 28, 1855, 121–22; Elliott, *Leathercoat,* 33–34.

31. Gammel, *Laws of Texas,* 3:72–79, 4:12; Texas House, *Journal, Sixth Legislature,* November 28, 1855, 121–22; Elliott, *Leathercoat,* 33–34.

32. Elliott, *Leathercoat,* 34–35; Texas House, *Journal, Sixth Legislature,* November 28, 1855, 121.

33. Elliott, *Leathercoat,* 36.

34. Texas House, *Journal, Sixth Legislature,* 290–91; Elliott, *Leathercoat,* 36.

35. Elliott, *Leathercoat,* 36.

36. Ibid., 37.

37. Ibid., 36–37; Gammel, *Laws of Texas,* 4:209.

38. Elliott, *Leathercoat,* 38.

39. Ibid.; Gammel, *Laws of Texas,* 4:474–75.

40. Ibid.

41. *Texas State Gazette,* December 6, 1851. The major issues discussed at this convention included, but were not limited to, the following questions: How would the

railroad be funded? Where would a transcontinental line bisect Texas–North Texas, Central Texas, or South Texas? Would land be granted to the railroad companies? The questions were important because they were taken up by the legislature between 1852 and 1857. Prominent Texas railroad men present at the convention included E. E. Lott (Smith County), W. T. Scott (Harrison County), S. A. Maverick (Bexar County), J. W. Flanagan (Rusk County), David C. Dickson (Grimes County), I. A. Paschal (Bexar County), Roger Q. Mills (Anderson County), and Jon W. Dancy (Fayette County).

42. *Texas State Gazette,* November 1, 1853; *Clarksville Northern Standard,* October 15, 1853.

43. *Texas State Gazette,* November 1, 1853; *Clarksville Northern Standard,* October 15, 1853. Special care of the state meant financial support to the road in the form of directing funding, donations of land, or taxation on the people for the purpose of railroad development.

44. *Texas State Gazette,* November 1, 1853; Armstrong, "Origins of the Texas and Pacific Railway," 497. Armstrong defines the Memphis, El Paso, and Pacific Railroad as "the forerunner of the Northern or, as it was sometimes called, the Transcontinental Division of the Texas and Pacific [after it was later made part of the Texas and Pacific]. The original company proposed to build from a point opposite Fulton, Arkansas, westward along the southern banks of the Red River, down to El Paso, and on to the Pacific Ocean." Construction was scheduled to begin in 1857, but plans were later abandoned when the Red River was blocked by an accumulation of driftwood, locally called the "great raft." The Memphis, El Paso, and Pacific was later acquired by the Southern Transcontinental Railroad Company, which in turn became part of the Texas and Pacific.

45. Armstrong, "Origins of the Texas and Pacific Railway," 491; Means, "East Texas and the Transcontinental Railroad," 49.

46. For more details concerning the debate over Throckmorton's proposed compromise regarding the Memphis, El Paso, and Pacific, see the following dates of the *Clarksville Northern Standard*: September 6, 13, and 20, 1856; October 11 and 25, 1856; November 29, 1856; September 12, 1857; October 10, 1857.

47. Means, "East Texas and the Transcontinental Railroad," 49–50.

48. Ibid., 50; Armstrong, "Origins of the Texas and Pacific Railway," 491–92.

49. Armstrong, "Origins of the Texas and Pacific Railway," 491; Means "East Texas and the Transcontinental Railroad," 50.

50. Means "East Texas and the Transcontinental Railroad," 50. Means identifies the Southern Pacific's board of directors as the following: Charles Stewart Todd, a newly arrived resident of Texas in 1850; Horatio Allen, a civil engineer from New York; Richard T. Archer, a planter from Mississippi; R. M. Diamond of Rhode Island; T. Butler King of Georgia; R. M. Stratton of New York; George D. Post of New York; R. J. Walker of Washington; Edwin Post of New York; Michael G. Bright of Indiana; S. F. Buttersworth of New York; W. Cook of New Jersey; William T. Schoot, M. J. Hall, J. P. Henderson, W. R. D. Ward, and J. Taylor of Texas.

51. Ibid., 50–51; Armstrong, "Origins of the Texas and Pacific Railroad," 492. Arm-

strong reveals that the home office was moved from New York to New Orleans in 1857 and George S. Yerger was named the company's new president.

52. Means, "East Texas and the Transcontinental Railroad," 51.

53. Ibid.; Armstrong, "Origins of the Texas and Pacific Railroad," 494–95.

54. Riegel, "Trans-Mississippi Railroads During the Fifties," 171.

55. Ibid.

56. Ibid., 171–72.

57. Tate, "Frontier Defense on the Comanche Ranges," 43–44. Tate defines the frontier line in 1849 as lying between Fort Worth and Fort Duncan. The initial forts on the 1849 frontier line included Graham, Gates, Croghan, Martin Scott, Lincoln, and Inge. By the end of the summer of 1852, the frontier line had moved farther west and a new line of forts was being constructed, including Fort Belknap, Phantom Hill, Chadbourne, McKavett, Mason, and Terret.

58. Tate, "Frontier Defense on the Comanche Ranges," 41–52. Tate's article offers a concise but very informative overview frontier defense prior to the Civil War.

59. Massey, "History of Collin County," 26.

60. Throckmorton to Peter H. Bell, July 30, 1852, Bell Records, TSL.

61. Ibid.

62. Ibid.

63. Ibid.

64. Ibid.

65. Tate, "Frontier Defense on the Comanche Ranges," 43–52. For further discussion of United States Indian policy in Texas prior to the Civil War, see Harmon, "United States Indian Policy in Texas."

66. Holbert, "Public Career of James Webb Throckmorton," 19; Texas House, *Journal,* Fourth Legislature, Extra Session, 11–37.

67. Spaw, *Texas Senate,* 1:263, 284–87.

## CHAPTER THREE

1. The most critical of these disturbances included the new fugitive slave laws incorporated in the Compromise of 1850, which forced people in northern states to aid in the capture and return of runaway slaves; Harriet Beecher Stowe's *Uncle Tom's Cabin* (1852), which fueled the abolitionist movement; the Kansas-Nebraska Act (1854), which ultimately negated the Compromise of 1820 and potentially allowed slavery to exist above the latitude of 36°30′; "bleeding Kansas" (1855–61), which pitted slave owners and Free Soil men in Kansas against one another in a bloody war for political dominance; the Ostend Manifesto (1854), which indicated the radical slave owners' desire to expand slavery into Latin America, further irritating abolitionists; Preston Brooks's caning of Charles Sumner on the floor of the U.S. Senate (1856), which further incited the fears of both the North and the South; the *Dred Scott* case (1857) in the Supreme Court, which appeared to be a significant legal victory for the South; John Brown's raid at Harper's Ferry, Virginia (1859), which caused widespread fear in the South that abolitionists were intent on initiating mass slave uprisings; and Abraham Lincoln's

election to the presidency (1860), which suggested that the South was losing political influence in the federal government. Each episode drove the northern and southern states farther apart until finally both sides realized that they were on the path of an irrepressible conflict.

2. Walter Buenger's "Texas and the Riddle of Secession" is one of the best article-length studies of the secession movement in Texas. Also see Hicks, "Texas and Separate Independence"; and Elliott, "Union Sentiment in Texas."

3. Buenger, *Secession and the Union in Texas,* 22–26.

4. Ibid., 23–24, 106; Buenger, "Stilling the Voice of Reason," 95–96. For more on Whig economic and political philosophy, see Holt, *Rise and Fall of the American Whig Party,* 67, 69–70, and 127–36; Brown, *Politic and Statesmanship,* 61, 64, 169, 187–88; and Howe, *Political Culture of the American Whigs,* 8, 13, 16, 31–32.

5. Buenger, *Secession and the Union in Texas,* 22–26; Holt, *Rise and Fall of the American Whig Party,* 957, 982–83.

6. Potter, *Impending Crisis,* 167–77, 238–41; Sandbo, "Beginnings of the Secession Movement," 48–49; Campbell, *Gone to Texas,* 236.

7. Haley, *Sam Houston,* 322.

8. Houston quoted in Haley, *Sam Houston,* 322; Sandbo, "Beginnings of the Secession Movement," 50–56.

9. Haley, *Sam Houston,* 341; Holt, *Rise and Fall of the American Whig Party,* 957; Holbert, "Public Career of James Webb Throckmorton," 9–10.

10. Smallwood, *History of Smith County,* 1:138–39.

11. "Proceedings of the State Convention of the Democratic Party of the State of Texas, which Assembled at Waco, Monday 4, 1857," TSL. H. R. Runnels was the convention's unanimous choice as the Democratic nominee for governor. This would have included Throckmorton's vote, but the actual vote was not included in the printed proceedings.

12. "Alexander W. Terrell's Reminiscence, 1912," 11, Terrell Papers.

13. Baum, *Shattering of Texas Unionism,* 10. For election returns broken down by counties, see Kingston, Attlesey, and Crawford, *Texas Almanac's Political History,* 54–57; Campbell, *Gone to Texas,* 237; and Sandbo, "Beginnings of the Secession Movement," 56–57.

14. James Swindells to Throckmorton, November 25, 1857, Throckmorton Papers, TSL; Texas Senate, *Journal,* Seventh Biennial Session, 368–72, 428; Texas Senate, *Journal,* Eighth Legislature, Extra Session, 44–45.

15. Throckmorton to John H. Reagan, August 17, 1859, Reagan Collection; Throckmorton to Reagan, September 9, 1859, Reagan Collection; Throckmorton to B. H. Epperson, August 18, 1859, Epperson Papers, Center for American History (CAH). Evidence of Throckmorton's support of Reagan is found in these letters.

16. Reagan, *Memoirs with Special Reference to Secession,* 73; Sandbo, "Beginnings of the Secession Movement," 59–63.

17. "Governor's Message to the Seventh Texas Legislature, January 20, 1858," Texas Senate, *Journal,* Seventh Biennial Session, 373–78; Elliott, *Leathercoat,* 41.

18. "Governor's Message to the Seventh Texas Legislature, January 22, 1858," Texas Senate, *Journal,* Seventh Biennial Session, 392–93.

19. "Governor's Message to the Seventh Texas Legislature, February 4, 1858," Texas Senate, *Journal,* Seventh Biennial Session, 529.

20. "Governor's Message to the Seventh Texas Legislature, January 26, 1858," Texas Senate, *Journal,* Seventh Biennial Session, 433.

21. Ibid., 434.

22. *Texas State Gazette,* April 30, 1859.

23. *Austin Southern Intelligencer,* June 15, 1859; *Texas State Gazette,* May 7, 1859, and May, 14, 1859; Elliott, *Leathercoat,* 42.

24. *Austin Southern Intelligencer,* May 11, 1859, and May 18, 1859. See these issues for commentary on the candidates nominated by the Houston Convention and for the views of those who opposed Runnels and favored Houston's candidacy.

25. Sandbo, "Beginnings of the Secession Movement," 63–65.

26. "Gen. Houston All Right on the Railroad Question," Broadside Collection, TSL.

27. *Austin Southern Intelligencer,* May 25, 1859.

28. *Texas State Gazette,* May 28, 1859.

29. *Austin Southern Intelligencer,* May 11, 1859.

30. Timmons, "Texas on the Road to Secession," 366; Elliott, *Leathercoat,* 43.

31. Texas Senate, *Journal,* Eighth Legislature, 44–47; Baum, *Shattering of Texas Unionism,* 10. For a breakdown of the vote by counties, see Kingston, Attlesey, and Crawford, *Texas Almanac's Political History,* 54–57. Baum makes an important observation about the 1859 gubernatorial election, stating that Houston's victory in part was attributable to the his success in winning new voters in the state and to Runnels's embrace of ultra-southern policies.

32. Elliott, *Leathercoat,* 42–43.

33. Throckmorton to Reagan, August 17, 1859, Reagan Collection; Elliott, *Leathercoat,* 43.

34. Throckmorton to Reagan, August 17, 1859, Reagan Collection; Elliott, *Leathercoat,* 43.

35. Throckmorton to Reagan, August 17, 1859, Reagan Collection; Elliott, *Leathercoat,* 43.

36. Throckmorton to Epperson, August 18, 1859, Epperson Papers, CAH.

37. Ibid.

38. Throckmorton to Reagan, September 9, 1859, Reagan Collection.

39. Ibid.

40. Ibid.; Elliott, *Leathercoat,* 45.

41. Throckmorton to Epperson, September 13, 1859, Epperson Papers, TSL; Elliott, *Leathercoat,* 44.

42. Buenger, *Secession and the Union in Texas,* 45–58.

43. Ibid., 45–46; Sandbo, "Beginnings of the Secession Movement," 68.

44. Smallwood, *History of Smith County,* 1:151–53.

45. Ibid.; Howell, *Henderson County, Texas,* 60.

46. Smallwood, *History of Smith County,* 1:153. For a detailed discussion of the Texas hysteria caused by the Texas fires, see Reynolds, *Editors Make War,* 97–117.

47. Sandbo, "First Session of the Secession Convention," 163–65.

48. Kingston, Attlesey, and Crawford, *Texas Almanac's Political History,* 75; Potter, *Impending Crisis,* 443–44; Sandbo, "First Session of the Secession Convention," 167–68. Lincoln received 1,864,735 votes; Douglas, 979,425 votes; Breckinridge, 669,472 votes; and Bell, 576,414 votes. Lincoln carried eighteen free states with 180 electoral votes; Breckenridge carried eleven slave states with 72 electoral votes; Bell carried the states of Kentucky, Tennessee, and Virginia with 39 electoral votes; and Douglas carried Missouri with 12 electoral votes. Breckenridge, usually considered the secession candidate, received 47,887 votes in Texas to 15,472 for Bell, the Constitutional Union candidate. Neither Lincoln nor Douglas received any votes in Texas.

49. Winkler, *Journal of the Secession Convention,* 9–13.

50. McCaslin, *Tainted Breeze,* 32; Timmons, "Texas on the Road to Secession," 577; Elliott, *Leathercoat,* 45–47; Sandbo, "First Secession of the Secession Convention of Texas," 178–80.

51. *Dallas Herald,* January 2, 1861, January 16, 1861, and January 23, 1861; Elliott, *Leathercoat,* 47–48.

52. U.S. Bureau of the Census, *Eighth Census, Schedule I,* 117; Stambaugh and Stambaugh, *History of Collin County,* 52, 82, 225, 252. The census reveals that Barnett owned real estate valued at $10,000 and that the value of his personal estate was $4,000. Barnett was forty-one years old when the census for Collin County was taken. The Stambaughs' study reveals that Barnett was a prominent businessman who came to Collin County in 1843. The Stambaughs also reveal that Barnett owned three slaves in the early 1860s.

53. *Dallas Herald,* January 16, 1861.

54. *Dallas Herald,* February 20, 1861; Throckmorton to Louis T. Wigfall, December 30, 1866, Throckmorton Papers, CAH; Elliott, *Leathercoat,* 48–49; Holbert, "Public Career of James Webb Throckmorton, 35–36; DeShields, *They Sat in High Places,* 271; Hendrickson, *Chief Executives of Texas,* 88.

55. *Austin Southern Intelligencer,* January 23, 1861; Elliott, *Leathercoat,* 49; Nunn, *Ten Texans in Gray,* 171.

56. Holbert, "Public Career of James Webb Throckmorton," 31–32.

57. Texas Senate, *Journal,* Eighth Legislature, Extra Session, 37; Elliott, *Leathercoat,* 50.

58. Owens, "Presidential Reconstruction in Texas," 156–57.

59. Texas Senate, *Journal,* Eighth Legislature, Extra Session, 45–46; Elliott, *Leathercoat,* 51.

60. Texas Senate, *Journal,* Eighth Legislature, Extra Session, 49–50; Spaw, *Texas Senate,* 1:319; Elliott, *Leathercoat,* 51–52.

61. Wooten, *Comprehensive History of Texas,* 99–103; Winkler, *Journal of the Secession Convention,* 46; Elliott, *Leathercoat,* 52–53; Wooster, "Analysis of the Membership," 322–35.

62. Winkler, *Journal of the Secession Convention,* 48–49; Wooster, *Secession Conventions of the South,* 130; Elliott, *Leathercoat,* 54–55; Chapin, "Presidential Reconstruction in Texas," 12–13; Holbert, "Public Career of James Webb Throckmorton," 36; Wooster, *Texas and Texans in the Civil War,* 13–14. For more information on the individuals who voted against secession in the convention, see Evelyn Calhoun Miller, "Seven Shouted

'No' When Secession Vote Taken Here," *Austin American-Statesman,* July 19, 1936, Throckmorton Papers, TSL.

63. Winkler, *Journal of the Secession Convention,* 48–49; Wooster, *Secession Conventions of the South,* 63–65.

64. Winkler, *Journal of the Secession Convention,* 48–49; Wooster, *Secession Conventions of the South,* 58–59, 85; *Clarksville Northern Standard,* April 20, 1861; Elliott, *Leathercoat,* 55–56.

65. "Proclamation by the Governor of the State of Texas, February 9, 1861," Broadside Collection, TSL; *Clarksville Northern Standard,* February 9, 1861; Ledbetter, "Slavery, Fear, and Disunion," 272–73.

66. *Dallas Herald,* February 20, 1861; *Austin Southern Intelligencer,* February 13, 1861.

67. *Austin Southern Intelligencer,* February 13, 1861.

68. Ibid.

69. Ibid.; Holbert, "Public Career of James Webb Throckmorton," 27–28, 37.

70. *Austin Southern Intelligencer,* February 13, 1861; McCaslin, *Tainted Breeze,* 33.

71. McCaslin, *Tainted Breeze,* 33–34.

72. Winkler, *Journal of the Secession Convention,* 48–49; Wooster, *Secession Conventions of the South,* 88–90, 133; Elliott, *Leathercoat,* 58; Stambaugh and Stambaugh, *History of Collin County,* 64; Wooster, *Texas and Texans in the Civil War,* 21; Buenger, "Stilling the Voice of Reason," 93–94, 96; Timmons, "Texas on the Road to Secession," 722–24; Ledbetter, "Slavery, Fear, and Disunion," 253–54; Timmons, "Referendum in Texas." Wooster in *Secession Conventions of the South* reveals that the figures in Winkler's volume were incorrect, but that the corrected figures appeared later in the *Texas State Gazette,* March 23, 1861. Both Wooster in *Texas and Texans in the Civil War* and Buenger reveal that one of the strongest areas of antisecession support came from the Red River counties. These scholars suggest that several factors contributed to the opposition vote in this area; most importantly, the inhabitants in this area were nonslaveholders and were small farmers from the Upper South or Midwest states where support for slavery and other institutions of the South was not as strident as that found in the Lower South states. Also, the authors point out that the inhabitants would be exposed to Indian raids if the federal troops were removed from the string of forts north of the Red River. Timmons reveals why Texas voters overwhelmingly supported secession: "the secessionists had a plan; they were ably led by a group in high position, though the movers of secession were generally outside the government; they controlled the important instrument of propaganda—the leading newspapers of the State and the State Democratic party machinery. They widely publicized their position in the press, in their private correspondence, in speeches, and in secessionist literature which was broadcast over the state—playing on the fears, emotions, and prejudices of a frightened people. They manipulated the election, and they coerced and silenced their opponents." For a discussion of potential voter fraud in the referendum election, see Baum, "Pinpointing Apparent Fraud in the 1861 Texas Secession Referendum."

73. *Dallas Herald,* March 20, 1861; *Houston Daily Post,* August 3, 1889; Elliott, *Leathercoat,* 58–59.

74. Haley, *Sam Houston,* 392–93; Sinclair, "Crossroads of Conviction," 186; Elliott, *Leathercoat,* 59–60; Holbert, "Public Career of James Webb Throckmorton," 41–42; Gould, *Alexander Watkins Terrell,* 31.

75. "Proclamation of Governor Sam Houston to the People of Texas in May, 1861, upon the Question of Texas Secession," broadside, TSL; Holbert, "Public Career of James Webb Throckmorton," 41; Timmons, "Texas on the Road to Secession," 730–31.

76. *McKinney Messenger,* October 18, 1861; Wooster, *Texas and Texans in the Civil War,* 23.

77. Wooster, *Texas and Texans in the Civil War,* 23.

78. Ibid.

79. Ibid.

80. Address delivered before the International Fair Association at San Antonio, Throckmorton Papers, TSL.

81. Ibid.

82. Ibid.

83. Ibid.

84. Ibid.

85. Ibid.

86. Ibid.

87. Baum, *Shattering of Texas Unionism,* 84; Baggett, "Rise and Fall of the Texas Radicals," 24–25; Griffin, "Connecticut Yankee in Texas," 167; Massey, "History of Collin County," 73; Crofts, *Reluctant Confederates,* 104–9. Crofts's work is the best single-volume study of Unionists in the Upper South written to date.

## CHAPTER FOUR

1. *Dallas Herald,* March 27, 1861; Baggett, "Rise and Fall of the Texas Radicals," 24–25; Lynch, "J. W. Throckmorton"; Owens, "Presidential Reconstruction in Texas," 156–57; Holbert, "Public Career of James Webb Throckmorton," 35–36; Elliott, *Leathercoat,* 63. For a general discussion of Unionist arguments in the Upper South states, see Crofts, *Reluctant Confederates,* 104–9. For a general discussion of Texans who chose to serve in the federal military, see Smyrl, "Texas in the Union Army."

2. Throckmorton to B. H. Epperson, January 19, 1862, Letters of Governor Throckmorton, CAH.

3. Schaefer, "Locational Choice in the Antebellum South," 163–64.

4. McPherson, *Battle Cry of Freedom,* 264–75.

5. Throckmorton to Epperson, January 19, 1862, CAH.

6. *Dallas Herald,* May 8, 1861, and July 22, 1865; Elliot, *Leathercoat,* 66.

7. McPherson, *Battle Cry of Freedom,* 274–78; Baum, *Shattering of Texas Unionism,* 84; Griffin, "Connecticut Yankee in Texas," 167; Elliott, *Leathercoat,* 64–66; Buenger "Stilling the Voice of Reason," 96. Buenger shows the close connection of North Texas to the Upper South states.

8. *Dallas Herald,* April 17, 1861; *Clarksville Northern Standard,* May 11, 1861; Elliott, *Leathercoat,* 64.

9. *Clarksville Northern Standard,* May 11, 1861; Elliott, *Leathercoat,* 64.

10. *Dallas Herald,* May 8, 1861; Jewett, *Texas in the Confederacy,* 74–75; Shook, "Federal Occupation and Administration," 162.

11. Throckmorton to Hamilton Bee, September 4, 1866, Throckmorton Letter Book, CAH.

12. *Texas Almanac, 1861,* 11–18. The almanac clearly shows that Texans in general felt that the federal government threatened the institution of slavery.

13. *Dallas Herald,* May 8, 1861; Alex Johnston to Governor Clark, April 30, 1861, Clark Records, TSL; Jewett, *Texas in the Confederacy,* 74–75; Smith, "Limits of Dissent and Loyalty in Texas," 25–26; Nunn, *Ten Texans in Gray,* 84.

14. John Crockett to Governor Clark, May 1, 1861, and Crockett to Governor Clark, May 5, 1861, Edward Clark Records, TSL.

15. Nunn, *Ten More Texans in Gray,* 173. Nunn explains that the Texans did not know that on April 16, 1861, Gen. Winfield Scott ordered U.S. Col. W. H. Emory to abandon all three forts and withdraw to Fort Leavenworth, Kan.

16. *Dallas Herald,* May 8, 1861. For the Union perspective on the abandonment of Fort Washita, Fort Arbuckle, and Fort Cobb, see *War of the Rebellion,* series 1, 1:648; Massey, "History of Collin County," 73; Holbert, "Public Career of James Webb Throckmorton," 44–45; Chapin, "Presidential Reconstruction in Texas," 15; Stambaugh and Stambaugh, *History of Collin County,* 64; McCaslin, *Tainted Breeze,* 42.

17. *Dallas Herald,* June 5, 1861, and June 19, 1861. The Union forces had retreated from the three forts in the Indian Territory that were closest to the Texas border. Also, Colonel Young reported that the Native Americans in the Indian Territory were currently involved in negotiating a peace with the Confederate authorities.

18. *Clarksville Northern Standard,* May 11, 1861.

19. *Clarksville Northern Standard,* June 1, 1861.

20. Ibid.; Smith, "Limits of Dissent and Loyalty in Texas," 78–79.

21. *Dallas Herald,* June 19, 1861.

22. Ibid.

23. *Clarksville Northern Standard,* June 20, 1861; J. W. Throckmorton to Governor Clark, July 9, 1861, Clark Records, TSL.

24. *Clarksville Northern Standard,* July 20, 1861.

25. *Clarksville Northern Standard,* July 13, 1861; *Dallas Herald,* July 10, 1861.

26. Nunn, *Ten Texans in Gray,* 26.

27. Throckmorton to Governor Clark, July 9, 1861, TSL.

28. *Dallas Herald,* August 28, 1861.

29. J. W. Throckmorton to Governor Clark, September 8, 1861, Clark Records, TSL. This letter indicates that Throckmorton's company of volunteers served in the Indian Territory between June 22, 1861, and August 31, 1861. Smith, "Limits of Dissent and Loyalty in Texas," 135–36.

30. *Dallas Herald,* September 11, 1861; *Supplement to the Official Records of the Union and Confederate Armies,* serial no. 79, pt. 2 (Record of Events), 752, 766; Elliott, *Leathercoat,* 66–70; Holbert, "Public Career of James Webb Throckmorton," 45.

31. *Supplement to the Official Records,* serial no. 79, pt. 2,766; *Dallas Herald,* September 25, 1861.

32. *Dallas Herald,* October 30, 1861; Nunn, *Ten More Texans in Gray,* 173.

33. Nunn, *Ten More Texans in Gray,* 174.

34. Carter, *As It Was,* 103–4. For a more detailed account of the Battle of Chustenahlah, see Hale, *Third Texas Cavalry,* 70–84.

35. *War of the Rebellion,* series 1, 8:27–28; Holbert, "Public Career of James Webb Throckmorton," 46.

36. *Dallas Herald,* January 15, 1862; Carter, *As It Was,* 104; Nunn, *Ten More Texans in Gray,* 174.

37. *Dallas Herald,* January 22, 1862; Holbert, "Public Career of James Webb Throckmorton," 46.

38. *War of the Rebellion,* series 1, 8:303. For a comprehensive examination of the Battle of Pea Ridge, see Hale, *Third Texas Cavalry,* 85–100; Holbert, "Public Career of James Webb Throckmorton," 46.

39. Holbert, "Public Career of James Webb Throckmorton," 46–47. General Van Dorn was partly blamed for the Confederate loss at Pea Ridge, and it is likely that Colonel Stone no longer maintained respect for Van Dorn's abilities as a military leader. For more information on the controversy, see Hale, *Third Texas Cavalry,* 98–100.

40. Holbert, "Public Career of James Webb Throckmorton," 46–47; Elliott, *Leathercoat,* 73; Lynch, "J. W. Throckmorton"; Nunn, *Ten More Texans in Gray,* 174.

41. Nunn, *Ten More Texans in Gray,* 174.

42. McCaslin, *Tainted Breeze,* 96; Elliott, *Leathercoat,* 73–74.

43. *Dallas Herald,* September 20, 1862; Elliott, *Leathercoat,* 73–74; Nunn, *Ten More Texans in Gray,* 174.

44. *Dallas Herald,* September 20, 1862.

45. McCaslin, *Tainted Breeze,* 39.

46. McCaslin, *Tainted Breeze,* 96; Wooster, *Texas and Texans in the Civil War,* 115; Wooster and Wooster, "A People at War," 10–11; Smith, "Limits of Dissent and Loyalty in Texas," 134–38; Elliott, *Leathercoat,* 74–75.

47. Wooster, *Texas and Texans in the Civil War,* 115; Elliott, *Leathercoat,* 75.

48. McCaslin, *Tainted Breeze,* 105–9.

49. Ibid., 108–9; *Clarksville Northern Standard,* November 1, 1862.

50. J. W. Throckmorton to Governor Lubbock, October 25, 1862, Lubbock Records, TSL; McCaslin, *Tainted Breeze,* 115–16.

51. Throckmorton to Governor Lubbock, October 25, 1862, TSL.

52. Ibid. Throckmorton would write Lubbock again regarding the matter of frontier defense in January 1863. See extract of letter from Throckmorton to Governor Lubbock, January 4, 1863, Lubbock Records, TSL. The January letter reiterates the problems of maintaining troops on the North Texas frontier.

53. Governor Lubbock tended to support the Confederate conscription law of 1862 and was not in favor of increasing the strength of the frontier regiments.

54. Holbert, "Public Career of James Webb Throckmorton," 47.

55. *Dallas Herald,* February 25, 1863, and March 25, 1863.

56. *Dallas Herald,* April 8, 15, 29, 1863, and May 13, 1863.

57. *Supplement to the Official Records,* serial no. 80, pt. 2, 354; *Dallas Herald,* June 10 and 24, 1863, and August 5, 1863; *Houston Tri-Weekly Telegraph,* July 10, 17, and 21,

1863; Holbert, "Public Career of James Webb Throckmorton," 47; Elliott, *Leathercoat,* 76–78.

58. McCaslin, "Wheat Growers in the Cotton Confederacy," 534–35; Roth, "Civil War Frontier Defense Challenges," 31.

59. *Houston Tri-Weekly Telegraph,* November 2, 1863; *Texas State Gazette,* October 28, 1863; Elliott, *Leathercoat,* 78–79.

60. *War of the Rebellion,* series 1, 26:352.

61. Day, *Senate Journal of the Tenth Legislature, Regular Session,* 95–99.

62. Gammel, *Laws of Texas,* 5:677–78; *Texas Almanac, 1862,* 47; *Texas Almanac, 1864,* 15; Day, *Senate Journal of the Tenth Legislature, First Called Session,* 8; Elliott, *Leathercoat,* 79–80.

63. For an overview of the frontier defense policy of Gov. Francis R. Lubbock, Murrah's predecessor, see *Houston Tri-Weekly Telegraph,* November 9, 1863; and Day, *Senate Journal of the Tenth Legislature, Regular Session,* 15–17, 47–55. For a brief but thorough discussion on the conscription controversy, see Smith, "Conscription and Conflict on the Texas Frontier."

64. Day, *Senate Journal of the Tenth Legislature, First Called Session,* 9–18; Yearns, *Confederate Governors,* 206. The Frontier Regiment was officially renamed the Mounted Regiment, Texas State Troops, in early 1863 during the Lubbock administration.

65. Day, *Senate Journal of the Tenth Legislature, First Called Session,* 17.

66. Ibid., 8–17; *War of the Rebellion,* series 1, 34, pt. 3:739–41; Yearns, *Confederate Governors,* 211.

67. *War of the Rebellion,* series 1, 34, pt. 3:779–80.

68. Ibid., 747–49; Yearns, *Confederate Governors,* 211; Nunn, *Ten Texans in Gray,* 129–30. For a thorough discussion of the problems that existed among frontier settlers, state officials, and the Confederate authorities, see Sutherland, *Guerrillas, Unionists, and Violence,* 104–47.

69. *Texas Almanac, 1864,* 31–32.

70. Throckmorton to B. H. Epperson, November 3, 1864, Letters of Governor Throckmorton, CAH; Shook, "Federal Occupation and Administration," 44–45.

71. Shook, "Federal Occupation and Administration," 44–45; Holbert, "Public Career of James Webb Throckmorton," 48–50; Nunn, *Ten More Texans in Gray,* 176; McCaslin, *Tainted Breeze,* 146–47.

72. Throckmorton to Epperson, November 3, 1864, CAH.

73. Ibid.

74. *War of the Rebellion,* series 1, 34, pt. 2:1011.

75. *Texas Almanac, 1864,* 43. The First Military District of the Frontier Organization included the following counties: Wise, Parker, Cooke, Montague, Jack, Palo Pinto, Stephens, and Young.

76. Sutherland, *Guerrillas, Unionists, and Violence,* 129–30; Overfelt, "Defense of the Texas Frontier," 64; Nunn, *Ten More Texans in Gray,* 177.

77. Sutherland, *Guerrillas, Unionists, and Violence,* 130–31. The Elm Creek raid, in Young County in October 1864, was one of the largest and most destructive raids witnessed on the Texas frontier.

78. *Texas Almanac, 1864,* 43; Nunn, *Ten More Texans in Gray,* 177.

79. J. W. Throckmorton to John Burke, February 22, 1865, Burke Records, TSL; Wooster, *Texas and Texans in the Civil War,* 153; Sutherland, *Guerrillas, Unionists, and Violence,* 136; Smith, "Elm Creek Raid," 134–35.

80. Throckmorton to Burke, January 29, 1865, Burke Records, TSL; Elliott, *Leathercoat,* 86–91; Smith, *Frontier Defense in the Civil War,* 138.

81. Throckmorton to Epperson, February 3, 1865, Letters of Governor Throckmorton, CAH.

82. Ibid.

83. Throckmorton to Epperson, March 12, 1865, Letters of Governor Throckmorton, CAH.

84. For Throckmorton's support of Reconstruction, see Throckmorton to Josiah Crosby, March 19, 1865, Letters of Governor Throckmorton, CAH.

85. Throckmorton to Epperson, April 6, 1865, Letters of Governor Throckmorton, CAH; *War of the Rebellion,* series 1, 48, pt. 2:1266–69; Nunn, *Ten More Texans in Gray,* 177; Lynch, "J. W. Throckmorton"; Elliott, *Leathercoat,* 93–96; Holbert, "Public Career of James Webb Throckmorton," 50–51; Smith, *Frontier Defense,* 142–43. For more on the magnitude of Indian depredations on the frontier, see Overfelt, "Defense of the Texas Frontier," 76–77.

86. *War of the Rebellion,* series 1, 48, pt. 2:1266–80.

87. *War of the Rebellion,* series 1, 48, pt. 2:1317–18.

88. Ibid.; Smith, *Frontier Defense,* 143; Elliott, *Leathercoat,* 93–96.

89. Overfelt, "Defense of the Texas Frontier," 77–78.

90. *War of the Rebellion,* series 1, 48, pt. 1:297–99; Nunn, *Ten Texans in Gray,* 133–34; Nunn, *Ten More Texans in Gray,* 177; Elliott, *Leathercoat,* 99.

## CHAPTER FIVE

1. Owens, "Presidential Reconstruction in Texas," 158. For a detailed examination of the differences between President Johnson and Congress over the issues of Reconstruction, see Foner, *Reconstruction,* 177–261.

2. Smallwood, *Time of Hope, Time of Despair,* 30–31; Richter, "The Army and the Negro," 11; Chapin, "Presidential Reconstruction in Texas," 5–6. Richter points out that many white Texans were determined to keep the freedmen in an inferior social and economic position.

3. Campbell, *Grass-Roots Reconstruction in Texas,* 7–26; Spaw, *Texas Senate,* 2:54.

4. Waller, *Colossal Hamilton of Texas,* 57–58; Sheridan, *Personal Memoirs,* 2:229–30; Hendrickson, *Chief Executives of Texas,* 85; Elliott, *Leathercoat,* 100.

5. Waller, *Colossal Hamilton of Texas,* 65–66; Baggett, "Rise and Fall of the Texas Radicals," 42; Elliott, *Leathercoat,* 101–2.

6. Throckmorton to Epperson, August 6, 1865, Letters of Governor Throckmorton, CAH; Chapin, "Presidential Reconstruction in Texas," 31–32; Owens, "Presidential Reconstruction in Texas," 118; McCaslin, *Tainted Breeze,* 162.

7. Throckmorton to Epperson, August 6, 1865, Letters of Governor Throckmorton, CAH; McCaslin, *Tainted Breeze,* 161–62; Moneyhon, *Republicanism in Reconstruction Texas,* 28–29.

8. Throckmorton to A. J. Hamilton, August 1865, Hamilton Records, TSL; Ramsdell, *Reconstruction in Texas,* 83–84.

9. *Dallas Herald,* January 13 and 20, 1866; Chapin, "Presidential Reconstruction in Texas," 47–48; Owens, "Presidential Reconstruction in Texas," 123; Massey, "History of Collin County," 74; Ramsdell, "Presidential Reconstruction in Texas," 300–317; Elliott, *Leathercoat,* 103–4.

10. Ramsdell, *Reconstruction in Texas,* 89.

11. *Dallas Herald,* January 27, 1866.

12. Reagan, *Memoirs,* 286–95. The letter is reprinted in Reagan's memoirs as appendix C.

13. Throckmorton to Epperson, January 21, 1866, Letters of Governor Throckmorton, CAH; Elliott, *Leathercoat,* 104–5.

14. Throckmorton to Epperson, January 21, 1866, CAH.

15. Ibid.

16. Ibid.

17. *Dallas Herald,* February 17, 1866; Moneyhon, *Republicanism in Reconstruction Texas,* 25, 34; Owens, "Presidential Reconstruction in Texas," 125; Hale, "Political Leadership in Texas During Reconstruction," 11; Ramsdell, *Reconstruction in Texas,* 89–90; Chapin, "Presidential Reconstruction in Texas," 57–58; Holbert, "Public Career of James Webb Throckmorton," 55–56; Stambaugh and Stambaugh, *History of Collin County,* 207; Elliott, *Leathercoat,* 105–6.

18. *Houston Telegraph* quoted in *Dallas Herald,* March 3, 1866.

19. *Tyler Journal* quoted in *Dallas Herald,* March 3, 1866.

20. *New Orleans Picayune* quoted in *Dallas Herald,* March 3, 1866.

21. "Message of Governor A. J. Hamilton to the Texas State Convention, February 10, 1866," Broadside Collection, CAH.

22. *Dallas Herald,* February 24, 1866.

23. Good, "John Henninger Reagan," 209; Elliott, *Leathercoat,* 105–8.

24. *Dallas Herald,* February 17, 1866; Elliott, *Leathercoat,* 108–9.

25. Brockman, "Railroads, Radicals, and Democrats," 11–13; Fowler, "Origins of the Texas Railroad Commission," 24; Elliott, *Leathercoat,* 110.

26. Elliott, *Leathercoat,* 110–11.

27. Ibid., 111–12.

28. *Dallas Herald,* March 24, 1866; Gray, "Edmund J. Davis," 88; Elliott, *Leathercoat,* 112–13.

29. *Dallas Herald,* March 10, 1866; Elliott, *Leathercoat,* 113.

30. Chapin, "Presidential Reconstruction in Texas," 84; Elliott, *Leathercoat,* 114. Elliott states, "Though he felt that the honor of Texas almost demanded a refusal to send men to Congress under such circumstances, he was not willing to advocate such a radical policy. In his heart he was one of the bitterest against the radical group and the so-called designated 'damned Yankees' in the convention or in Texas; but his good sense put him in a compromising attitude, and he never went as far as he would have gone had it not been for his desire to create harmony and to make political friends in both parties."

31. Ibid., 115–16.

32. Ibid., 116.

33. Throckmorton to Epperson, April 17, 1866, Letters of Governor Throckmorton, CAH.

34. Ibid.

35. Ibid.

36. Throckmorton to Epperson, April 17, 1866, and April 25, 1866, Letters of Governor Throckmorton, CAH; *Dallas Herald,* April 14, 1866, May 5, 19, and 26, 1866; Good, "John Henninger Reagan," 209; Moneyhon, *Republicanism in Reconstruction Texas,* 44; Owens, "Presidential Reconstruction in Texas," 131; Nunn, *Ten More Texans in Gray,* 179; Ramsdell, *Reconstruction in Texas,* 108–09; Chapin, "Presidential Reconstruction in Texas," 84–89; Holbert, "Public Career of James Webb Throckmorton," 65–66; Gray, "Edmund J. Davis," 94; Elliott, *Leathercoat,* 119–25.

37. Baggett, "Rise and Fall of the Texas Radicals," 51–52; Owens, "Presidential Reconstruction in Texas," 134; Ramsdell, *Reconstruction in Texas,* 111; Smallwood, *Time of Hope, Time of Despair,* 130; Baum, *Shattering of Texas Unionism,* 145–46; Holbert, "Public Career of James Webb Throckmorton," 75–77; Elliott, *Leathercoat,* 125–29.

38. Throckmorton to Epperson, May 30, 1866, Letters of Governor Throckmorton, CAH; *Dallas Herald,* June 16, 1866; Nieman, "Andrew Johnson," 399–401; Moore, "Radical Reconstruction," 21; Moneyhon, *Republicanism in Reconstruction Texas,* 44–49; Baggett, "Rise and Fall of the Texas Radicals," 51–53; Owens, "Presidential Reconstruction in Texas," 132–34; Ramsdell, *Reconstruction in Texas,* 11–12; Kingston, Attlesey, and Crawford, *Texas Almanac's Political History,* 61; Smallwood, *Time of Hope, Time of Despair,* 130; Baum, *Shattering of Texas Unionism,* 146–47; Holbert, "Public Career of James Webb Throckmorton," 68–78; Ramsdell, "Presidential Reconstruction in Texas," 204–7; Elliott, *Leathercoat,* 125–29.

39. *Dallas Herald,* August 18, 1866; Ramsdell, *Reconstruction in Texas,* 113; Holbert, "Public Career of James Webb Throckmorton," 79.

40. *Dallas Herald,* August 18, 1866; "Transcription of Inaugural Ceremonies of James W. Throckmorton, August 13, 1866," Throckmorton Collection, CAH.

41. *New York Times,* August 16, 1866; *Dallas Herald,* August 18, 1866; "Transcription of Inaugural Ceremonies," Throckmorton Collection, CAH.

42. *New York Times,* August 16, 1866; *Dallas Herald,* August 18, 1866; "Transcription of Inaugural Ceremonies," Throckmorton Collection, CAH.

43. *Dallas Herald,* August 25, 1866; "Transcription of Inaugural Ceremonies," Throckmorton Collection, CAH; *New York Times,* August 22, 1866; Owens, "Presidential Reconstruction in Texas," 134, 159; Ramsdell, *Reconstruction in Texas,* 113, 126; Chapin, "Presidential Reconstruction in Texas," 119–20; Holbert, "Public Career of James Webb Throckmorton," 80–81.

44. Roberts, "Experiences of an Unrecognized Senator," 87–89; Richter, *Army in Texas,* 57; Moneyhon, *Republicanism in Reconstruction Texas,* 49–50; Ramsdell, *Reconstruction in Texas,* 115–18; Holbert, "Public Career of James Webb Throckmorton," 81–82.

45. Crouch, "All the Vile Passions"; Moneyhon, *Republicanism in Reconstruction Texas,* 49–50; Smallwood, *Time of Hope, Time of Despair,* 130–31; Baum, *Shattering*

*of Texas Unionism,* 160–61. Crouch's work is the single best study on the Texas Black Codes.

46. Richter, *Army in Texas,* 59–61.

47. *Dallas Herald,* September 1, 1866.

48. Sheridan, *Personal Memoirs,* 2:232–33.

49. *Dallas Herald,* September 1, 1866.

50. Shook, "Federal Occupation and Administration," 167.

51. Throckmorton to J. J. Diamond, September 12, 1866, Throckmorton Letter Book, CAH.

## CHAPTER SIX

1. *Dallas Herald,* October 13, 1866; Ramsdell, *Reconstruction in Texas,* 126. The best general account of Throckmorton's role in Reconstruction Texas is Carl Moneyhon, *Texas After the Civil War: The Struggle of Reconstruction.*

2. Throckmorton to Col. W. W. Cochran, E. Stewart, and others, August 8, 1866, Throckmorton Letter Book, CAH; Parker, "Indian Affairs and the Frontier of Texas," 33–34.

3. Parker, "Indian Affairs and the Frontier," 23–24; Ramsdell, *Reconstruction in Texas,* 136–37; Holbert, "Public Career of James Webb Throckmorton," 83–84; Elliott, *Leathercoat,* 133–34; *Dallas Herald,* August 18, 1866; "Transcription of Inaugural Ceremonies," Throckmorton Collection, CAH.

4. Elliott, *Leathercoat,* 134.

5. T. Smiley to Hon. J. W. Throckmorton, August 14, 1866, Throckmorton Records, TSL.

6. T. L. Jackson and others to Governor J. W. Throckmorton, August 15, 1866, Throckmorton Records, TSL.

7. T. Smiley to Governor J. W. Throckmorton, August 16, 1866, Throckmorton Records, TSL.

8. For a statistical analysis of the violence perpetrated against the freedmen and white Unionists, see Cantrell, "Racial Violence and Reconstruction Politics," 333–55.

9. Parker, "Indian Affairs and the Frontier," 15, 29–30; Chapin, "Presidential Reconstruction in Texas," 121; Elliott, *Leathercoat,* 135.

10. Major General Wright to Throckmorton, August 14, 1866, Throckmorton Records, TSL; Richter, *Army in Texas,* 54.

11. *Dallas Herald,* October 6, 1866. This issue of the *Herald* contains extracts from letters received by Governor Throckmorton. The governor apparently allowed the correspondent to view a letter sent to General Sheridan that contained copies of letters that the governor had received since the beginning of his administration, regarding Indian depredations on the frontier.

12. Throckmorton to President Johnson, August 25, 1866, Throckmorton Collection, CAH; Ramsdell, *Reconstruction in Texas,* 137–38; Chapin, "Presidential Reconstruction in Texas," 119–20; Holbert, "Public Career of James Webb Throckmorton," 101; Elliott, *Leathercoat,* 136–37.

13. Major General Wright to Throckmorton, August 21, 1866, Throckmorton Records, TSL.

14. Major General Sheridan to Throckmorton, September 3, 1866, Throckmorton Records, TSL; Richter, *Army in Texas,* 67; Morris, *Sheridan,* 276–77.

15. *New York Times,* January 17, 1867; Spaw, *Texas Senate,* 2:67.

16. Baylor to Throckmorton, September 1, 1866, Throckmorton Records, TSL; Elliott, *Leathercoat,* 138–39.

17. J. J. Cureton to Throckmorton, September 2, 1866, Throckmorton Records, TSL.

18. Throckmorton to Capt. J. J. Cureton, September 8, 1866, Throckmorton Collection, CAH.

19. J. F. Mosby to T. F. Barrets, September 2, 1866, Throckmorton Records, TSL. This letter was undoubtedly forwarded to the governor's office by the recipient.

20. Throckmorton to Major General Sheridan, September 27, 1866, and Throckmorton to E. M. Stanton, September 29, 1866, Throckmorton Collection, CAH.

21. General Sheridan to Throckmorton, October 16, 1866, Throckmorton Records, TSL; Elliott, *Leathercoat,* 138–39. Sheridan's letter to Throckmorton makes reference to the governor's request that colored troops be removed from the interior of the state. The general informed Throckmorton that federal troops would be placed in Texas wherever they were needed without discrimination between colored and white troops.

22. Throckmorton to General Getty, October 3, 1866, and Throckmorton to U. S. Grant, October 6, 1866, Throckmorton Collection, CAH; Elliott, *Leathercoat,* 139–40. Also, see Grant to Throckmorton, October 20, 1866, Throckmorton Records, TSL. Grant advised against raising state troops and promised more U.S. troops would be sent to the state if circumstances warranted their deployment.

23. General Phil Sheridan to Throckmorton, October 1, 1866, and General Sheridan to Throckmorton, October 9, 1866, Throckmorton Records, TSL; Parker, "Indian Affairs and the Frontier," 29–31; Holbert, "Public Career of James Webb Throckmorton," 102–3; Elliott, *Leathercoat,* 140–42.

24. See various letters from Throckmorton to George B. Pickett, Jack Cureton, J. B. Barry, J. B. Davis, C. R. Perry, W. C. Durand, J. W. Sansome, T. P. C. Hambrick, W. H. Harris, J. B. Earhart, and others. Letters located in the Throckmorton Collection, CAH, and in the Throckmorton Records, TSL. Letters from Throckmorton are dated October 6, 1866. Letters received by the governor are found between October 9, 1866, throughout November 1866.

25. Throckmorton to Thos. F. Mosby, November 26, 1866, Throckmorton Collection, CAH.

26. Sheridan to Throckmorton, October 16, 1866, Throckmorton Records, TSL; Parker, "Indian Affairs and the Frontier," 29–31; Holbert, "Public Career of James Webb Throckmorton," 102–3; Elliott, *Leathercoat,* 140–42.

27. Major General Sheridan to Throckmorton, October 25, 1866, and November 3, 1866, Throckmorton Records, TSL.

28. Morris, *Sheridan,* 280; Elliott, *Leathercoat,* 142.

29. Elliott, *Leathercoat,* 142.

30. General Sheridan to General Heintzelman, November 6, 1866, Throckmorton Records, TSL.

31. General Heintzelman to Throckmorton, November 13, 1866, Throckmorton Records, TSL; Elliott, *Leathercoat,* 142–43.

32. Elliott, *Leathercoat,* 144–46.

33. Ibid., 147.

34. Ibid.

35. Brevet Major General Kiddoo to Throckmorton, August 23, 1866, Throckmorton Records, TSL.

36. Throckmorton to Maj. Gen. J. B. Kiddoo, August 20, 1866, Throckmorton Collection, CAH; Elliott, *Leathercoat,* 148.

37. Owens, "Presidential Reconstruction in Texas," 174; Elliott, *Leathercoat,* 149.

38. Brevet Major General Kiddoo to Throckmorton, September 13, 1866, Throckmorton Records, TSL; Owens, "Presidential Reconstruction in Texas," 174; Elliott, *Leathercoat,* 149.

39. Richter, *Overreached on All Sides,* 116–25.

40. Ibid., 133–34.

41. W. E. Goodrich to Throckmorton, October 8, 1866, Throckmorton Records, TSL; Richter, *Overreached on All Sides,* 132–35; Elliott, *Leathercoat,* 149–50.

42. Richter, *Overreached on All Sides,* 133–34.

43. Carson to Throckmorton, September 19, 1866, and Mullins (District Clerk of Victoria County) to Throckmorton, October 27, 1866, Throckmorton Records, TSL; Throckmorton to Major General Heintzelman, September 8, 1866, Throckmorton Collection, CAH; Richter, *Army in Texas,* 63; Elliott, *Leathercoat,* 152–53. Mullins sent a copy of the murder indictment against Smith and Stanley, which was filed August 22, 1866.

44. Throckmorton to General Heintzelman, September 25, 1866, Throckmorton Collection, CAH.

45. Brevet Major General Heintzelman, September 29, 1866, Throckmorton Records, TSL.

46. For the military's explanation of the murder of William Walker, see the military's report from the Headquarters Post in Victoria, Tex., November 29, 1866, and Sheriff H. Garnett to Throckmorton, January 11, 1867, Throckmorton Records, TSL.

47. *New York Times,* September 20, 1866; Richter, "Brenham Fire of 1866"; Morris, *Sheridan,* 278; Elliott, *Leathercoat,* 153–54. Richter's work is the best single source on the Brenham fire.

48. *New York Times,* October 5, 1866; Major General Sheridan to Throckmorton, September 20, 1866, Throckmorton Records, TSL; "Address of Throckmorton to the Texas House of Representatives, September 13, 1866," Throckmorton to Colonel Mason, September 14, 1866, and Throckmorton to General Sheridan, September 28, 1866, Throckmorton Collection, CAH; *Dallas Herald,* October 6, 1866; Elliott, *Leathercoat,* 154.

49. Throckmorton to Henry Stanbery, October 12, 1866, Throckmorton Collection, CAH.

50. Throckmorton to Henry Stanbery, October 19, 1866, Throckmorton Collection, CAH.

51. Attorney General Henry Stanbery to Throckmorton, November 6, 1866, Throckmorton Records, TSL.

52. Holbert, "Public Career of James Webb Throckmorton," 93–95; Elliott, *Leathercoat,* 155.

53. Morris, *Sheridan,* 278–79.

54. Ibid., 279.

55. Richter, "Brenham Fire of 1866," 311.

56. Richter, *Army in Texas,* 64; Ramsdell, *Reconstruction in Texas,* 131–32.

57. "Resolutions Adopted at a meeting in Belton, Bell County, Texas, August 13, 1866," Throckmorton Records, TSL; Throckmorton to Major Starr, September 11, 1866, and Throckmorton to General Heintzelman, September 24, 1866, Throckmorton Collection, CAH; E. S. C. Robertson to Throckmorton, December 7, 1866, Throckmorton Records, TSL; J. W. Fishburn and W. Taylor to E. S. C. Robertson, December 7, 1866, Throckmorton Records, TSL; Throckmorton to J. W. Fishburn and Taylor, December 12, 1866, Throckmorton Collection, CAH; General Saylors to Throckmorton, December 15, 1866, and James H. Miller to Throckmorton, December 17, 1866, Throckmorton Records, TSL; Richter, *Army in Texas,* 64; Ramsdell, *Reconstruction in Texas,* 131–32.

## CHAPTER SEVEN

1. John H. Reagan to Throckmorton, October 12, 1866, Throckmorton Records, TSL; *Dallas Herald,* November 10,1866; *New York Times,* November 8, 1866; Good, "John Henninger Reagan," 299–301; Chapin, "Presidential Reconstruction in Texas," 124–25.

2. President Andrew Johnson to Throckmorton, October 30, 1866, Throckmorton Records, TSL; *New York Times,* November 11, 1866.

3. Throckmorton's message to the Texas Legislature, October 31, 1866, and William Seward to Throckmorton, December 6, 1866, Throckmorton Records, TSL; *New York Times,* November 7, 1866; Chapin, "Presidential Reconstruction in Texas," 126–30; James, "Southern Reaction," 483–85.

4. Throckmorton to H. G. Hendricks, November 27, 1866, Throckmorton Letter Book, CAH.

5. Ibid.

6. Throckmorton to C. R. Breedlove, November 30, 1866, Throckmorton Letter Book, CAH.

7. Throckmorton to B. H. Epperson, December 10, 1866, Throckmorton Letter Book, CAH.

8. Throckmorton to William Fitzhugh, December 16, 1866, Throckmorton Letter Book, CAH.

9. Throckmorton to Charles R. Breedlove, December 21, 1866, Throckmorton Letter Book, CAH.

10. W. C. Phillips to Throckmorton, December 14, 1866, Throckmorton Records, TSL; Elliott, "Freedmen's Bureau in Texas," 21.

11. Brevet Major General Heintzelman to Throckmorton, December 1, 1866, Throckmorton Records, TSL.

12. Throckmorton to the Judge of the County Court of Caldwell County, Texas, December 19, 1866, Throckmorton Collection, CAH; Elliott, *Leathercoat,* 157–58.

13. William Sinclair to Throckmorton, January 17, 1867, Throckmorton Records, TSL; Throckmorton to Judge of the County Court of Wharton County, January 28, 1867, Throckmorton Collection, CAH.

14. A. F. Manning to General Kiddoo, January 20, 1867, Chamberlin to Throckmorton, January 22, 1867, Flint and Chamberlin to Throckmorton, February 5, 1867, and Charles Pearce (District Attorney) to Throckmorton, February 6, 1867, Throckmorton Records, TSL; Holbert, "Public Career of James Webb Throckmorton," 100–101.

15. Brevet Major General Griffin to Throckmorton, January 28, 1867, Throckmorton Records, TSL.

16. First Lieutenant Kirkman to Manning, February 7, 1866, Throckmorton Records, TSL.

17. Richter, *Overreached on All Sides,* 170; Campbell, *Grass-Roots Reconstruction,* 170–71.

18. McCaslin, *Tainted Breeze,* 173–74; Holbert, "Public Career of James Webb Throckmorton," 104.

19. McCaslin, *Tainted Breeze,* 173–74; Holbert, "Public Career of James Webb Throckmorton," 104–5; Elliott, *Leathercoat,* 158–59.

20. Throckmorton to R. B. Hubbard, February 12, 1867, Throckmorton Letter Book, CAH.

21. *Galveston Daily News,* March 30, 1867; Morris, *Sheridan,* 285; Hale, "Political Leadership in Texas," 24; Schroeder-Lein and Zuczek, *Andrew Johnson,* 264; Elliott, *Leathercoat,* 160.

22. Richter, *Army in Texas,* 90; Chapin, "Presidential Reconstruction in Texas," 141; Owens, "Presidential Reconstruction in Texas," 172.

23. Throckmorton to County Judge in Marshall, Harrison County, March 4, 1867, Throckmorton Collection, CAH.

24. Wheeler (County Attorney) to Throckmorton, March 1, 1867, Throckmorton Records, TSL; Throckmorton to Major General Griffin, March 5, 1867, Throckmorton Collection, CAH.

25. Throckmorton to Major General Griffin, March 5, 1867, Throckmorton Collection, CAH.

26. Throckmorton to Ashbel Smith, March 11, 1867, Throckmorton Letter Book, CAH.

27. Major General Sheridan to Throckmorton, March 29, 1867, Throckmorton Records, TSL; Morris, *Sheridan,* 285–86; Holbert, "Public Career of James Webb Throckmorton," 106–7.

28. Jacob Raney to J. W. Throckmorton, May 3, 1867, Throckmorton Collection, CAH; *New York Times,* May 25, 1867; Moneyhon, *Republicanism in Reconstruction Texas,* 64.

29. Brevet Major General Griffin, April 26, 1867, Throckmorton Records, TSL; McCaslin, *Tainted Breeze,* 176–77.

30. Governor Throckmorton reply to General Griffin as quoted in Elliott, *Leathercoat,* 162.

31. Throckmorton to Hon. Jno. Good, April 29, 1867, Throckmorton Letter Book, CAH.

32. Throckmorton to County Judge, Parker County, April 29, 1867, Throckmorton Letter Book, CAH.

33. A. J. Hunter to Throckmorton, May 24, 1867, Throckmorton Records, TSL. Hunter's communication to the governor gives a general overview of the events in the county from the local authorities' perspective.

34. Richter, *Overreached on All Sides,* 160.

35. Throckmorton to Hon. Jno. Ireland, April 30, 1867, Throckmorton Letter Book, CAH; 2nd Lt. H. C. Peterson to 1st Lt. S. C. Plummer, March 31, 1867, Throckmorton Records, TSL.

36. Richter, *Army in Texas,* 84–85; Chapin, "Presidential Reconstruction in Texas," 123–24.

37. Holbert, "Public Career of James Webb Throckmorton," 107–9.

38. Brevet Major General Griffin to Throckmorton, May 4, 1867, Throckmorton Records, TSL; Holbert, "Public Career of James Webb Throckmorton," 107–9; Elliott, *Leathercoat,* 170.

39. Brevet Major General Griffin to Throckmorton, April 4, 1867, Throckmorton Records, TSL; *Dallas Herald,* April 20, 1867.

40. Throckmorton to the County Judge of——— County, April 8, 1867, Throckmorton Letter Book, CAH; *Dallas Herald,* April 20, 1867; Elliott, *Leathercoat,* 171.

41. Holbert, "Public Career of James Webb Throckmorton," 109.

42. Richter, "Tyrant and Reformer," 232; Morris, *Sheridan,* 287; Baggett, "Rise and Fall of the Texas Radicals," 72–73; Moneyhon, *Republicanism in Reconstruction Texas,* 68; Chapin, "Presidential Reconstruction in Texas," 142–43; Elliott, *Leathercoat,* 171.

43. Holbert, "Public Career of James Webb Throckmorton," 109.

44. *Galveston Daily News,* May, 3, 1867; Richter, "Tyrant and Reformer," 233–34; McCaslin, *Tainted Breeze,* 177. Richter's work contains a solid overview of Circular Order No. 13.

45. *New York Times,* May 15, 1867; Throckmorton to Judge of———, May 2, 1867, Throckmorton Letter Book, CAH; Campbell, "District Judges of Texas," 369. Throckmorton's letter was sent to county judges throughout the state.

46. Throckmorton to President Andrew Johnson, May 2, 1867, Throckmorton Letter Book, CAH.

47. Holbert, "Public Career of James Webb Throckmorton," 110.

48. Ibid., 111.

49. Morris, *Sheridan,* 279; Elliott, *Leathercoat,* 173.

50. Thomas Brown to Throckmorton, May 5, 1867, Throckmorton Papers, TSL; Holbert, "Public Career of James Webb Throckmorton," 114–15. Brown's letter reaffirms Epperson's position that Throckmorton is in political trouble and will undoubtedly be removed from office.

51. Chapin, "Presidential Reconstruction in Texas," 143–44.

52. Texas Legislature, *Report of the Special Committee on Lawlessness and Violence in Texas* (Austin: Texas Legislature, 1868), also printed as *Letter of the President of Constitutional Convention of Texas Communicating the Report of Special Committee on Lawlessness and Violence in that State,* 40th Cong., Senate, 2nd sess., 1868, Misc. Doc. No. 109.

53. *New York Times,* August 1, 1867; Morris, *Sheridan,* 292; Moneyhon, *Republicanism in Reconstruction Texas,* 68; Holbert, "Public Career of James Webb Throckmorton," 116; Massey, "History of Collin County," 74; Chapin, "Presidential Reconstruction in Texas," 144; Hale, "Political Leadership in Texas," 24; Gray, "Edmund J. Davis," 103.

54. Special Order No. 105, July 30, 1867, Throckmorton Collection, CAH; *New York Times,* July 31, 1867.

55. Throckmorton to Epperson, July 31, 1867, Throckmorton Collection, CAH.

56. *Dallas Herald,* August 24, 1867; Holbert, "Public Career of James Webb Throckmorton," 116–17; Ramsdell, *Reconstruction in Texas,* 170; William L. Richter, "General Phil Sheridan," 147. The "Address to the People of Texas" printed in the *Dallas Herald* reprinted much of the correspondence between Throckmorton and the military authorities, especially General Griffin and General Sheridan.

57. *Dallas Herald,* September 28, 1867.

58. Richter, *Army in Texas,* 113–14.

59. *Dallas Herald,* October 5, 1867. A complete summary of Throckmorton's administration is found in this issue of the *Dallas Herald.*

## CHAPTER EIGHT

1. Throckmorton to Epperson, December 19, 1867, Letters of Governor Throckmorton, CAH; *Dallas Herald,* November 2 and 9, 1867; Horton, *Samuel Bell Maxey,* 49; Lynch, "J. W. Throckmorton"; Baggett, "Rise and Fall of the Texas Radicals," 3. For a brief but comprehensive examination of African American political contributions, see Crouch, "Hesitant Recognition," 41–58. Baggett points out that even though there were more black Republicans than white Republicans in Texas after 1867, black political domination was impossible in the state. The highest political position achieved by an African American in Texas was state senator and only three blacks attained that office. Nevertheless, Throckmorton undoubtedly knew, as did most white Texans, that African American voters could effectively help white Radical Republicans win office, especially since many white Democrats remained disenfranchised by the Reconstruction Acts. Horton reveals that Throckmorton was the member of a law firm in Bonham, Fannin County, Texas. The ex-governor was a law partner with Samuel A. Roberts and Thomas J. Brown. The *Dallas Herald* states that Throckmorton was a partner in the Throckmorton and Brown Law Firm in McKinney, Texas.

2. Throckmorton to Epperson, September 5, 1867, and Throckmorton to Rev. J. W. P. McKenzie, September 10, 1867, Letters of Governor Throckmorton, CAH; Elliott, *Leathercoat,* 181–82.

3. James Waller to Throckmorton, September 29, 1867, Throckmorton Papers, TSL; *New York Times,* November 2, 1867.

4. Throckmorton to Epperson, September 5, 1867, Letters of Governor Throckmorton, CAH; *Dallas Herald,* November 9, 1867; Elliott, *Leathercoat,* 183–84; Perman, *Reunion Without Compromise,* 335.

5. *Dallas Herald,* November 16, 1867; Cantrell, "Racial Violence and Reconstruction," 348–49; Hendrickson, *Chief Executives of Texas,* 92; Elliott, *Leathercoat,* 184–86; Moneyhon, *Texas After the Civil War,* 82–83.

6. Moneyhon, *Texas After the Civil War,* 83–84; *Dallas Herald,* February 1, 1868; Cantrell, "Racial Violence and Reconstruction," 348–49; Hendrickson, *Chief Executives of Texas,* 92; Elliott, *Leathercoat,* 186–87.

7. Russ, "Radical Disfranchisement in Texas," 45–46; Ramsdell, *Reconstruction in Texas,* 199; Elliott, *Leathercoat,* 186–87.

8. *Dallas Herald,* June 20, 1868; Baggett, "Birth of the Texas Republican Party," 19–20; Norvell, "Reconstruction Courts of Texas," 145–46; Hendrickson, *Chief Executives of Texas,* 92; Moneyhon, *Republicanism in Reconstruction Texas,* 82–86.

9. *Dallas Herald,* June 20, 1868; Moneyhon, *Republicanism in Reconstruction Texas,* 86–92.

10. Moneyhon, *Republicanism in Reconstruction Texas,* 86–92, *Dallas Herald,* June 20, 1868.

11. Moneyhon, *Republicanism in Reconstruction Texas,* 93.

12. Norvell, "Reconstruction Courts of Texas," 146–47; Moneyhon, *Republicanism in Reconstruction Texas,* 101–2; Russ, "Radical Disfranchisement," 46–48; Elliott, *Leathercoat,* 187–88.

13. Moneyhon, *Republicanism in Reconstruction Texas,* 103.

14. Russ, "Radical Disfranchisement," 50; Elliott, *Leathercoat,* 188.

15. *Dallas Herald,* May 30 and June 6, 1868; Good, "John Henninger Reagan," 311; Elliott, *Leathercoat,* 188–89.

16. *Dallas Herald,* July 18, 1868; Chamberlain, "Two-Thirds Rule,"11; Good, "John Henninger Reagan," 311–12; Elliott, *Leathercoat,* 189.

17. *Dallas Herald,* July 25, 1868.

18. *New York Herald* quoted in *Dallas Herald,* August 14, 1869.

19. *Dallas Herald,* June 19, 1869.

20. Norvell, "Reconstruction Courts," 147–48; Hendrickson, *Chief Executives of Texas,* 92; Elliott, *Leathercoat,* 190.

21. Norvell, "Reconstruction Courts," 147–48; Russ, "Radical Disfranchisement," 51; Hendrickson, *Chief Executives of Texas,* 93; Elliott, *Leathercoat,* 190; Campbell, *Gone to Texas,* 280.

22. Baum, *Shattering of Texas Unionism,* 183–228.

23. Raines, *Six Decades in Texas,* 605; Miller, "State Finances of Texas," 91; Degler, *The Other South,* 251–52; Hendrickson, *Chief Executives of Texas,* 93. One of the clearest signs that whites were hostile to the state police primarily because it was a biracial force is the case of Capt. L. H. McNelly. As an officer of the state police, McNelly was widely considered a disgrace, but later, when he joined the Texas Rangers, an all-white organization, he was heralded a hero.

24. *Dallas Herald,* July 30, 1870; Baggett, "Rise and Fall of the Texas Radicals," 137–38.

25. *Dallas Herald,* August 6, 1870; Gray, "Edmund J. Davis," 271; Baggett, "Rise and Fall of the Texas Radicals," 137–38; Elliott, *Leathercoat,* 191–92.

26. Throckmorton to G. W. Sulthen, March 22, 1869, Letters of Governor Throckmorton, CAH. This letter reveals that Throckmorton became the director of the Memphis, El Paso, and Pacific Railroad Company. For more on Throckmorton's involvement with the railroad, see the following letters: Throckmorton to Benjamin Epperson, November 17, 1869, February 1, 1871, and August 2, 1871, Letters of Governor Throckmorton, CAH. An article in the *New York Times,* September 13, 1870, reveals that Throckmorton stayed at the St. Nicholas Hotel in New York, suggesting that he was indeed out of the state.

27. *Dallas Herald,* November 5, 1870; Elliott, *Leathercoat,* 192.

28. *Dallas Herald,* September 30, 1871; *Austin Daily State Journal,* September 22, 1871; Elliott, *Leathercoat,* 192–93.

29. *Austin Daily State Journal,* September 23, 1871; Elliott, *Leathercoat,* 193.

30. *Dallas Herald,* October 21, 1871; *Austin Daily State Journal,* September 23, 1871; *Austin Democratic Statesman,* September 23, 1871; Miller, "State Finances of Texas," 95; Elliott, *Leathercoat,* 194.

31. *Austin Democratic Statesman,* September 26, 1871; Waller, *Colossal Hamilton of Texas,* 135; Wooten, *Comprehensive History of Texas,* 2:193–94; Elliott, *Leathercoat,* 195.

32. *Austin Democratic Statesman,* September 26, 1871.

33. Ibid.

34. Ibid.

35. Ibid., September 28, 1871.

36. *Austin Daily State Journal,* October 1, 1871; Elliott, *Leathercoat,* 198.

37. *Austin Democratic Statesman,* October 3, 1871; Elliott, *Leathercoat,* 199.

38. *Austin Democratic Statesman,* October 3 and 5, 1871; Elliott, *Leathercoat,* 196.

39. Elliott, *Leathercoat,* 204.

40. Ibid., 204–5.

41. *Houston Union,* October 14, 1870. The term "Fusion" refers to a coalition formed between conservative Democrats and conservative, or moderate, Republicans.

42. *Houston Union,* November 9, 1870; Elliott, *Leathercoat,* 206.

43. Elliott, *Leathercoat,* 206.

44. Throckmorton to Epperson, February 1, 1871, Epperson Papers, CAH.

45. Throckmorton to Epperson, February 6, 1871, Epperson Papers, CAH.

46. *Houston Union,* May 12, 1871.

47. *Bonham News,* April 28, 1871, quoted in the *McKinney Enquirer,* May 6, 1871.

48. *Houston Union,* May 12, 1871.

49. *Dallas Herald,* June 24, 1871.

50. Throckmorton to Epperson, April 9, 1871, and June 7, 1871, Letters of Governor Throckmorton, CAH; *Dallas Weekly Herald,* June 24, 1871.

51. Ramsdell, *Reconstruction in Texas,* 310; Elliott, *Leathercoat,* 210.

52. *Dallas Herald,* January 6 and 27, 1872, February 3, 10, 17, and 24, 1872, March 16, 1872, April 20, 1872; *Sherman Patriot* and *Denton Monitor* quoted in *Dallas Herald,* January 20, 1872; Elliott, *Leathercoat,* 211.

53. *Dallas Herald,* May 11, 18, and 25, 1872; Elliott, *Leathercoat,* 211–12.

54. *Dallas Herald,* June 22, 1872; John H. Reagan, *Memoirs,* 241; Chamberlain, "Two-Thirds Rule," 13–14; Elliott, *Leathercoat,* 212.

55. *Sherman Courier* quoted in *Dallas Herald,* July 6 and September 28, 1872.

56. *Dallas Herald,* May 31, 1873.

57. *Austin Democratic Statesman* quoted in *Dallas Herald,* September 6, 1873.

58. *New York Times,* September 4, 1873; Raines, *Six Decades in Texas,* 605; Norvell, "Reconstruction Courts of Texas," 149; Moneyhon, *Republicanism in Reconstruction Texas,* 188; Hendrickson, *Chief Executives of Texas,* 97; Campbell, *Gone to Texas,* 285–86, 295.

## CHAPTER NINE

1. *Austin Daily Journal,* January 29, 1874; Elliott, *Leathercoat,* 214.

2. Elliott, *Leathercoat,* 214–15.

3. *Austin Daily Journal,* January 29, 1874; Elliott, *Leathercoat,* 216–17.

4. *Fort Worth Daily Democrat,* June 13, 1874; *Dallas Weekly Herald,* June–October 1874 passim.

5. *Denison Daily News,* July 6, 1874.

6. *Dallas Weekly Herald,* July 4, 1874; Elliott, *Leathercoat,* 219.

7. Elliott, *Leathercoat,* 223–27; *Dallas Weekly Herald,* July 18, 1874.

8. Norton's *Union Intelligencer,* December 21, 1874; Elliott, *Leathercoat,* 232. Throckmorton received 6,000 votes; H. B. Sumner (Republican) received 70 votes; and I. P. Valentine (Independent) received 280; 333 votes were scattered among various other candidates.

9. House Committee, "Report No. 139," 44th Cong., 2nd sess., January 24, 1877; Elliott, *Leathercoat,* 235–36.

10. *Galveston Daily News,* May 3, 4, 24, and June 10, 1876.

11. *Weatherford Times,* May 27, 1876.

12. *Fort Worth Democrat,* August 5, 1876; Elliott, *Leathercoat,* 237–38; Barr, *Reconstruction to Reform,* 32–34.

13. Barr, *Reconstruction to Reform,* 34; *Dallas Weekly Herald,* September 2, 1876; *Galveston Daily News,* December 25, 1876; Elliott, *Leathercoat,* 240–42.

14. House Committee, "Report No. 139"; Elliott, *Leathercoat,* 244–45.

15. Elliott, *Leathercoat,* 243.

16. House Committee, "Report No. 139, Part II, Minority Report," 44th Cong., 2nd sess., January 24, 1877.

17. *Galveston Daily News,* October 26, 1877.

18. *Congressional Record,* 45th Cong., 3rd sess., appendix, 8(3):115–19; Elliott, *Leathercoat,* 248–49.

19. Wooten, *Comprehensive History of Texas,* 2:324; DeShields, *They Sat in High Places,* 271; Hendrickson, *Chief Executives of Texas,* 90; Elliott, *Leathercoat,* 214–76; Barr, *Reconstruction to Reform,* 39–41.

20. *Galveston Daily News,* April 23, 1880; Elliott, *Leathercoat,* 279–80.

21. Elliott, *Leathercoat,* 281–83; Barr, *Reconstruction to Reform,* 61.

22. Elliott, *Leathercoat,* 284–86.

23. Wooten, *Comprehensive History of Texas,* 2:324; DeShields, *They Sat in High Places,* 271; Hendrickson, *Chief Executives of Texas,* 90; Elliott, *Leathercoat,* 214–76; Barr, *Reconstruction to Reform,* 118–19.

24. Elliott, *Leathercoat,* 293–94.

25. "Throckmorton Dead," newspaper clipping located in Throckmorton Scrapbook, Throckmorton Collection, CAH.

# BIBLIOGRAPHY

PRIMARY SOURCES

Bell, Peter Hansborough. Governor's Correspondence. Texas Office of the Governor. Archives Division, Texas State Library, Austin.

Burke, John. Records. Adjunct General Correspondence. Archives Division, Texas State Library, Austin.

Clark, Edward. Records. Governor's Correspondence, Texas Office of the Governor. Archives Division, Texas State Library, Austin.

Day, James M., ed. *Senate Journal of the Tenth Legislature, First Called Session of the State of Texas, May 9, 1864–May 28, 1864.* Austin: Texas State Library, 1965.

———. *Senate Journal of the Tenth Legislature, Regular Session of the State of Texas, November 3, 1863–December 16, 1863.* Austin: Texas State Library, 1964.

Epperson, Benjamin H. Papers. Center for American History, University of Texas at Austin.

———. Archives Division, Texas State Library, Austin.

Gammel, Hans Peter Nielson, comp. *Laws of Texas.* 10 vols. Austin, 1898.

"Gen. Houston All Right on the Railroad Question." Broadside. Archives Division, Texas State Library, Austin.

Hamilton, Andrew J. Records. Governor's Correspondence, Texas Office of the Governor. Archives Division, Texas State Library, Austin.

Lubbock, Francis Richard. Records. Texas Office of the Governor. Archives Division, Texas State Library, Austin.

"Message of Governor A. J. Hamilton to the Texas State Convention, February 10, 1866." Broadside Collection, 1866–1867. Center for American History, University of Texas at Austin.

"Proceedings of the State Convention of the Democratic Party of the State of Texas, which Assembled at Waco, Monday 4th, 1857." Archives Division, Texas State Library, Austin.

"Proclamation of Governor Sam Houston to the People of Texas in May, 1861, Upon the Question of Texas Secession." Broadside Collection. Archives Division, Texas State Library, Austin.

"Proclamation by the Governor of the State of Texas, February 9, 1861." Broadside Collection. Archives Division, Texas State Library, Austin.

Reagan, John H. Collection. Archives Division, Texas State Library, Austin.

*Supplement to the Official Records of the Union and Confederate Armies.* Serial nos. 79 and 80, pt. 2: *Record of Events.* Wilmington, N.C.: Broadfoot Publishing Company, 1998.

Terrell, Alexander W. Papers. Archives Division, Texas State Library, Austin.

*Texas Almanac, 1861.* Galveston: Galveston Weekly News Printing Office, 1862.

*Texas Almanac, 1862.* Galveston: Galveston Weekly News Printing Office, 1863.

*Texas Almanac, 1864.* Galveston: Galveston Weekly News Printing Office, 1865.

Texas. House of Representatives. *Journal of the Texas House of Representatives,* Fourth Legislature, Austin, 1851–1852.

———. *Journal of the Texas House of Representatives,* Fourth Legislature, Extra Session, Austin, 1853.

———. *Journal of the Texas House of Representatives,* Sixth Legislature, Austin, 1855–1856.

Texas. Senate. *Journal of the Senate of Texas,* Seventh Biennial Session, Austin, 1857.

———. Senate. *Journal of the Senate of Texas,* Eighth Legislature, Austin, 1859.

———. Senate. *Journal of the Senate of Texas,* Eighth Legislature, Extra Session, Austin, 1859.

———. Senate. *Journal of the Senate of Texas,* Eighth Legislature, Extra Session, Austin, 1861.

Texas. State Legislature. *Members of the Texas Legislature, 1846–1980.* Austin: Legislature, 1980.

Throckmorton, James Webb. Collection. Center for American History, University of Texas at Austin.

———. Letter Book. Center for American History, University of Texas at Austin.

———. Letters of the Governor, 1862–1876. Center for American History, University of Texas at Austin.

———. Papers. Center for American History, University of Texas at Austin.

———. Papers, 1857–1940. Manuscript Collection. Archives Division, Texas State Library, Austin.

———. Records. Governor's Correspondence, Texas Office of the Governor. Archives Division, Texas State Library, Austin.

U.S. Bureau of the Census. *Eighth Census of the United States, 1860: Schedule I and II.* National Archives, Washington, D.C.

———. *Seventh Census of the United States, 1850.* Washington, D.C.: Robert Armstrong, Public Printer, 1853.

U.S. Congress. *Congressional Globe.* 29th Cong., 1st sess. Washington, D.C.: Government Printing Office, 1846.

———. *Congressional Record.* 45th Cong., 3rd sess., 1879. Appendix. Vol. 8, pt. 3, 115–19.

U.S. Congress. House Committee. "Report No. 139" and "Report No. 139, Part II, Minority Report." 44th Cong., 2nd sess., January 24, 1877.

U.S. War Department. *War of the Rebellion: A Compilation of the Official Records of the Union and Confederate Armies.* Series 1. Washington, D.C.: Government Printing Office, 1880–1898.

## SECONDARY SOURCES

Armstrong, A. B. "Origins of the Texas and Pacific Railway." *Southwestern Historical Quarterly* 56 (April 1953): 489–97.

Babb, Valerie. *Whiteness Visible: The Meaning of Whiteness in American Literature and Culture.* New York: New York University Press, 1998.

Baggett, James A. "Birth of the Texas Republican Party," *Southwestern Historical Quarterly* 78 (July 1974): 1–20.

———. "The Rise and Fall of the Texas Radicals." Ph.D. diss., North Texas State University, 1972.

Barr, Alwyn. *Reconstruction to Reform: Texas Politics, 1876–1906.* Austin: University of Texas Press, 1971. Reprint, Dallas: Southern Methodist University Press, 2000. Page references are to the reprint edition.

Baum, Dale. "Pinpointing Apparent Fraud in the 1861 Texas Secession Referendum." *Journal of Interdisciplinary History* 22 (Autumn 1991): 201–21.

———. *The Shattering of Texas Unionism: Politics in the Lone Star State during the Civil War Era.* Baton Rouge: Louisiana State University, 1998.

Bergeron, Paul H., Stephen V. Ash, and Jeanette Keith. *Tennesseans and Their History.* Knoxville: University of Tennessee Press, 1999.

Berlin, Ira. *Many Thousands Gone: The First Two Centuries of Slavery in North America.* Cambridge: Belknap Press of Harvard University Press, 1998.

Brands, H. W. *The Age of Gold: The California Gold Rush and the New American Dream.* New York: Doubleday, 2002.

Brockman, John Martin. "Railroads, Radicals, and Democrats: A Study in Texas Politics, 1865–1900." Ph.D. diss., University of Texas at Austin, 1975.

Brown, Thomas. *Politics and Statesmanship: Essays on the American Whig Party.* New York: Columbia University Press, 1985.

Buenger, Walter L. *Secession and the Union in Texas.* Austin: University of Texas Press, 1984.

———. "Stilling the Voice of Reason: Texans and the Union, 1854–1861." Ph.D. diss., Rice University, 1979.

———. "Texas and the Riddle of Secession." *Southwestern Historical Quarterly* 87 (October 1983): 151–82.

Calvert, Robert, Arnoldo De Leon, and Gregg Cantrell, *The History of Texas.* 3rd ed. Wheeling, Ill.: Harlan Davidson, 2002.

Campbell, Randolph B. *Gone to Texas: A History of the Lone Star State.* New York: Oxford University Press, 2003.

———. "The District Judges of Texas in 1866–1867: An Episode in the failure of Presidential Reconstruction." *Southwestern Historical Quarterly* 93 (January 1990): 357–77.

———. *Grass-Roots Reconstruction in Texas, 1865–1880.* Baton Rouge: Louisiana State University Press, 1997.

Cantrell, Gregg. "Racial Violence and Reconstruction Politics in Texas, 1867–1868." *Southwestern Historical Quarterly* 93 (January 1990): 333–55.

Carrier, John Pressley. "A Political History of Texas During the Reconstruction, 1865–1874." Ph.D. diss., Vanderbilt University, 1971.

Carroll, E. Malcolm. *Origins of the Whig Party.* Durham, N.C.: Duke University Press, 1925.

Carter, Douglas John. *As It Was: Reminiscences of a Soldier of the Third Texas Cavalry and the Nineteenth Louisiana Infantry.* Austin: State House Press, 1990.

Carter, W. A. *History of Fannin County, Texas.* Bonham, Tex.: privately printed, 1885.

Chamberlain, James Clark. "The Two-Thirds Rule in Texas State Democratic Conventions." M.A. thesis, Texas Technical College, 1933.

Chapin, Walter Tribble. "Presidential Reconstruction in Texas, 1865–1867." M.A. thesis: North Texas State University, 1979.

Cole, Arthur C. *The Whig Party in the South.* Washington, D.C.: American Historical Association, 1912.

Connor, Seymour V. *Adventure in Glory.* Austin: Steck-Vaughn, 1965.

———. *Kentucky Colonization in Texas: A History of the Peters Colony.* Baltimore: Genealogical Publication Co., 1983.

———. *The Peters Colony of Texas: A History and Biographical Sketches of the Early Settlers.* Austin: Texas State Historical Association, 1959.

Cooper, William J., Jr., and Thomas E. Terrill. *The American South: A History.* 2nd ed. New York: McGraw-Hill, 1996.

Crofts, Daniel W. *Reluctant Confederates: Upper South Unionists in the Secession Crisis.* Chapel Hill: University of North Carolina Press, 1989.

Crouch, Barry A. "All the Vile Passions: The Texas Black Codes of 1866." *Southwestern Historical Quarterly* 97 (July 1993): 13–34.

———. *Freedmen's Bureau and Black Texans.* Austin: University of Texas Press, 1992.

———. "Hesitant Recognition: Texas Black Politicians, 1865–1900." *East Texas Historical Journal* 31 (Spring 1993): 41–58.

———. "'Unmanacling' Texas Reconstruction: A Twenty-Year Perspective." *Southwestern Historical Quarterly* 93 (January 1990): 275–302.

Degler, Carl. *The Other South: Southern Dissenters in the Nineteenth Century.* New York: Harper and Row, 1974.

DeShields, James T. *They Sat in High Places: The Presidents and Governors of Texas.* San Antonio: The Naylor Company, 1940.

Doane, Ashley, and Eduardo Bonilla-Silva, eds. *White Out: The Continuing Significance of Racism.* New York: Routledge, 2003.

Dunning, William A. *Reconstruction, Political and Economic, 1865–1877.* New York: Harper & Brothers, 1907.

Elliott, Claude. "The Freedmen's Bureau in Texas." *Southwestern Historical Quarterly* 56 (July 1952): 448–77.

———. *Leathercoat: The Life of James W. Throckmorton.* San Antonio: Standard Printing Co., privately printed, 1938.

———. "Union Sentiment in Texas, 1861–1865." *Southwestern Historical Quarterly* 50 (April 1947): 448–77.

Fleming, Walter. *Civil War and Reconstruction in Alabama.* New York: P. Smith, 1949.

Foner, Eric. *Reconstruction: America's Unfinished Revolution, 1863–1877.* New York: Harper and Row, 1988.

Fowler, Pamela McDougald. "The Origins of the Texas Railroad Commission." M.A. thesis, Rice University, 1982.

Fulmore, Z. T. *The History and Geography of Texas As Told in County Names.* Austin: Press of E. L. Stech, 1915.

Good, Benjamin Harvey. "John Henninger Reagan." Ph.D. diss., University of Texas at Austin, 1932.

Gould, Lewis L. *Alexander Watkins Terrell: Civil War Soldier, Lawmaker, Diplomat.* Austin: University of Texas Press, 2004.

Gray, Ronald Norman. "Edmund J. Davis: Radical Republican and Reconstruction Governor of Texas." Ph.D., diss.: Texas Tech University, 1976.

Grégoire de Roulhac Hamilton, Joseph. *Reconstruction in North Carolina.* New York: Columbia University, 1914.

Griffin, Roger Allen. "Connecticut Yankee in Texas: A Biography of Elisha Marshall Pease." Ph.D. diss., University of Texas at Austin, 1973.

Hale, Charles. "Political Leadership in Texas During Reconstruction." M.A. thesis, Lamar State College of Technology, 1965.

Hale, Douglas. *The Third Texas Cavalry in the Civil War.* Norman: University of Oklahoma Press, 1993.

Haley, James L. *Sam Houston.* Norman: University of Oklahoma, 2002.

Harmon, George D. "The United States Indian Policy in Texas, 1845–1860." *Mississippi Valley Historical Review* 17 (December 1930): 377–403.

Harrison, Arlene. "J. W. Throckmorton's Administration." M.A. thesis, East Texas State University, 1971.

Hendrickson, Kenneth E., Jr. *The Chief Executives of Texas: From Stephen F. Austin to John B. Connally, Jr.* College Station: Texas A&M University Press, 1995.

Hicks, Jimmie. "Texas and Separate Independence, 1860–61." *East Texas Historical Journal* 4 (Fall 1966): 85–106

Holbert, Ruby Crawford. "The Public Career of James Webb Throckmorton, 1851–1867." M.A. thesis, University of Texas at Austin, 1932.

Holt, Michael F. *The Rise and Fall of the American Whig Party: Jacksonian Politics and the Onset of the Civil War.* New York: Oxford University Press, 1999.

Horton, Louise. *Samuel Bell Maxey: A Biography.* Austin: University of Texas Press, 1974.

Howe, Daniel Walker. *The Political Culture of the American Whigs.* Chicago: University of Chicago Press, 1979.

Howell, Kenneth W. *Henderson County, Texas: An Antebellum History, 1846–1861.* Austin: Eakin Press, 1999.

———. "James Webb Throckmorton: The Life and Career of a Southern Frontier Politician, 1825–1894." Ph.D. diss., Texas A&M University, 2005.

James, Joseph B. "Southern Reaction to the Proposal of the Fourteenth Amendment." *Journal of Southern History* 22 (November 1956): 477–97.

Jewett, Clayton E. *Texas in the Confederacy: An Experiment in Nation Building.* Columbia: University of Missouri Press, 2002.

Jones, Billy. *The Search for Maturity.* Austin: Steck-Vaughn, 1965.

Kingston, Mike, Sam Attlesey, and Mary G. Crawford. *The Texas Almanac's Political History of Texas.* Austin: Eakin Press, 1992.

Kolchin, Peter. "Whiteness Studies: The New History of Race in America." *Journal of American History* 89 (June 2002): 154–74.

Ledbetter, Billy D. "Slavery, Fear, and Disunion in the Lone Star State: Texans' Attitudes Toward Secession and the Union, 1846–1861." Ph.D. diss., North Texas State University, 1972.

Lynch, James D. "J. W. Throckmorton." Unpublished manuscript. James Webb Throckmorton Papers, 1857–1940. Manuscript Collection, Archives Division, Texas State Library.

Massey, Harold E. "A History of Collin County." M.A. thesis, Southwestern University, 1948.

McCaslin, Richard. "Wheat Growers in the Cotton Confederacy: The Suppression of Dissent in Collin County, Texas, during the Civil War." *Southwestern Historical Quarterly* 96 (April 1993): 526–39.

———. *Tainted Breeze: The Great Hanging at Gainesville, Texas, 1862.* Baton Rouge: Louisiana State University Press, 1994.

McDonald, Forrest, and Grady McWhiney. "The Antebellum Southern Herdsman: A Reinterpretation." *Journal of Southern History* 41 (May 1975): 147–66.

McPherson, James M. *Battle Cry of Freedom: The Civil War Era.* New York: Oxford University Press, 1988.

Means, Emilia Gay. "East Texas and the Transcontinental Railroad." *East Texas Historical Journal* 25 (Fall 1987): 49–59.

Miller, E. T. "The State Finances of Texas During the Reconstruction." *Southwestern Historical Quarterly* 14 (October 1910): 87–112.

Moneyhon, Carl. *Republicanism in Reconstruction Texas.* 1980. Reprint, College Station: Texas A&M University Press, 2000.

———. *Texas After the Civil War: The Struggle of Reconstruction.* College Station: Texas A&M University Press, 2004.

Moore, Richard. "Radical Reconstruction: The Texas Choice." *East Texas Historical Journal* 16 (Spring 1978): 15–23.

Morris, Roy, Jr. *Sheridan: The Life and Wars of General Phil Sheridan.* New York: Crown Publishers, 1992.

Nieman, Donald G. "Andrew Johnson, the Freedmen's Bureau, and the Problem of Equal Rights, 1865–1866." *Journal of Southern History* 44 (August 1978): 399–420.

Norvell, James R. "The Reconstruction Courts of Texas, 1867–1873." *Southwestern Historical Quarterly* 62 (October 1958): 141–63.

Nunn, William C., ed. *Ten More Texans in Gray.* Hillsboro, Tex.: Hill Junior College Press, 1980.

———, ed. *Ten Texans in Gray.* Hillsboro, Tex.: Hill Junior College Press, 1968.

———. *Texas Under the Carpetbaggers.* Austin: University of Texas, 1962.

Otto, John Solomon. "The Migration of the Southern Plain Folk: An Interdisciplinary Synthesis." *Journal of Southern History* 51 (May 1985): 183–200.

Otto, John Solomon, and N. E. Anderson. "Slash-and-Burn Cultivation in the Highlands South: A Problem in Comparative Agricultural History." *Comparative Studies in Society and History* 24 (January 1982): 131–47.

Overfelt, Robert C. "Defense of the Texas Frontier: 1861–1865." M.A. thesis, Baylor University, 1968.

Owens, Nora Estelle. "Presidential Reconstruction in Texas: A Case Study." Ph.D. diss., Auburn University, 1983.

Parker, Bruce Logan. "Indian Affairs and the Frontier of Texas, 1865–1880." M.A. thesis, University of Texas at Austin, 1925.

Perman, Michael. *Reunion Without Compromise: The South and Reconstruction, 1865–1868.* New York: Cambridge University Press, 1973.

———. *The Road to Redemption: Southern Politics, 1869–1879.* Chapel Hill: University of North Carolina Press, 1984.

Phillips, Margaret. *The Governors of Tennessee.* Gretna, La.: Pelican Publishing Company, 1978.

Pitts, Alice Ellison, and Minnie Pitts Champ, *Collin County, Texas, Families.* 2 vols. Fort Worth: Landmark Publishing, Inc., 1998.

Potter, David M. *The Impending Crisis, 1848–1861.* New York: Harper and Row, 1976.

Raines, C. W., ed. *Six Decades in Texas: The Memoirs of Francis R. Lubbock, Confederate Governor of Texas.* Austin: Pemberton Press, 1968.

Ramsdell, Charles W. "Presidential Reconstruction in Texas." *Southwestern Historical Quarterly* 11 (April 1908): 204–30.

———. *Reconstruction in Texas.* 1910. Reprint, Austin: University of Texas Press, 1970.

Reagan, John H. *Memoirs with Special Reference to Secession and the Civil War.* New York: Neale Publishing Company, 1906.

Reynolds, Don. *Editors Make War.* Nashville: Vanderbilt University Press, 1966.

Richardson, James D., comp. *A Compilation of the Messages and Papers of the Presidents.* Washington, D.C.: Bureau of National Literature, 1911.

Richardson, Rupert N., Adrian Anderson, Cary Wintz, and Ernest Wallace, *Texas: The Lone Star State.* 8th ed. Upper Saddle River, N.J.: Prentice Hall, 2001.

Richter, William L. "The Army and the Negro during Texas Reconstruction, 1865–1870." *East Texas Historical Journal* 10 (Spring 1972): 7–19.

———. *The Army in Texas During Reconstruction, 1865–1870.* College Station: Texas A&M University Press, 1987.

———. "The Brenham Fire of 1866: A Texas Reconstruction Atrocity." *Southern Studies* 14 (Fall 1975): 287–314.

———. "General Phil Sheridan, The Historians, and Reconstruction," *Civil War History* 33 (1987): 131–54.

———. *Overreached on All Sides: The Freedmen's Bureau Administrators in Texas, 1865–1868.* College Station: Texas A&M University Press, 1991.

———. "Tyrant and Reformer: Charles Griffin Reconstructs Texas, 1865–66." *Prologue* 10 (1978): 225–41.
Riegel, Robert E. "Trans-Mississippi Railroads during the Fifties." *Mississippi Valley Historical Review* 10 (September 1923): 153–72.
Roberts, O. M. "The Experiences of an Unrecognized Senator." *Southwestern Historical Quarterly* 12 (October 1908): 87–147.
Roth, Jeffery M. "Civil War Frontier Defense Challenges in Northwest Texas." *Military History of the West* 30 (2000): 21–44.
Russ, William A., Jr. "Radical Disfranchisement in Texas, 1867–1870." *Southwestern Historical Quarterly* 38 (July 1934): 40–52.
Russel, R. R. "A Revaluation of the Period Before the Civil War: Railroads." *Mississippi Valley Historical Review* 15 (December 1928): 341–54.
Sandbo, Anna Irene. "Beginnings of the Secession Movement in Texas." *Southwestern Historical Quarterly* 18 (July 1914): 41–82.
———. "The First Session of the Secession Convention of Texas." *Southwestern Historical Quarterly* 19 (October 1914): 162–94.
Saxon, Gerald D. "The Politics of Expansion: Texas as an Issue in National Politics, 1819–1845." Ph.D. diss., North Texas State University, 1979.
Schaefer, Donald F. "Locational Choice in the Antebellum South." *Journal of Economic History* 49 (March 1989): 145–65.
Schlameus, Barron. "Secessionist Thought in Texas." M.A. thesis, Southwest Texas State University, 1971.
Schroeder-Lein, Glenda R., and Richard Zuczek. *Andrew Johnson: A Biographical Companion.* Santa Barbara: ABC-CLIO, 2001.
Schutte, Gerhard. *What Racists Believe: Race Relations in South Africa and the United States.* Thousand Oaks, Calif.: Sage Publications, 1995.
Seager, Robert, II, ed. *The Papers of Henry Clay.* Lexington: University Press of Kentucky, 1988.
Sellers, Charles G., Jr. "Who Were the Southern Whigs?" *American Historical Review* 59 (January 1954): 335–46.
Sheridan, P. H. *Personal Memoirs of P. H. Sheridan.* Vol. 2. New York: Charles L. Webster and Company, 1888.
Shook, Robert W. "Federal Occupation and Administration of Texas, 1865–1870." Ph.D. diss., North Texas State University, 1970.
Sinclair, Oran Lonnie. "Crossroads of Conviction: A Study of the Texas Political Mind, 1856–1861." Ph.D. diss., Rice University, 1975.
Smallwood, James. *The History of Smith County, Texas: Born in Dixie.* 2 vols. Austin: Eakin Press, 1999.
———. *Time of Hope, Time of Despair: Black Texans During Reconstruction.* Port Washington, New York: Kennikat Press, 1981.
Smith, David P. "Conscription and Conflict on the Texas Frontier, 1863–1865," *Civil War History* 36 (1990): 250–61.
———. "The Elm Creek Raid, 1864: State and Confederate Defense and Response." *Military History of the Southwest* 19 (1989): 121–36.

———. *Frontier Defense in the Civil War: Texas' Rangers and Rebels.* College Station: Texas A&M University Press, 1992.

———. "The Limits of Dissent and Loyalty in Texas." In *Guerillas, Unionists, and Violence on the Confederate Home Front,* ed. Daniel Sutherland, 133–50. Fayetteville: University of Arkansas Press, 1999.

Smyrl, Frank H. "Texas in the Union Army, 1861–1865." *Southwestern Historical Quarterly* 65 (October 1961): 234–50.

Spaw, Patsy McDonald. *The Texas Senate,* vol. 1: *Republic to Civil War, 1836–1861.* College Station: Texas A&M University Press, 1990.

———. *The Texas Senate,* vol. 2: *Civil War to the Eve of Reform, 1861–1889.* College Station: Texas A&M University Press, 1999.

Spurlin, Charles, comp. *Texas Veterans in the Mexican War: Muster Rolls of Texas Military Units.* Victoria, Tex.: privately printed, 1984.

Stambaugh, J. Lee, and Lillian J. Stambaugh. *A History of Collin County, Texas.* Austin: Texas State Historical Association, 1958.

Stegmaier, Mark J. *Texas, New Mexico, and the Compromise of 1850: Boundary Dispute and Sectional Crisis.* Kent, Ohio: Kent State University Press, 1996.

Sutherland, Daniel, ed. *Guerrillas, Unionists, and Violence on the Confederate Home Front.* Fayetteville: University of Arkansas Press, 1999.

Tate, Michael L. "Frontier Defense on the Comanche Ranges of Northwest Texas, 1846–1860." *Great Plains Journal* 11 (1971): 41–56.

Throckmorton, C. Wickliffe. *A Genealogical and Historical Account of the Throckmorton Family in England and the United States with Brief Notes on Some of the Allied Families.* Richmond, Va.: Old Dominion Press, 1930.

Throckmorton, Gary. Unpublished genealogical register for William Edmund Throckmorton (updated April 23, 2003). Printed copy in author's possession.

Timmons, Joe T. "The Referendum in Texas on the Ordinance of Secession, February 23, 1861: The Vote." *East Texas Historical Journal* 11 (Fall 1973): 12–28.

———. "Texas on the Road to Secession." Ph.D. diss., University of Chicago, 1973.

Tutorow, Norman E. *Texas Annexation and the Mexican War: A Political Study of the Old Northwest.* Palo Alto, Calif.: Chadwick House, 1978.

Wallace, Ernest. *Texas in Turmoil.* Austin: Steck-Vaughn Company, 1965.

Wallace, Ernest, David Vigness, and George B. Ward, eds. *Documents of Texas History.* Austin: State House Press, 1994.

Waller, John. *Colossal Hamilton of Texas: A Biography of Andrew Jackson Hamilton.* El Paso: Texas Western Press, 1968.

Wilbarger, J. W. *Indian Depredations in Texas.* Austin: Hutchinson Printing House, 1889. Reprint, Austin: Pemberton Press, 1967. Page references are to the reprint edition.

Wilkins, Frederick. *The Highly Irregular Irregulars: Texas Rangers in the Mexican War.* Austin: Eakin Press, 1990.

Wilson, Clyde N., ed. *The Papers of John C. Calhoun.* Vols. 13 and 14. Columbia: University of South Carolina Press, 1980, 1981.

Winfrey, Dorman H., and James M. Day, eds. *The Indian Papers of Texas and the Southwest, 1825–1916.* Vol. 1. Austin: Pemberton Press, 1966.

Winkler, William, ed. *Journal of the Secession Convention of Texas 1861.* Austin: Austin Printing Company, 1912.

Wooster, Ralph A. "An Analysis of the Membership of the Texas Secession Convention." *Southwestern Historical Quarterly* 62 (January 1959): 322–35.

———. *The Secession Conventions of the South.* Princeton: Princeton University Press, 1962.

———. *Texas and Texans in the Civil War.* Austin: Eakin Press, 1995.

Wooster, Ralph A., and Robert Wooster. "A People at War: East Texans During the Civil War." *East Texas Historical Journal* 28 (Spring 1990): 3–16.

Wooten, Dudley G., ed. *A Comprehensive History of Texas, 1685 to 1897.* 2 vols. Dallas: William G. Scarff, 1898. Reprint, Austin: Texas State Historical Association, 1986. Page references are to the reprint edition.

Wortham, Louis J. *A History of Texas: From Wilderness to Commonwealth.* 4 vols. Fort Worth: Wortham-Molyneaux-Company, 1924.

Yearns, W. Buck, ed. *The Confederate Governors.* Athens: University of Georgia Press, 1985.

# INDEX

ISBN-13: 978-1-60344-040-0
ISBN-10: 1-60344-040-2